On Music
and
Musicians of
Hindoostan

On Music and Musicians of Hindoostan

ASHOK D. RANADE

NEW DELHI
PROMILLA & CO., PUBLISHERS

Ranade, Ashok Damodar, 1937-

 On music and musicians of Hindoostan / Ashok D. Ranade. —
1st ed. — New Delhi : Promilla, 1984.
 [10], 208 p., [1] leaf of plates : ports. ; 23 cm.
 Includes bibliographical references and index.

 1. Music, Hindustani—History and criticism. 2. Musicians, Hindustani.
3. Music—India—History and criticism. 4. Music and literature.

First Edition 1984

Publishers

Promilla & Co.
'Sonali'
C-127 Sarvodaya Enclave
New Delhi 110 017   India

Printers

Bela Pack n Print
225 Okhla Industrial Complex
Phase I
New Delhi 110 020   India

Dedicated to
Hemangini

Preface

To all appearances the following pages present a collection of papers and evaluative articles. To an extent, each individual piece is independent and self-sufficient.

However, it is hoped that taken together the writings succeed in projecting the immense variety of Indian music, the extreme complexity of the Hindustani art-music and the inevitable necessity of using a multi-criteria method in approaching problems of evaluation.

I am deeply grateful to Dr. Aroon Tikekar and Professor D.H. Butani for planting the idea of the effort. Without Mr. Arun Naik's help I could not have persevered with the task of completing the manuscript!

Pune   ASHOK D. RANADE

CONTENTS

List of Illustrations

1

Literature and music in India

Introduction

In any society and at any particular point of time, the prevailing culture is a sum total of diverse civilizing forces acting on the collective psyche, either simultaneously or successively. Along with other civilizing forces, the fine arts, the performing arts, and the composite arts also function as shaping powers that determine the eventual form of a culture. This is the reason why a connected view of the arts often serves as an efficient indicator of the quality of the societal mind.

However, to obtain a connected view of the arts is more easily said than done. Firstly, in spite of their cultural contribution—that being their common feature—arts vary in respect of their ways, paces and proportions in which such a contribution is realized. It is therefore advisable to further subgroup the arts.

If we contrast the arts with other cultural forces like science and religion, the arts seem to function as cognate entities. A study of interrelationship of various arts therefore assumes importance in the context of cultural dynamics.

There is one more, narrower ground for examining arts in combination : arts often flower in combination. For instance, literature and music came specially close in medieval India; devotional music *(bhakti sangeet)* and saint-poets (creators of *sant-kaavya*) were the resultant unique contributions to the arts of music and literature. Similarly, drama and music became special partners in nineteenth century Maharashtra; music-drama, as well as stage-music, were the specific gains registered in dramatics and music. The sixteenth century vogue of the *raagamaalaa* paintings is again attributed to a rare joint expression of arts with diverse individual appeals, one audio and the other visual.

Examination of the arts in combination is, in reality, an attempt to analyse the possibilities of mutual influence with reference to two or more arts. Such an analysis proves invaluable as a part of a larger cultural enquiry. It is intended here to consider literature and music in India in respect of their mutual influences.

Interrelationship of arts : general principles

In its root-sense, 'influence' is a 'flowing of effects'. There are various ways of studying these effect-flows. An enumeration of the ways in which arts can act on each other is a virtual impossibility, but a single specific art or a group of arts can be studied in relation to another specific art or a group of arts. Further, we can concentrate on a particular society even as we are examining the relationship of specific arts. More ambitiously, arts might also be examined as aesthetic phenomena governed by one single dominant tendency or a set of tendencies. In case we fail to find a common moving principle in arts even during a particular period, it might be possible to state the principles of evolution of one single art viewed in its entirety by keeping it at the centre all the time. In this way, the moment the arts are considered together, challenges of almost equal intensities are posed.

In the Indian context, complexities are further compounded because more than a dozen regional literatures and musics flourish today in India. In addition, two fully developed active systems of art-music operate side by side while the tribal world remains by and large uncharted! In face of this bewildering multiplicity we can briefly state four general principles involved in a study of the interrelationship of arts and then proceed to study literature-music relationship in a particular culture (that is, the Indian).

Firstly, all art-interrelationships are structured on a fundamental though changeable dependence or independence. This fundamental feature of dependence/independence comes into play on account of medium, material and genre-traditions of the arts concerned. There is thus something intrinsic about it. Medium, material and other factors mean that there is something in every art which is specially *within* it and this 'something' further leads to something else which *follows*. Due to these 'within' factors, certain arts are naturally dependent on each other while certain others are naturally independent of each other. For example, literature and architecture are naturally independent of each other while sculpture can be said to be naturally dependent on painting.

Secondly, the threefold classification of arts (viz., fine arts, performing arts and composite arts) indicates that arts falling within the same group can be assumed to have closer interrelationships. In this connection, instances of music and dance, drama and music, etc. will easily come to mind.

Thirdly, it would be seen that in particular societies, at particular developmental stages and at particular periods, non-art forces from the political, social, religious and economic spheres of life prove extraordinarily decisive in respect of the nature, extent and effect of interrelationship of the various arts.

Finally, the revolution in communications in the present century is so comprehensive, rapid and qualitative that all theoretical formulations concerning interrelationships are likely to turn out to be mere tentative probings! It is a writing on the wall that the communications-revolution has threatened the validity of every consecrated art-theory. Art theories have been truly reduced to an endangered species!

Literature: a wider connotation

As this stage it would have been logical to trace literary development juxtaposed with musical developments and then grapple with the problem of mutual action and reaction. Such an inquiry would have been based on historical-chronological data.

However there are three discouraging factors. Problems posed by the sheer multiplicity of regional literatures and musics of folk-variety are to be contended with. Our legendary indifference to chronological exactness also acts as a damper. The major difficulty to be reckoned with, however, is conceptual. The question: 'What is literature?' evokes baffling responses. Literature is customarily understood to be the whole body of imaginative prose and poetry in written form in a particular society and often in a particular period. What happens when this well-established connotation is viewed in the Indian context? The connotation no doubt retains its relevance but certainly not before a qualifying note has expanded its scope.

The term 'literature' is etymologically tied up with the word 'letter', that is, a written or a printed sign which stands for a particular sound. (It is interesting to note that a learned man is often described as a man of letters.) In India, the two terms are treated as capable of striking correspondence with the term 'literature'. They are *vaangmaya* and *saahitya* respectively. It is clear that none of them carries any suggestion of the process of 'being written' or 'writing'. In fact, the term *vaangmaya* is directly related to *vaak* (voice). Further, it is on record that though the existence of imaginative prose and poetry dates back to the Vedic period (2750 B.C. — 500 B.C.), the term *saahitya* came in use only around the seventh century. It was during this period that poetry was defined as शब्दार्थौ सहितौ काव्यम् and therefore the science dealing with poetry was called *saahitya*.[1] A yet another interesting detail is found in *Kaamasootra* by Vatsyayana (200 A.D.). In his computation of the human arts, he mentions poesy and writing (*lipishaastra*) as separate arts.[2] In all probability, the term *lipishaastra* referred to the art of decorative writing or calligraphy—may be, to proficiency in the physical act of writing.

Whatever the meaning, two general inferences are inescapable:
1. No approach that insists on literature being 'written' can do justice to the Indian situation. The Indian literary impulse has generated overwhelming oral manifestations: these are to be taken into account while defining terminology or determining methodology.
2. Even at the risk of appearing abaxial in our treatment, we might have to seek answers to 'literary' questions—having widened the scope of the term to include oral manifestations—in music, because *no other discipline in India has been so thoroughly oral-aural as music*. Further, considering that Indian musical expression is primarily vocal, the way Indian music has dealt with its own musical problems might turn out to be a relevant strategy for tackling issues so far preempted by reliance on written expression.

The oral tradition in India
Oral tradition has been usually defined in too literary a fashion, without any conceptual justification. As a result, literary thinkers have regarded the ability to read and write and the oral mode of literary expression as mutually exclusive.[3] This is hardly tenable: the Indian context compels us to reject such a simplistic definition.

In India, oral tradition spreads over a wide range: from music to medicine and from philosophy to actual judicial practices. It is not easily appreciated that the pervasive pursuance of the oral tradition was not a case of making virtue out of necessity. The cultivation of oral tradition had not become necessary because India suffered from ignorance of penmanship. Writing and cognate processes existed abundantly in ancient India. B.S. Naik has pointed out numerous facts which prove the existence of writing even in Rigvedic times.[4] In later times, the evidence is conclusive:

(a) Paanini (800 B.C.) mentions *lipi, lipikaar*, etc.[5]

(b) *Arthashaastra* by Kautilya (400 B.C.) warns that efficacy of writing in keeping knowledge secure is doubtful.[6]

(c) Around 300 B.C., there were two major scripts circulating in India, namely, the Braahmi and the Kharoshti. In fact *Lalitavistaar*, an ancient Buddhist manuscript, mentions the names of 60 scripts.[7]

To conclude, oral tradition does not rule out the existence, knowledge or use of writing. It means coexistence of the written and the spoken word. However, the latter is clothed with a special sanction and validity. Winternitz has rightly observed:

> From such facts one would conclude that at the time, that is, in the fifth century B.C., the idea of the possibility of writing books had not as yet occurred at all. Such a conclusion, however, would be too hasty, for it is a strange phenomenon that in India, from the oldest times, up till the present day, the spoken word, and not writing, has been the basis of the whole literary activity ... Not out of manuscripts or books does one learn the texts, but from the mouth of the teacher, today as thousands of years ago ... Authority is possessed only by the spoken word of the teacher.[8]

Thus it is not the absence of being 'written' that makes the tradition 'oral' but the significance attached to the oral-aural processes by the communicators concerned that makes it so. The deep-seated and widely detected preference for the oral tradition is due to many reasons but ignorance of writing is certainly not one of them.

Another authority, A. A. Macdonell, agrees that oral tradition and knowledge of writing can co-exist but argues that this happened at a later stage when the oral tradition was already entrenched in India. He says:

> Even modern poets do not wish to be read, but *cherish the hope*

that their works may be recited. This immemorial practice indeed
shows that the beginnings of Indian poetry and science go back
to the time when writing was unknown, and the system of the
oral tradition, such as is referred to in the *Rigveda*, was developed before writing was introduced. The latter could, therefore,
have been in use before it began to be mentioned.[9]

In addition to its peaceful co-existence with the art of writing
and the consequences flowing thereof, the oral tradition also
incorporates the feature of being 'aural'. In other words, the
tradition not only employs the organ of hearing but also the
evaluative criteria following from the process. Thus it used (and
still uses) the touchstone of *how it sounds to the ear* for evaluating the expressions falling within its purview.

As a consequence, the hearers and the sense of hearing do
not remain mere concomitants in an action but also become
conditioning factors and the resulting product shows unmistakable
traces of their operation. One of Winternitz's observations is
meaningful in this regard. He says: 'The works of the poets, too,
were in India never intended for readers, but always for hearers.'[10]
Reference to the aural aspect clearly brings out an essential
aspect of the Indian situation: the chances are that *an Indian
litterateur may turn out to be a performer like a musician.* Thus it
would be natural for him to gear up to features like improvisation,
audience-participation, stylization in sound, etc., like a musician.
It therefore follows logically that for evaluating literary products
with a reasonable finality, and, in fact, in every attempt aimed at
getting to their total import, the musico-literary mode of their gestation and consequent presentation must be kept in mind.

Guru, the preceptor, has a special role to play in the oral tradition. He is an indispensable link in the process of communication, irrespective of the content of the message involved. Unless
he undertook to decode the message, the texts were reduced to a
body of almost unintelligible letters. The institution of a *guru* was
not confined to subjects considered obscure, nor were the teaching-
learning processes understood to be mere exchanges or transactions
of commodities. Whether it was in the home of the *guru,* as in the
early times, or as in the renowned educational centres like
Vaaraanasi or Takshasheelaa during Buddhist times, education
was *guru*-oriented.

Though Winternitz uses the term 'transmission' to describe the

educational processes initiated by the *guru*, the import of his statement does not fail to bring out the wider scope of the process
better described as communication. The sacredness associated
with the office of the *guru* is also amply reflected in what he says:

> Therefore, to a teacher, as the bearer and preserver of know-
> ledge, the highest veneration is due, according to the ancient
> Indian law; as the spiritual father he is venerated, now as an
> equal, now as a superior of the physical father, he is looked
> upon as an image of God Brahman, and to him who serves the
> teacher faithfully and humbly, Brahman's heaven is assured . . .
> A book existed only when and only so long as there were
> teachers and pupils, who taught and learned it.[11]

In all probability the didactic element prevalent in Indian
literature is genetically connected with oral tradition. *The line of
literary development in India passes virtually through music* because
music illustrates all the facets of oral tradition to the utmost.
However, this does not mean that there is no direct connection
between literature and oral tradition. For example, the *sootra*
literature in India shows a direct relationship without the inter-
mediary role of music. Because of the extraordinary compression
of meaning and the consequential essential role of the *guru* as the
interpreter – the *sootras* form a link with the oral tradition and its
norms. Winternitz remarks:

> . . . The pupil memorized only these aphoristic sentences receiv-
> ing the necessary explanations from the teachers . . . This
> peculiar *sootra* style originated in the prose of the Brahmanas.[12]

He also points out elsewhere that the abundant use of phrases
which are literally translatable as 'this here' indicates the oral
presentation of the material.[13] This is an instance of literature
establishing a direct link with the oral tradition to formulate
a stylistic device successfully.

However, throughout history taken as a whole, Indian literary
development was not influenced in equal measure by oral tradition. Perhaps this phenomenon of partaking of each other's
characteristics showed a continuous decline, as individual arts
became more and more differentiated and the genetic links
weakened. However, there is no doubt that the oral tradition
and its direct consequences provided cultural and creative arche-
types to successive generations of Indian artists. Effects of the
perpetuated oral tradition merit attention due to a number of

reasons: the vastness of the country, illiteracy of the majority of the population, together with the twists and turns of media-operations, are bound to make the spoken word more important, culturally as well as educationally.

Pre-history : the Harappans and the Aryans

Pre-Aryan civilization, generally known as the 'Indus', met its final doom sometime around 2750 B.C. Having entered India during the period 3300 B.C. – 3200 B.C., the Aryans succeeded in estab-lishing a firm foothold in Brahmaavarta by 3102 B.C.[14] Thus the Harappan and the Aryan cultures co-existed for about five hundred years, though perhaps in a warring state.

Under the circumstances, is it justifiable to comment on the pre-Aryan culture as a separate culture? Is it not possible to main-tain that the consideration of pre-Aryan and Aryan cultures virtually means dealing with a joint manifestation? The chrono-logical overlap encourages such a view. One more speculative observation could be mentioned. Conquests have invariably led to greater cultural exchanges: this too might have made the pre-his-torical Indian culture a less differentiated entity. Whatever may be the case, the musico-literary source-material pertaining to this period is scanty. Yet one can hardly write-off the Harappans culturally, as Basham seems to have done. He says: 'They were not on the whole an artistic people. No doubt they had literature, with religious epics similar to those of Sumer and Babylon, but these are forever lost to us.'[15] Considering the prosperity enjoyed and the intense trading activity carried on by the Harappans, and taking into account their achievements in glyptic and modelling arts and their ritualistic religion, it is reasonable to assume that conditions were not unfavourable for a thriving artistic life, and very likely, music and literature must have enjoyed their share. In fact the Lothal excavations seem to have unearthed a bridge of a two-stringed instrument and organologically viewed, the find indi-cates a finer musical culture.   Yet, it has to be admitted that the enquiry into the musico-literary relationship assumes significant proportions only when one considers the Vedic period proper.

Vedic literature and music

Vedic literature is coextensive with the four *Veda*(s), the *Brahmana*(s), the *Aaranyaka*(s) and the *Upanishad*(s). Due to their content and their overall purpose, the latter three literatures are independent of music. Of the four *Vedas*, *Saamaveda* is, in all respects, a music-oriented redaction of the *Rigveda*, though some of its verses were of more ancient origin, that is, they were pre-Vedic. In fact, out of the total 1,810 verses, about 75 are *not* from the *Rigveda*. *Saamaveda* is a case of influence of music on literature. As Winternitz comments:

> The *Saamaveda samhitaa*s are nothing but collections of texts which have been collected for the uses of the *udgaatr*s, not for their own sake, but because of the melodies—the bearers of which they were.[16]

What is a *saama*? G.H. Taralekar has referred to two meaning-ful explanations. According to one explanation, साम is derived as सा+अम where सा refers to the verse-component and अम to the musical notes attached to it. This explanation patently draws our attention to the tonal or melodic aspect reflected in the *saama*-composition. The second explanation derives the word from the term समता (*samataa*) which means equality or equalization. The equalization referred to here is equalization of diverse metres like *gaayatri*, *birhati*, *jagati* and *trishtubh* employed during the various sacrificial rites. Different metres can hardly be equalized unless a substantial rhythmic manipulation is effected. In this manner, both the tonal and the rhythmic aspects are taken care of in a *saama*—the musical *avataar* of a literary metre. Even the *Chhandogya* and the *Brihad-aaranyaka Upanishad*s assert the musical *raison d'tre* of the *saama*.[17] Under the circumstances, it stands to reason that a *richaa* (hymn) would undergo many changes in recitation. Not only were the changes allowed but they were later duly codified. In this respect, the following eight codified categories of changes are worth noting:

1. विकार   = modification (ओऽग्नाइ of अग्ने)
2. विश्लेषण = dissolution (वोइतोयाऽऽइ of वीतये)
3. विकर्षण = suspension (याऽऽइयि of ये)
4. अभ्यास   = repetition (तोयाऽऽइ)
5. विराम   = pause (ग्णानोह् व्यदागेया instead of ग्णानो ह्व्यदातये)
6. स्तोभ   = insertion (औ होवा हा उ हा इ)
7. लोप   = disappearance (प्रचोह्आंदयो आ instead of प्रचोदयात्)
8. आगम   = augmentation (वरेणियोम in place of वरेण्यम्)

On examination, it becomes apparent that the codified changes are extremely varied and far-reaching in scope. This could happen because music had become the controlling agency. Music held the reins to such an extent that no facet of the verse was left untouched. Without going into further details of a very elaborately constructed system of *saaman*-singing, two points need special attention because they are direct spill-overs from the system as it evolved through the broader framework of the oral tradition.

i) Firstly, the nature of the Vedic accent was musical and continued to be so till the seventh century A.D.[18]

ii) Secondly, many of the *saama*-hymns were sung according to much older melodies or tunes.[19] This means that the tonal moulds were provided by the non-Vedic, pre-Aryan culture and the texts alone were of Vedic origin. It is logical to deduce that the popularity enjoyed by these melodies was such that they could easily become dominant partners in the evident marriage of music and literature. This phenomenon, recorded so early in Indian cultural history, will be seen to have an arresting recurrence in Indian literary development. Prosody and other related areas felt the impact of music; and these areas deserve closer analysis. In all probability, the varying degrees of musicality customary accent of specific literary forms, abundant use of certain stylistic devices, a detectable reluctance to move away from the Sanskrit traditions and such other features, will appear in a new light when the pervasive role of music in literary development is properly understood.

It is precisely due to the all-embracing influence of music that even the not-so-musical aspects of *Saamaveda* reveal the music-literature relationship under discussion. The whole Vedic republic of letters is characterized by general tendencies that are attributable to music. Winternitz obviously perceived the general layer of musicality that the *saama*-way of literary conception brought to notice; hence he expressed the opinion that the term *saama* means 'rhythmical speech'.[20] It is in the context of this 'general musicality' that the following three trends in the entire Vedic literature become important: i) tendency towards versification, ii) crystallization of pitch-patterns, and iii) pervasiveness of the incantatory element. These three literary effects can be directly ascribed to music. There are some more which are traceable to the oral tradition, but they are beyond our present brief. The three effects need some discussion.

i) Tendency towards versification

Verse is distinguished from prose because, due to its very nature, the former is more measured. On the other hand, verse is also separable from a metrical expression because it is not as regular as the latter. In this manner, verse carries a suggestion of metrical expression and at the same time, registers a movement away from the linearity of prose. It is therefore an instance of a double-edged non-conformism. Of our immediate interest is the fact that, irrespective of the content and the exact chronological placement of the works involved, the entire Vedic literature is suffused with the measured accent which, as we have seen, is the hallmark of verse. In case of Vedic literature this was logical and inescapable because basically Vedic literature is an 'utterance' in expression. It can be inferred, therefore, that in it, the controlling factor was the breath-unit of the users. As vocal music has been the primary manifestation of the Indian musical impulse, music and inclination towards versification become causally connected.

At this point, a general underlying principle needs to be noted. All performing arts create two causal chains: one of them is manifest in the living tradition of the actual performances (which may be artistic successes or failures) and the second is witnessed in the efficiency displayed by the performers in facing and solving problems of co-ordinating various physical and psychological forces in the operation. The former causal chain remains chiefly relevant only to the art and the artists concerned (in the present instance it is music and the musicians). However, the latter chain becomes germane to other activities which need all, or some, of the same, or similar physical and psychological forces. This is so because this latter chain from the performing arts necessarily evolves definite efficient formulae to meet specific challenges or needs. This is why (and how) solutions for co-ordination of breathing, movement, pronunciation, ascending and descending modes of vocalization, etc.—originally formulated by musicians—spill over to language and literature. Further, in addition to the natural extension of musical solutions to non-musical fields (on account of the similarity of problems faced by both activities) the general spread of the oral tradition as such also makes its presence felt.

Against this background we can maintain that, in the context of Vedic literature, the literary utterances organized themselves into verse *because* they were compelled to take notice of the breathing-patterns. The functional formulae thus arrived at, were then perceived as 'pattern' and this could be described as the first appearance of the musical impulse on the scene. In its turn, the impulse created further prosodic potentialities. To versify is to give way to the musical urges of the speakers of language. It is therefore, a sure sign of the ascendency enjoyed by musical sensibility over literary ability.

After the initial creation of the measured accent, the same impulse subsequently leads to a metrical use of the available linguistic resources. Metrical manifestation naturally means a more strictly controlled and deliberately directed operation of the musical impulse. The Vedic scene may be scrutinised in this light.

On examination, the Vedic literary scene reveals that about fifteen meters were employed. Seven of them were noticeably in circulation while three meters could be almost described as popular in the sense of being more frequent in use. It is significant that these three, namely, *anushtubh, trishtubh* and *jagati* were the most flexible of them all. From the point of musical aesthetics, a suggestion of regularity has always proved more conducive to musical quality than a strict adherence to the norms set by a rigid sense of regularity.

In short, music won the day. It is no wonder that the metrical sparseness of the Vedic literary corpus in respect of the number of metres employed and their accommodative structures, is in direct contrast to the literature of the classical age. The latter boasted of about eight hundred and fifty meters and also fathered about one hundred and fifty treatises on prosody! Thus, rigidity in prosodic thinking was directly responsible for these features: loss of musicality and abundance of individual prosodic items. Considered in this light, the Epic period of Sanskrit literature was the nadir of metrical musicality.[21] It is therefore evident that Vedic literature performed a difficult feat of moving away from prose and yet keeping out the rigidity of a strict metricality. A fuller exploration of the musical possibilities of versification could therefore be attempted.

ii) Crystallization of pitch-patterns

Logically viewed, pervasiveness of versification and the importance accorded to recitation go together. Recitation is a purposeful and methodical reproduction of sound-structures patterned in memory prior to the act of recitation. In musical activity taken as a whole, it is seen that recitation is assiduously practiced in case of all types of basic frameworks concretized in melodic compositions as well as in the rhythmic and language-based compositions. Taken together, these fundamental frameworks provide artists with the necessary stable structures employed for introducing improvised variables. This feature of Indian music remains unaltered even today.

Going back to the Vedic scene, it would not be unwarranted to say that the post-Vedic codification of Vedic recitation is an indication of the importance attached to it by the users. Codification is always a consolidation of long standing practices, hence it is always subsequent to the actual practice. The entire *shikshaa* literature (c. 1000 B.C. to 600 B.C.), consisting of five *shikshaa*s and five *praatishaakhyaa*s collectively form a monumental exercise in the scientification of an elusive phenomenon like recitation.

Vashistha Narayan Jha has noted that (as mentioned in the *Taittiriyopanishad)* the *shikshaa*s dealt with the following six items:

1) *Swara* (note)
2) *Varna* (phoneme)
3) *Maatraa* (phonetic quantity)
4) *Bala* (stress)
5) *Saama* (Vedic hymn)
6) *Santaan* (conjunctions)[22]

Of the six items, the first five display an unambiguous musical thrust. The entire *shikshaa*-based training process employed in respect of recitation thus reveals a natural orientation towards musicality. It is significant that even today one of the *shikshaa*s, the *Naaradiya Shikshaa*, is regarded as a seminal work of musicological import. This is an interesting instance of reciprocity conveyed across aeons of time. Antiquity recognized and accentuated musical elements in recitation while modernity detected and accepted musicological noteworthiness of an ancient work on recitation.

Apart from an unhesitant application of musical categories, the Vedic recitation-system also employed musical techniques of skeletal notation in training as well as in actual performance. In addition, a gesture-language was also pressed into service to accompany the notation. It is in this connection that the

Naaradiya Shikshaa refers to the human body itself as *gaatra-veenaa*.[23]

The intrinsic relationship existing between gestures and musical expression should be properly understood. Both are inevitably connected for two reasons. Firstly, because singing is, to all purposes, a deliberate deviation from the sound-patterns used in day-to-day speech. However, deviated speech-patterns hardly prove adequate in themselves unless they are combined with the corresponding gesture-patterns. On the other hand, it should be remembered that gesture-patterns are also results of efforts—the coordinated and willed body-responses. Further, gestures also discharge the function of relieving psycho-physiological tensions created by the efforts involved. This is the second reason why gestures are bound to accompany singing—an activity which makes extra demands on the psycho-physical resources normally at one's command. As a cumulative result of the two requirements (of having matching patterns and tension-reliefs), the hand-body gestures accompanying Vedic-recitation fixed the accompanying or associated pitch-patterns and thus made them prominently perceived. In this manner, Vedic Sanskrit became a language of musical accents and as a consequence versified pitch-patterns proved unavoidable. That the entire Vedic literature taken as a whole, should get permeated with these features was only to be expected.

iii) *Pervasiveness of the incantatory element*

We have seen that versification was a manifestation of one aspect of the initial musical impulse. The other aspect was a crystallization of pitch-patterns. Yet another musical aspect which percolated into the non-musical areas of language and literature, was the incantatory use of sound. One of the explanations of how and why Vedic culture was also a *mantra*-culture, with all its ramifications like ascendency of priesthood, ritualism etc. is to be sought here. It is easy to see how incantation-practices could thus get entrenched in India without difficulty because oral tradition had already become well-established and comprehensive. The same set of reasons also led to the primacy of vocal music in India.

In fact we can go a little further. Considering the totality of circumstances, it is not surprising that *musical expression finally came to hold a sort of co-ordination portfolio in Ancient India.* The function of bringing about a cohesion of various communicative components like language, movement, gestures was also delegated to music. In this manner, all non-material and aesthetically oriented human endeavour of the Vedic period turned into a musical package—a *gestalt* with music as a dominant partner.

Coming back to *mantra* it is helpful to understand the role of incantation as the original permeating phenomenon because *mantra* is an epitome of all the tendencies that appear in an incantation. *Mantra* has been defined in various ways and the definitions unfailingly highlight the chief facets of musico-literary relationship realized through the medium of sound. The following definitions and descriptions are noteworthy:

☐*Mantra* is a Sanskrit syllable or a group of syllables, used to concentrate cosmic and psychic energies.[24]

☐Thus *mantra*s correctly uttered or sung become part of the liturgy of the sacrifice which gave them an additional authority, as well as ensuing communication with the chosen deity.[25a]

☐The *mantra*s of the *Rigveda* are composed in an artificial style, full of poetic archaisms and poetic constructions and complicated, well defined metrical forms . . . and under the influence of a fully developed literary convention.[25b]

☐The efficiency of a *mantra* in post-Vedic times was not dependent on its meaning, but rather on the subjective effect of the mental discipline involved in its utterance, and the accompanying mode of breathing.[25c]

Certain deductions follow from the emphases on various characteristics of *mantra* contained in the definitions given above. These features bring out the heavy musical bias of the literary expression concerned:

(i) In a *mantra*, the basic linguistic and semantic unit was kept short (to facilitate quicker memorizing). Repetition being the essence of the practice of a *mantra*, the lack of longer duration of an individual unit was, to an extent, compensated.

(ii) Measured accent was insisted upon and breathing processes, as well as utterances, were controlled according to established norms.

(iii) The ultimate aim of the *mantra*-iteration was communication and the subjective forces were to be deliberately disciplined to achieve the objective.

(iv) *Mantra*-patterns were sound-patterns and were to be intentionally evolved and used. Further, it was not mandatory that the patterns be meaningful because *mantra*s recognised 'sound' as an efficient and legitimate channel of expression *per se*.

In this manner, *love of sound for its own sake* becomes relevant and natural in certain developmental stages of literature. Iteration, assonance, echo, rhyme, onomatopoeism and similar literary devices possess attraction and authority because they are touched by musical qualities. Application of these devices affects the listeners because sound appears in them as an entity perceived through hearing (and not through reading). In them, sound is felt immediately. Sound which requires to be read and understood can hardly prove equally potent. Literary expression exploiting these devices is a concrete instance of musical sensibility coming into operation. Due to its function, an otherwise 'dry' literary experience gains an edge. Experience involved becomes less indirect and to that extent, less contingent.

It is not fortuitous that Bhagwaan Krishna identified himself with the *Saamaveda*. It is also symptomatic that among the Western attempts to bring the *Veda*s into the modern version of literary traditions, *Saamaveda* was the first to be edited in its entirety. (Stevenson, a missionary, brought out the earliest edition in 1842.[26]) Evidently, *Saamaveda* is rightfully recognized as the conclusive voice of the Vedic literary sensibility viewed as a whole.

Indian culture has been shaped by oral tradition and hence music has influenced its various manifestations *naturally*. The musical forces which so actively controlled the Vedic phase of Indian literature were, in fact, never obliterated. Through the successive high tides and low ebbs of love for sound *per se*, taste for finer manipulations of pitches, skilled use of flexible rhythms, and finally, through the longing for the abstract aesthetic identity of form and content, music continued to hold its sway. No doubt, the pattern of musico-literary relationships went on becoming more and more complex because regional languages, literatures and music(s) started claiming individual attention. They also set differing developmental paces. However, the processes initiated in the pre-Aryan ages could hardly be totally written-off. They submerged and resurfaced later, though with many new features. However, this is anticipating the upheaval that occurred after the Epic period in Indian literary tradition.

The epic age

The post-Vedic world of letters consisted of the *sootra*s, the epics, the *Puraana*s and the *smriti*s. Of these, the epics alone are directly relevant for musico-literary examination. The very nature of the subject-matter of the other three genres prevents any substantial connection with music. For example, the *sutra*s dealt with six items, namely, *shikshaa* (phonetics); *chhandas* (metre); *vyaakarana* (grammar); *nirookta* (etymology); *kalpa* (religious practices) and *jyotisha* (astronomy). In their normal format the *Purana*s treated five set topics: *sarga* (creation); *prati-sarga* (recreation after dissolution); *vamsha* (geneology of gods, sages or teachers); *manvantara* (groups of great ages) and lastly the *vamshacharita* (the history of royal dynasties). And finally, the *smriti*s were the law-books that laid down norms governing various aspects of social life.

However, the *sutra*s merit some attention. Firstly, because manuals of recitation like *Naaradiya Shikshaa* fall in the *sootra* category, and chiefly because *sootra* was a mode of *composing* literature. As a compositional mode, *sootra* meant a stringing together of rules, briefly and succinctly stated, pertaining to a particular area of knowledge. The aim of the mode was to effectively preserve the concerned material through a systematic use of the faculty of memory. The practices and procedures perfected by the oral tradition were thus fully exploited by this mode. For example, repetition was liberally employed and strongly advocated in the study-procedures adopted. In fact, an ability to remember (which was expected to get strength through repetition) was used as a criterion to grade students. However, the *sootra*-mode does not exhibit any exciting or enduring traces of relationship with music. It was, to all musical purposes, too abrupt and discontinuous to attain either melodic or rhythmic stature. Therefore, it was the epic mode which became the resonating frequency for the musico-literary expression of the post-Vedic period.

Examined composition-wise, an epic turns out to be much more complicated than is commonly understood. The commonly understood meaning of the term 'epic' refers usually to the two great epics—the *Raamaayana* and the *Mahaabhaarata*. In reality, this commonly understood denotation constitutes only one of the three meanings of the epic-mode. The two other meanings are suggested by the terms 'ballad', and 'narrative poem', respectively. As in the case of *mantra*s and the *sootra*s, ballads, narratives and epics indicate three *separate* modes of literary composition and expression.

As a consequence, they offer three individual formulae of co-ordinating the various elements present in the communication-processes of the oral tradition. Of course, the three modes enjoyed the usual overlaps and exemplified different extents of musico-literary dependencies. However, the pervasiveness of the oral tradition ensured their continued interrelationship.

The ballads are often songs in praise of men (*gaathaa naaraashamsi*): Winternitz rightly calls them 'precursors of the great epics': 'These old, heroic songs, whose existence we must take for granted, have not all vanished without trace; in remnants and fragments some of them have been preserved in our two great epics.'[27] Indian ballad-singers were known as *soota*s. They were professional, itinerent singers who composed their own songs and passed them on by oral tradition from generation to generation. They memorized the songs, sung them to lute accompaniment in public concerts.[28] *Soota*s were attached to kings, warriors, etc., whom they often accompanied during battles. The first-hand experience thus gained was the raw-material which they transformed into their compositions.

In a slightly different fashion, Macdonell too has made distinctions relevant to our purpose. He writes:

Sanskrit epic poetry falls into two main classes. That which comprises old stories goes by the name of *itihaasa* (legend), *aakhyaana* (narrative), or *puraana* (ancient tale), while the other is called *kaavya* or artificial epic. The *Mahaabhaarata* is the chief and oldest representative of the former group, the *Raamaayana* of the latter.[29]

For our purpose, the ballad deserves more attention because, of them all, the ballad is the most music-influenced. Customarily, ballad-singing was accompanied by *veenaa*, a string-instrument which demanded careful tuning and smoother handling. Naturally, the stylistic texture of the verse must have possessed matching sound-qualities. The balladeers were professionals and were therefore highly solicitous about the 'success' of their performances. As a result, they employed all the devices and techniques employed by a musician in a performance of music. This was so because both the manifestations sought similar results and depended on the same resources. The balladeers therefore improvised the texts to suit the needs of the audience present at a particular performance. They also took into account the requirements of the regions in which they were presenting their art. Though Winternitz has commented on these features,[30] he has not referred to the motivation provided by the deliberate, aesthetic inclination of the performers. The balladeers were professionals and thus made their living by the effectiveness of their art. This did not fail to have a bearing on the development of the epic-mode.

When aspects like language, style and meter of the epic-mode are considered, this same 'musical' concern for a successful performance should be examined as a controlling factor. The lack of uniformity in respect of language, style and meter which the *Mahaabhaarata* exhibits is directly traceable to the people who 'presented' the epics and faced the exigencies of performance. The archaic quality of the language evident in some parts showed great affinity with the Vedic language because of the presence of the bardic element. This element was part of a wider oral tradition which, after all, is a continuous process. Similarly, parts of the linguistic and stylistic texture recalled the Pali-heritage, which of course represented the popular stratum of the total literary reality. That the epic-style was much less embellished and ornate than the later *kaavya* style is also causally related to the bardic elements. A performer has to be intelligible as well as audible. A bard was perforce inclined to use simpler language. He was also compelled to ensure that his sentence-structures, line-lengths, etc., remained conducive to manipulation of the breathing and the phonating apparatuses.

It is highly significant that a more rigid adherence to the *shloka*-metre characterizes the *Raamaayana* rather than the *Mahaabhaarata*. The latter shows traces of the more flexible Vedic metres like *trishtubh*; it also finds a place for the older rhythmical prose that sometimes alternated with verse. In this respect too, the causation is clear. It is the reciter who needs variety in metres— the temporal frameworks in which the literary content is to appear. Rhythmic variety is one of the important means in a reciter's *repertoire* for capturing and sustaining the interest of listeners. The heterogeneity displayed by the *Mahaabhaarata* owes its origin to its being part of a greater performing tradition which shared many features with music.

It is incorrect to try to place both the epics in a 'pure' literary tradition, with equal confidence. Winternitz remarks rather ruefully: 'This very thing constitutes the peculiarity of the

Mahaabhaarata in its present form: it is neither proper warrior-poetry nor proper religious poetry; it is no longer an epic, but not yet a real puraana.'[31] It was inevitable that the *Raamaayana* presented a contrast to the *Mahaabhaarata*, because it is, in Macdonell's words: '. . . in the main, a work of a single poet, homogeneous in plan and execution, composed in the East of India'.[32] From a slightly changed angle, Winternitz made a similar point when he observed that the *Raamaayana* was, for all purposes, a beginning of the classical, ornate Sanskrit poetry.[33] This is the reason why in spite of its original bardic leanings, qualitatively, the *Raamaayana* comes nearer poetry which almost belongs to another milieu. One can therefore deduce the following performing conditions for the *Raamaayana*: it had an audience that was more cohesive and *elite*. The reciters of the *Raamaayana* were more systematically trained, the poem itself was the result of a cooler and a more deliberate act of composing. The venue of the performance was enclosed or was at least well-covered. As yet, its poetry was a poetry that was 'heard' but the days were not far when poetry would be preferably read. It was then that the influence of music via the oral tradition would suffer considerable erosion. In that phase, music would affect literature but only at a subtler level and in an indirect manner. Compared to the later *kaavya* literature, the epic literature showed an immediate and also an intrinsic type of relationship with music—a relationship almost organically necessary for its emergence as a literary expression.

Summing up, the period ranging from the pre-Vedic to the Vedic was one of close relationship between music and literature, with the latter leaning heavily on the former. The basic cause was a very comprehensive oral tradition which controlled expressions both in music and literature. Of the two, music made its orientation clear chiefly by remaining vocal to a large extent. On the other hand, literature declared its basic loyalty through music—by relying on recitation, prosodic formations depending on sound-patterns' and *alankaara*s sustained through enjoying sound for its own sake. In the final synthesis, language, style, metres and other literary constituents combined with body-movements, gestures, breath-patterns and other aspects of vocalization and performance to produce a musico-literary *gestalt*.

NOTES

1. Kane, P.V., *Saahityadarpan*, pub. self, Bombay, 1923, p. CXLI.
2. Walimbe, R.S., *Praachin Bhaaratiya Kalaa*, Joshi and Lokhande, Pune, 1959, pp. 39-47.
3. Preminger, Alex, *Princeton Encyclopedia of Poetry and Poetics*, Princeton University Press, 1974, p. 591.
4. Naik, B.S., *Devanagari Mudraaksharlekhan Kala*, Maharashtra Rajya Sahitya Sanskriti Mandal, Mumbai, 1980, pp. 5-7.
5. Ibid, p. 5.
6. Ibid, p. 7.
7. Ibid, p. 6.
8. Winternitz, M., *A History of Indian Literature*, University of Calcutta, 1962, Vol. 1, Part I, p. 29.
9. Macdonnell, A. A., *A History of Sanskrit Literature*, Munshiram Manoharlal, New Delhi, 1961,   p. 16.
10. Winternitz, op cit, p. 29.
11. Winternitz, op cit, pp. 31-32.
12. Winternitz, op cit, p. 236.
13. Ibid, p. 182.
14. Deshmukh, P.R., *Sindhu Sanskriti, Rgveda va Hindu Sanskriti*, Pradnya Paathshaalaa, Wai, 1966, p. 324.
15. *The Wonder that was India*, Fontana Books, Calcutta, 1971, p. 20.
16. Winternitz, op cit, p. 142.
17. 'Bharatiya Sangeet', *Praachin Bhaaratiya Vidyeche Punardarshan*, ed. Dandekar, R.N. and Kashikar, C.G. Vedashaastrottejak Sabhaa, Pune, 1978, p. 426.
18. Macdonnell, op cit, p. 52.
   The nature of the Vedic accent was musical, depending on the pitch of the voice, like that of the ancient Greeks . . . But just as the old Greek musical accent, after the beginning of our era, was transformed into a stress accent, so by the seventh century A.D. (and probably long before) the Sanskrit accent had undergone a similar change.
19. Winternitz, op cit, pp. 146-47.
   The number of known melodies must have been a very large one, (footnote: a later author gives the number of *saman*s as 8000! R. Simon, Loc. Cit., p. 31) and already at a very early period every melody had a special name . . . The priests and theologians certainly did not invent all these melodies themselves.   The oldest of them were presumably popular melodies, to which in very early times semi-religious songs were sung at solstice celebrations and other national festivals, and yet others may date back as far as that noisy music with which pre-brahmanical wizard-priests not unlike the magicians, *saman*s and medicine-men of the primitive peoples, accompanied their wild songs and rites. Traces of this popular origin of the *saman*-melodies are seen already in the above-mentioned *stobha*s or shouts of joy, and especially in the fact that the melodies of the *Samaveda* were looked upon as possessing magic power even as late as in brahmanical times.

20. Winternitz, op cit, p. 147, footnote.

The primary meaning of *saman* is probably 'propitiatory song', 'a means for appeasing gods and demons'. The word *saman* also occurs in the sense of mild, soothing words. In the older literature, when the *Saamaveda* is quoted, it is usually with the words : "The Chandogas say." Chandoga means Chandas singer, and *chandas* combines in itself the meanings 'magic song', 'sacred text' and 'metre'. The fundamental meaning of the word must be something like 'rhythmical speech'; it might be connected with the root *chand*, to please, to satisfy or to cause to please, (of *chand*, 'pleasing, alluring, inviting').

21. Mukherjee, Amulyadhan, Sanskritmadhil Chandaanchaa Ekaa Navin Drishtikonatun Abhyas, *Praachin Bhaaratiya Vidyeche Punardarshan*, ed. Dandekar, R.N. et. al., p. 98.

22. Ibid, pp. 77-78.

23. *Naaradiya Shiksha*, I-7-3, 4.

24. Rawson, Philip., *The Art of Tantra*, Thames and Hudson, London, 1978, p. 211.

25. (a, b, c,.) Stutley, Margaret and James., *A Dictionary of Hinduism*, Allied Publishers Pvt. Ltd., Bombay, 1977, p. 180.

26. Macdonnell, op cit, p. 174.

27. Winternitz, op cit, p. 276.

28. Ibid, pp. 276-77.

29. Macdonnell, op cit, p. 283.

30. Winternitz, op cit, p. 409.

. . . the rhapsodists, among whom the heroic songs must have been transmitted orally during the centuries, probably took every possible liberty in the presentation of their songs: they lengthened scenes which pleased their audiences, and abridged others which made less impression. But the greatest alterations, by means of which the ancient heroic poem gradually became a compilation, which offered much and therefore every one something, can probably be explained by the fact that the transmission and preservation of the ancient heroic songs passed from the original singers to other classes, that the songs themselves were transplanted to other regions, and adapted to other times and changing public.

31. Winternitz, op cit, p. 410.

32. Macdonnell, op cit, p. 283.

33. Winternitz, op cit, p. 418.

2

Indian oral tradition
and Hindustani music

Wide range of oral tradition

There are special reasons for examining the phenomenon of oral
tradition in the Indian context.

Firstly, many features of music are directly and deeply related
to oral tradition. In India, oral tradition has significantly influenced the education, performance, creation, appreciation as well as
propagation of music.

Oral tradition assumes greater importance in the Indian context
because it is not confined to music: this is the second reason for
its discussion. Oral tradition in India is found to play noteworthy
roles in arts such as literature and drama; in disciplines such as
philosophy, *Aayurveda*, *Yoga*, linguistics, grammar, as also in areas
of day to day life such as administration of justice, education and
civic administration.

The variety of areas in which oral tradition remains active is
sufficient to persuade social thinkers to take a close look at it. In
fact, every ameliorative move is likely to remain fruitless unless the
total make-up of the societal psyche is taken into consideration
before chalking out strategies of reform. In the Indian context
therefore, the oral tradition must be understood as a legitimate
and powerful philosophy of life possessing contemporary relevance.
References made here to the historical aspect of the tradition
should not be misinterpreted as an instance of the historicist
fallacy. Oral tradition is shown here to have a history because
continuation is the essence of tradition. History is not quoted here
at the cost of or as a substitute for contemporary validity and

modern relevance. In fact, the author is inclined to believe that *the oral tradition is a living cultural force.* We cannot overlook phenomena like information-explosion, mass-media-impact and the growing interactions of the formerly isolated human groups. In all these factors oral communication (alongwith its parent-tradition) is important.

In the case of India, following the oral tradition is also expedient. The Indian scene today is not very encouraging in respect of the spread of literacy and reformist attitudes. In view of the size of the country and the continued population growth, our efforts to become a largely literate nation may succeed only in the distant future. However, it is not necessary to tie up pro-reform attitude with total literacy. Even though literacy-level does not reach the required standards, progressive thinking can be propagated by resorting to the oral tradition.

And if we could envisage a situation wherein the tools provided by the print-culture and the oral tradition could be combined, our literacy drives and the adult education programmes are sure to gain in efficacy.

To sum up, our educational methods and the institutional set-ups, intended to bring about cultural upliftment, must find a place for the oral tradition. Unfortunately, we seem to be witnessing today a curious spectacle in which attempts are made to impose a written culture on a *societal mind that is well-tuned to oral culture.* Probably, we forget that to lay down literacy as a pre-condition for being progressive is also an instance of being superstitious!

Against this background, to ignore the claims of the oral tradition as a strategy in our programmes of all-round development is a serious mistake. Those who make constant references to total revolution, comprehensive reforms and deeper societal change will do well to give a thought to oral tradition.

To an extent, the foregoing remarks were made *en passant* but they provide the necessary background for our immediate concern: to study the relationship of the oral tradition in general and a specific musical manifestation in India, that is, Hindustani music.

There is an easily understandable propriety in the musician's lead to put forward a strong plea, advocating an active role for the oral tradition. In modern times the need to stress the quality-aspect in thinking, planning and execution has been repeatedly voiced. Music in India follows the oral tradition precisely because of its *pronounced quality-orientation* which results from the interpersonal aspect inherent in it. Music thus indicates a resolve for upholding quality and resisting in the process the pressure of sheer numbers which alarmingly obfuscates our vision.

Towards definition

How are we to define oral tradition? Of course the phenomenon has been widely noticed and defined. Before consulting these well-established definitions, some preliminary remarks may be essential in the light of our approach.

Firstly, many, who discuss oral tradition today, operate with an anthropological bias: as a consequence, the non-art and the non-aesthetic aspects of culture get a wide scope. This is logical as the anthropologist's aim is to examine the total fabric of life. However, it cannot be denied that due to this stance, the two main cultural endeavours, namely, the aesthetic and the ethical, receive a rather sparse treatment. Of the two, the aesthetic thinking has, in addition, remained largely 'bookish'. As a result, oral tradition is considered by the anthropologists only in parts; and it has been practically ignored by the aestheticians. The thrust of the established definitions should not therefore be accepted too readily.

Secondly, the anthropologists, very frequently, tend to bracket oral tradition with pre-literate or folk cultures. It is sheer prejudice to confine possession of culture to the literate and equate the pre-cultured state with the non-literate. A deeper look into the origin, development and function of the oral tradition does not allow such a negative presumption. When we are confronted with cultures such as that of India, oral tradition is not necessarily linked with folk-culture. It is desirable to avoid unjustifiable restrictions on the scope of the oral tradition. This should convince us of *its potentialities in contexts that are both modern and sophisticated*. This tradition is important *because* it answers some basic human needs; because there are intrinsic bonds between creativity and oral tradition.

In this context, the five definitions taken from various sources, may be considered.

☐ Tradition which is the cumulative social heritage in the form of habits, customs, attitudes and ways of life is transmitted from generation to generation either through written scriptures or through word of mouth. The tradition transmitted through word of mouth is called the oral tradition.[1]

S. L. Srivastava

☐ Oral tradition is now defined as verbal testimony transmitted from one generation to the next one or a later one.[2]

Jan Vansina

☐ Oral poetry is poetry composed in oral performance by people who cannot read or write. It is synonymous with traditional and folk poetry . . . All oral poetry is sung, or, at the very least, chanted . . .[3]

Alex Preminger

☐ . . . for it is a strange phenomenon in India, from the oldest times, up till the present day, the spoken word and not writing has been the basis of the whole of the literary and scientific activity . . . The written text can at most be used as an aid to learning, as a support to the memory, but no authority is attributed to it. Authority is possessed only by the spoken word of the teacher . . . The works of the poets too, were in India never intended for readers but always for hearers. Even the modern poets do not desire to be read, but their wish is that their poetry may become an adornment for the throats of the experts.[4]

M. Winternitz

☐ The Vedic system of oral teaching . . . was the only authoritative system to be pursued through the subsequent ages in spite of all material facilities they might bring in their course . . .There was a traditional opinion absolutely condemning the acquisition of knowledge from written sources.[5]

R. K. Mookerji

The definitions cited above are illustrative of representative positions, concerning the scope and nature of the oral tradition. It is logical that definitions from Indian authorities are comparatively scarce and recent. A culture truly believing in the oral tradition can hardly be expected to document its definition unless it is confronted with a need to do so. However, even though a

society does not define its faith it can live according to it. This
has been so with Indian society which continues to function according to the norms laid down by the oral tradition. Thus the uses
are the proofs of definitions. Usages which follow the oral tradition are to be detected in different walks of life in India. Various
characteristics of the oral tradition are exemplified in various
areas of life. A careful examination of the seemingly isolated
instances of the oral tradition in operation certainly reveals a
pattern. It functions as a mode of communication understood in
a wider sense. Knowledge of this phenomenon helps us to understand its potentials, even in the modern context.

Oral tradition : the chief characteristics

1. Prestige of the 'word'

Perhaps the most easily discernible of the characteristics is the
significance attached to 'word' as such. (In this context a word is
to be understood as any meaningful acoustic signal forming itself
into a communicatory unit.) When a word is reduced to writing
it is transformed and the transformation is achieved with the help
of accepted signs known as letters. The point is that Indian
culture, due to its acceptance of the oral tradition, holds 'word' in
high regard in its unwritten form.

For example:

☐ In day-to-day life, interpersonal relationships are controlled
by the act of giving one's word as a promise etc. In the near
past, promises were given and received with great faith in their
meaningfulness for the giver and reliability for the receiver. It
is known that till 1870 an orally made 'will' was not considered
illegal and invalid.[6] Even today, oath-taking or swearing-in
etc. carry significance.

☐ Oral communications and undertakings were guarantees of
completion of transactions.[7]

☐ Literary art came into being as a manifestation of voice or
vaak and was received and appreciated as such. The term
saahitya, understood today as synonymous with 'literature' did
not gain currency till the seventh century.[8]

☐ In religion, basic texts were recognized as expressions of
vaak; the deities in charge of learning and arts are described as
expressing themselves through vaak; and theological and philosophical thinking largely developed through the medium of

discussion. Even today *keertan* (i.e., musico-philosophical discourse), *puraana* (i.e., narrative of mythological tales), *pravachana* (i.e., philosophical lectures) are pervasive modes of communication, representing a strong current in the total oral tradition.

The two main architects of the Science of Longevity (i.e., *Aayurveda*, the indigenous system of medicine in India) were Vaagbhat and Sushruta. The names carry unmistakable reference to oral tradition.

2. *The oral and the aural*

It is common knowledge that articulation and hearing of sound are physiologically interdependent processes. Oral tradition exemplifies this mutual dependence through its insistence on the importance of the listener's role. It makes a critical distinction between hearing and listening, laying stress on attention as the factor that distinguishes listening from hearing.

It is therefore not surprising that oral tradition holds the audience almost in veneration. From saint-poets like Dnyaneshwar to actor-singers like Balgandharva, all have repeatedly referred to the invaluable contribution of the audience. The audience is patron, participant, critic, inspirer, all rolled into one. The high status enjoyed by the audience is obviously due to the essential oral-aural nature of the oral tradition. The underlying logic perhaps needs a brief explanation.

Due to their physiological interdependence both hearing and articulation processes are granted significant places in the oral tradition. In the present context articulation consists of speaking and singing.

Further, the process of listening is made concrete through a specific material agency, the audience. It stands to reason that objectivised in this manner, the audience becomes worthy of a separate treatment. In fact the qualifications of good auditors have been minutely described. In the absence of qualified listeners, the oral tradition is bound to fail as an efficient channel of communication. All those belonging to the performing tribe—speakers, actors, musicians, dancers—have realized time and again that the quality of their presentation depends a great deal on the quality of the auditors who are the receivers. To that extent and in that sense, performing arts are 'dependent beauties'. This is clearly in contrast to literary and fine arts.

In addition to a detailed discussion of a 'qualified' listener, the oral tradition prescribes norms of behaviour the audience is expected to follow in a concert etc. These norms mainly relate to the modes of expressing approval/disapproval of a performance. To a great extent, this is the manner in which any audience can become an active constituent in the total performing process which is ultimately expected to lead to aesthetic experience. Audience is a participant with a definite function to discharge and a matching code of conduct. Had it been regarded merely as a passive entity undergoing an experience, the deliberate laying down of norms of behaviour would have been unwarranted. As early a work as *Naatyashaastra* had discussed this aspect with customary thoroughness. Referring to the judges of a drama-competition, the *Naatyashaastra* points out that the judges have to take into consideration the response of the audience in order to evaluate the quality of a performance. Bharata has enumerated the ways and means in which the audience registers its responses.[9]

It is interesting to note that even today very similar channels are used for expressing responses to a work experienced. The existence of norms to govern the audience is unmistakably evident.

For example, contemporary *mushaira*s (meets of poets composing in Urdu)[10], *kavi sammelan*s (meets of poets composing in Hindi)[11] are eloquent instances where the audience contributes by its participation and further, where participation is governed by definite, though unwritten norms. Tandon's description of the traditional story-telling offers another example of how an auditor is assigned a definite role in order to complete the communication-process which a story-teller is trying to realize.[12]

The twin-processes of articulation and hearing need a coordinated *avataar* in the oral tradition. This is the reason why an elaborate code of conduct emerges to deal with the question: how to listen?

3. Co-existence with the 'written'

Quite often it is incorrectly suggested that the oral tradition rules out the existence of writing and the written, by definition. The oral and the written are regarded as mutually exclusive; and as a consequence it is erroneously held that the oral tradition necessarily prospers when

    a) writing, printing, etc., are not possible, or

   b) when writing, etc., is not known to a particular culture, or

   c) when the particular culture in question finds the writing-methods, etc., extremely difficult to execute and hence turns to them very rarely.

This point of view is obviously vitiated by an either/or attitude which is hardly justifiable. Such an attitude excludes the possibility of a group's deliberate choice of the oral mode of communication in preference to the written mode in spite of the fact that the group possesses the requisite knowledge and technique of writing. There are circumstances where the choice is therefore to be interpreted as an instance of a communal cultural preference for one particular mode out of the many at its disposal. The decision is a cultural strategy which in itself is an outcome of a prolonged collective thinking that takes into consideration factors like relative need of the various social strata for written records, pervasiveness and currency of the prevailing symbolism, efficacy of one or more languages in meeting the needs of inland and international commerce and other channels of exchange.

It is clear that the mounting evidence of Asian cultures underscores the co-existence of the oral tradition and writing. The strategy adopted by these cultures is based on the conviction that the process of writing tends to reduce the quality of learning. Further, it is believed that dependence on writing and silent reading leads to a diluted mastery over any subject. Finally, the underlying faith firmly regards information and knowledge to be two separate entities and holds that the former is sustained through the written and the latter through the oral tradition. This is the reason why the oral tradition in India perfected a communication mode which assigned specific though limited tasks to writing and the written. However, the process of writing and the written versions were both viewed as secondary because communication of content which could take place through these was not considered truthful, adequate and durable. Therefore, the use of writing and books was not indiscriminately prohibited but it was unambiguously restricted to *storage of information* and skeletal knowledge. Books were accepted and respected but not as equal partners of the oral communication in the total activity. They were allowed as memory-aids or as devices of checking distortions. Their claims as shortcuts to knowledge were firmly rejected. Permeation with the subject or art studied was the ultimate aim, and *recourse to writing was an accessory procedure.* There is no reason to suspect that dependence on the oral tradition is or was an act resulting from any inability or cultural helplessness.

4. *The guru*

Emergence of *guru* as an institution and his supremacy in the oral tradition is a cumulative effect of the three features discussed earlier, namely, significance of word, importance of listening and the audience, and finally, the coexistence of the written-oral. It is the *guru* who transforms word-meanings into content, converts information into knowledge and replaces isolated facts with related, coherent wholes. It is to be remembered that all these critical actions or procedures are to be flexibly applied according to the capacity, requirements, etc., of the individual recipient. This is the reason why a *guru's* role is not confined to the field of education alone. In fact, oral tradition holds the entire act of communication as a process that seeks to percolate to the unconscious levels of those who receive. Seen in this perspective, the *guru* comes forth as a force that operates in a framework much wider than the one available to a teacher. In correspondence to the *guru's* wide framework, a disciple also works in a perspective larger than the one available to a student. As a consequence, what transpires between a *guru* and his *shishya* is qualitatively different from what usually takes place in a teacher-student relationship. Oral tradition does not fail to accord recognition to this unique relationship which elevates a transaction or an exchange into a communication and at the same time aims at transmuting facts into information, information into knowledge and knowledge into deeper insight.

The elevated stature of the entire process as well as the extraordinary role assigned to the institution of *guru* is illustrated in the following features of the Indian context:

* The *guru* is regarded to be so comprehensive an entity that both God and the parents are described to have been accomodated in him.

* It was laid down that a *guru* is not to accept money from his disciples. A disciple can give his *guru* only an offering, i.e., *dakshinaa.*

* Every disciple is expected to 'serve' his *guru.* In this context, to serve means to offer *sevaa,* a very inclusive concept. Thus what a disciple is supposed to offer to his *guru* is as abstract as that which

is imparted to the disciple by the *guru*. In both cases, equally intangible entities are being dealt with; hence the relationship is pitched on a nearly metaphysical plane.

5. *The* sootra *way*

It is difficult to translate the term *sootra*. In a broad sense, it means 'a versified formula'. Oral tradition preserves and passes on the 'content' by using such formulae. In order to understand how . a *sootra* operates, it is helpful to examine its structure.

The first thing that strikes one about a *sootra* is that it is never self-explanatory. Communication of content of a *sootra* is never complete unless it is enunciated as well as explained. Oral tradition further ensures that the explanation is provided through the medium of discussion. In other words, a *sootra* in itself is only a text which supplies the basis of discussion expected to take place between the educated and the educator. As it flows between two individuals, the discussion changes in tenor according to the nature, need and quality of participation of the disciple involved.

In a way, the *sootra* is the foundation on which the structure of the *guru-shishya* dialogue is raised. (In the present context 'dialogue' appears to be a better term than discussion as the former brings out clearly the personality-orientation of the activity involved.) A *sootra* is designed to contain the basic, the unchangeable and the universal while the explanation is to take care of the corollories, the subjective and the incidental. It follows that a *sootra* can afford to being subjected to the process of writing which is an impersonalized method of storage, while the explanation has to be received from the *guru*. *Sootra*s consist of conclusions as they form the final and the stable part of any communication. On the other hand, the explanations are the haven of variable and less permanent portions of all communication.

Apart from the nature of the content of a *sootra*, the way a *sootra* is formulated also needs attention. Firstly, though *sootra*s vary in length, they generally tend to be short. In most cases, a *sootra* can boast of possessing an acoustic attraction because of its pronounced use of assonance, alliteration, rhyme and other similar devices. In addition, *sootra*s are so grouped together that sequence and classification of the thought-structures are reflected in the grouping. In this manner if the content of a *sootra* holds appeal for the intellect, the way it is composed could be said to have an appeal to the ear as well as to the phonating mechanism. The sound-patterns perform this double-duty admirably.

It is evident that a *sootra* is designed to accommodate the total idea in a seed-form; the full development of the idea is expected to emerge only through the inter-personality exchanges made possible through the *guru-shishya* dialogues. Hence a *sootra* simultaneously proves to be an indication of the importance of the *guru* and a confirmation of the significant role played by the faculty of memory in oral tradition.

6. *Memory and the oral tradition*

It has been seen that *sootras* function as centres created to facilitate the focussing of intellection. Therefore, *sootras* need memorizing to enable the explanations to come up as and when required. According to oral tradition, isolated facts serve no useful purpose unless they appear as members of the total complex of related ideas. It is also deemed necessary that the ideas are not divested of their emotional associations and colourings when they come into action. In all probability the vague but unfailing association of sounds with emotions is exploited in the *sootra*-construction to complement its intellectual substance. The point is that even though *sootras* analyse the knowable in the interests of comprehension, the knowable is not allowed to disintegrate while being brought into action. Knowledge is not to be compartmentalized and the emotional (as well as the non-rational) aspect must be allowed to play its part in the process of knowing. The *sootra*-way, combined with the operation of memory, attempts to ensure that knowledge is imparted both as a segmental and a total reality.

In this context, it is logical that mnemonic aids and methods of developing memory should constitute an inevitable part of the oral tradition. The following features of the oral tradition are worth noting in this respect.

☐ Repetition is accorded a high place in study-procedures. What is more, it is laid down that repetition is not to be practiced at random. Detailed instructions are given as to how the device of repetition is to be employed. It is interesting to note that *abhyaas* means repetition in Sanskrit: today it means 'study' in most of the regional languages. It is obvious that the intrinsic relationship between repetition and study is reflected in the usage.

☐ Features like gestures, symbols, etc., are also pressed into service as mnemonic aids. However, these remain outside the scope of the oral tradition in its exact literal connotation.

☐ In order to heighten the importance of memory, external sanctions are invoked in the case of memory-lapses. For example, forget-
fulness is regarded as a sin or equated with the loss of professional
prestige, or with lack of proper education, etc. God's displeasure,
self-imposed punishments and penance, ridicule of others, etc., constitute the other authorized sanctions.

☐ Subtler strategies are also used. For example, the item to be
memorized is temporarily removed from its original context and
repeated in a different framework. Thus the item acquires an
additional mnemonic co-ordinate and as a consequence is firmly
entrenched.

7. Ritualism

The oral tradition displays definite leanings towards ritualism. It
is expressed through the insistence that recitation and other para-
mount manifestations follow the norms laid down regarding the
manner, temporal placement, gestural accompaniment or similar
external parameters. Ritualism is expected to ensure that the oral
tradition gets particularized in each of its multiple aspects. If and
when developed in this manner, the oral tradition becomes more 'real'
vis-a-vis other life-forms. The physio-mental action through which
ritualism seeks to operate is known as samskaara, a term which
has great prestige in the oral tradition. Ritualism carries out the
twin-task of registering an impact on the conscious and effect a
permeation of the unconscious in a synchronous move. As a help
in completing this complicated psychological manoeuvre, other
action-areas like the wearing of dresses, seating-arrangements, per-
formance-timings, and the like are also rigidly controlled while
they accompany recitation, etc. In a way these areas are loosely
related to the act of recitation itself. Yet they are sought to be
controlled because the entire drive is towards creating an overall
atmosphere conducive to the specific act performed. The primary
motive is to achieve an efficient concentration of all helpful factors
drawing on them from other seemingly unrelated or indirectly
related life-areas. The role of ritualism in general is to channelize
the psychological forces, not otherwise accessible. The realm of
ritualism begins where the reign of explanations, guidance, verbalization, writing, etc., ends. No human activity is totally realized through intelligibility, rationality and objectivity. If one
is to grapple with the total reality, emotivity, contradiction and
subjectivism must be granted the place they deserve in the total

life-pattern. Ritualism is employed to reconcile forces that are apparently contradictory.

8. *The prestige of sound*

Sound enjoys an elemental importance in the oral tradition. It is therefore valued in its essence, as well as in its various physical manifestations. For our purpose, language and music are the two major sound-generated expressions that need examination. Due to their common regard for the generic principle of sound, both language and music are found to use a large number of identical terms of major import.

In the Indian context, the following facts are noteworthy:

☐ The Sanskrit alphabet is accepted as an excellent example of highly and subtly developed phonology. This would not have been possible without holding the principle of sound in high critical esteem.[13]

☐ Prakrit languages are influenced by a musical inclination in their very formation.

On account of the comprehensive oral tradition both the Sanskrit and the Prakrit manifestations held the spoken word in high esteem. As a consequence, classical Sanskrit (also) came to prefer adjectives to verbs; and the Prakrit languages displayed extreme metrical flexibility. These aspects are traceable to the prestige enjoyed by sound *per se*.

☐ Oral tradition and the prestige accorded to sound both logically lead to a *mantra*-culture. It is known that in *mantras*, meaningfulness soon ceases to be an indispensable quality. In *mantras* it is the hypnotic property of sound that is sought to be exploited to its fullest.[14]

9. *Multiplicity of communicators*

The multiplicity or the variety found among communicators is a factor of considerable importance in the oral tradition. It is the variety of communicators which proves the richness of the oral tradition. The variety exists because the tradition evolves over a period and covers a large number of specialized categories of practitioners. It is inevitable because the tradition is operative in a number of diverse areas and each of these areas has numerous specific claims on the tradition. In addition to the overall numerous claims, there are different sub-species of demands too. As a consequence, a reasonable division of labour is formalized. Further, the tradition also develops particular techniques of communication in accordance with the functions associated with a particular area. Thus religion, arts, judiciary and such other areas have different communicators acting according to their own particular norms. According to their respective functions these communicators evolve specific techniques of communication. The roles of specialization and division of labour are thus clearly demarcated.

Combined with specialization, the variety of communicators achieves two things. Firstly, due to the greater number of participants involved in the process, the variety makes it possible to maintain a considerable degree of authenticity regarding its manifold aspects. In addition, counterchecking the authenticity of each of the individual components becomes practicable. In a way, this is what makes it possible to transmit the total experience to posterity. An experience is rich only if it is structured with diverse and multiple facets of reality. The experiential richness is greatly ensured when experience is passed on to the receiver as a total package. Depletion in quality is avoidable only if the experience is passed on as a whole. Secondly, the division of labour and the accompanying specialization also secure greater participation and social involvement. A majority of persons and agencies come to enjoy a sense of belonging. Each of the participants has a definite and meaningful place in the execution of the total activity and the result is significant from the angle of social cohesion.

Oral tradition in Hindustani music
The chief characteristics of the oral tradition have been so far described in a general perspective. Some interesting examples from the Indian life-context have also been briefly dealt with. However, our chief concern is to examine the tradition of Hindustani music in this context. The general features obtain specific reinforcements from the world of music because music in India is one of the major expressions of the oral tradition.
1. Importance of the word
Word of mouth is revered in Hindustani music. Therefore notation is employed only in respect of composition-skeletons: nothing comparable to a musical score (as understood in the Western tradition of music) exists in Indian music. In view of the reliance on improvisation (elaboration of the basic musical material)

notation becomes a virtual impossibility. It is of course simplistic to maintain that notation becomes irrelevant because Hindustani music is too complicated to be reduced to the notating activity. With greater validity it could be held that trying to write down musical nuances is likely to hamper the spontaneous element which breathes through Hindustani music. It is of interest to note that all attempts to subject Hindustani musical elaboration to notation were made only after the advent of British rule.

It seems that during the modern period, workers in the field of culture were pulled in two opposite directions. Due to the nascent nationalism they often tended to hold that Indian culture was too sophisticated, etc., to be encompassed by Western concepts and methods. For instance, it was argued that music of India possessed such qualities of excellence, subtlety, etc., that it could not be notated (unlike the conquerer's Western music). On the other hand, it was also felt that Indian superiority could hardly be proved unless Indians performed everything that the 'whites' did. Hence the Indian musician's claims to high status could hardly be substantiated unless he carried out everything that his Western counterpart achieved. Hence, from the latter half of the nineteenth century we encounter attempts of elaborate notation of Hindustani music. Maulabux Ghise Khan (Baroda, the 1890s), Pandit Vishnu Digambar (Maharashtra, the 1890s) and such other personalities easily come to mind in this context. A similar situation prevailed in respect of positions which the Hindustani musicians adopted in matters like resorting to the principle of harmony, use of orchestration, utility of institutionalized music-education, etc.

2. Significance of listening

Listening is considered vital to the study and performance of music. For example, *swarasaadhanaa* consists of early-morning exercises of a vocalist. *Swarasaadhanaa* is chiefly confined to the lower octave and a special feature of it is the time mandatorily allowed to elapse between the completion of emitting one single note and the beginning of the subsequent. The intervening time-span is meant for concentrated listening of the drone. Another telling example is the phenomenon known as *aas*. *Aas* can be defined as a lingering tonefulness of a musician who has virtually ceased to produce the tone or sound in question. A musician who excels in this effect is rated high. Abrupt or staccato effect does not enjoy good reputation in Hindustani music because continuity is regarded as central. It is obvious that the *aas*-effect essentially involves alert listening both on the part of the musicians as well as the audience. It is also common knowledge that Hindustani musicians keep a premium on '*kaan taiyaar karnaa*' (to prepare one's ears). The 'preparation' naturally refers to a high degree of receptivity or sensitivity expected of every musician. It is significant that as ancient a text as *Dattilam* (c. 200 A.D.) lists *avadhaana* (that is, hearing accompanied by attention) as an important component of *Gaandharva* music.[15]

Equally noteworthy are the attempts of the Hindustani music-world to secure the right type of listeners. In fact all efforts of organized music-listening are directed to enable the performers to give their best. It is to be understood that court-concerts, ticketed concerts, music circles, music conferences etc. constitute in reality mechanisms created deliberately for channelizing listeners of high quality. The underlying logic is simple: listeners participate in music-making and therefore good listeners are to be necessarily collected into a receptive gathering which an audience is supposed to be.

3. Co-existence

In a manner of speaking, oral tradition is like an unwritten constitution. That is, it emphasizes the unwritten, relies on it, but hardly imposes a blanket ban on writing and the written. It consistently proclaims the primacy of the oral and the unwritten, though their opposites are not voted out of existence. For instance, Hindustani musical tradition *does* accommodate writing down of composition-skeletons (e.g., *cheez*s, *paltaa*s, *alankaar*s as well as *bol, paran*). It even encourages writing down of elaboration-sketches of certain *raag*s. Tomes comprising these are handed down from generation to generation. The written volumes are carefully preserved and extreme secrecy is maintained about their very existence. Sons of the musicians or their favoured disciples are allowed access to these 'treasures'. However, the point is that these documents are utilized only to aid the musician's memory. They are regarded as supplementary and are held important only because they facilitate transmission of the frameworks of knowledge to posterity.

It needs to be emphasized that nothing becomes a part of the oral tradition, only by virtue of being unwritten. Hence items like instruments, amulets, cures for voice-disorders, etc., do not deserve

a place in our discussion. Orality is a decision of a certain sophistication; it remains high above items which could only claim to be
unwritten. Oral tradition is not a manifestation of superstition.

4. *The guru*

By all accounts, Hindustani musical tradition extols the *guru* in a
manner which could only be rivalled by the esteem he is held in
the fields of metaphysics, *yoga*, etc. For instance, a very high per-
centage of the *cheez*s refer to or describe the indispensable function of the *guru* and his supremacy.

It is a fundamental premise that the final authority in everything 'musical' is of the *guru*. It is assumed that every musician's
corpus is in fact determined solely by what his *guru* has taught
him. The hard core of a musician's total learning is made up of
his *guru*'s teachings. Of course, a disciple is not prohibited from
learning by listening to others, or by composing his own *cheez*s, etc.
But the potency of this latter portion of his corpus is however
invariably suspected. Unless learnt from the *guru*, a disciple is
hardly allowed to claim authenticity for his learning: a *guru* is the
ultimate sanction behind everything that a disciple is inclined to
include in his effective repertoire. This is the reason why the
philosophy of *gharaanaa*s has *guru* as the point of musical conver-
gence. Every *ghaaranaa* is represented in its totality by the *guru*:
it is this which enables his disciples to belong to the inner and
self-sufficient subtraditions existing within the larger framework of
the oral tradition in music.

Generally speaking one cannot become a *guru* by heredity.
*Guru*ship is not an empty honour but an authority to be earned.
*Guru*s can be classified. For example, those formally accepted
belong to one class, those only informally recognised and those
who are respected as *guru*s are the remaining classes. In conclusion,
*guru*ship seems to be a subjective assessment and subsequent
behaviour based on it. A disciple evaluates the existence and the
extent of benefits he receives from a particular person and if he
finds them weighty enough, *guru*ship becomes a reality.

5. *The sootra way*

Many of the directive principles that govern musical arts are
aphoristically expressed. These are instances of the *sootra* mode
in operation. Musical aesthetics, musical studies, listening as a
participating activity and such other areas of music are covered by
these *sootra*s. All participants in the music-making processes res-

pond to different contingencies. Some of these responses are verbalized, and result into *sootra*s. Taken together, the *sootra*s provide very significant examples of the common cognitive foundation of Hindustani musical heritage taken as a whole. In spite of the multiplicity of the *guru*s, disciples, *gharaanaa*s and styles, a large number of *sootra*s are almost universally referred to. Such a common reference-back becomes possible because in a majority of cases, perceptions of musical reality have been the same. As explained earlier, *sootra*s contain the essence: they become full-fledged musical insights only after the *guru* has added his explications. In all probability, an exhaustive listing of such *sootra*s will prove to be a fascinating and rewarding study of the collective mind that moves Hindustani music. Given below is a free translation of some of the *sootra*s:

1. If one is achieved, everything is achieved; if everything is achieved, all is lost.
2. Going false in beat is to lose a hair, going out of tune is to lose the head.
3. Initiation, education and examination: these are the stages.
4. You need to perfect the camel-posture if you want to realize an *aalaap*.
5. One who works, becomes a master,
   One who does not, becomes a disciple.
6. Without a voice a *raag* gets burnt up.
7. To be born with, to have an inclination to and to have a nature.
8. Those who appreciate are our slaves. We are the slaves of those who do not appreciate.
9. To a goldsmith's hundred strokes, one by a blacksmith (is equal).
10. A *guru* desires defeat from his own disciple.
11. Only a swan knows a swan's gait.
12. One should have a string (instrument) in the voice and a voice in the string (instrument).
13. The real, the imitation and the fashionable.
14. What can practice not achieve? It can parade the incorrect as the correct.
15. One who eats is the one who sings.
16. May be, may be . . . that is the name of the *raag*!
17. Every artist is good—in his own place.

18. Sing today's *yaman*, not yesterday's!
19. Fame is greater than Sanskrit.
20. Firstly to eat, then to dress and then, only then, to look after your home.
21. Oh brother: A Ghulam Ali who cannot sing is worthless.
22. Regularly singing, is the voice.
    Regularly watered, is the orchard.
23. Oh, he is only a 'learned' man!
24. The pinnacle preceding the foundation! (a *taan* before the *aalaap*.)
25. Significance in words.
    Significance in notes.
    and significance in significance is to be created.
26. Pure *raag*, nay, realized *raag*.
27. Do grind, but do not pulverize.

Another interesting instance of the *sootra*-way is the *dohaa*. *Dohaa* is a popular metre in which a great number of saint-poets have composed. *Dohaa*s are employed in Hindustani musical tradition to versify the *raag*-grammar. No doubt, grammatical information of a *raag* is also stored in *lakshanaa geet* (i.e., songs describing characteristics of a particular *raag* composed in the same *raag*). However, the difference between the two is easily discernible. As the *lakshanaa geet* is a tune it is more musical but cannot care for the *raag*-mood, etc., because its main function is to store information. On the other hand, *dohaa* is a step away from mere prose but it has no musical role to perform; hence it is recited. Another metrical mould like *aaryaa* with its minimal musical contours is also used in a similar manner.[16] To an extent, the oral tradition makes the *sootra*-way slightly more musical as exemplified by *dohaa*s and the *aaryaa*s. The *sootra*s are nearer to prose than the *dohaa*s which through recitation remain midway between prose and *lakshanaa geet*.

6. *Mnemotechny and Hindustani music*

In Hindustani music what is written down amounts to a mere skeleton of the total musical reality. All the elaboration-moulds are remembered; the actual elaboration is improvised. Where a major portion of the elaboration is written down (e.g., in respect of developed rhythm instruments like *tablaa*, *pakhaawaj*, etc.) improvisation is reduced almost to nil. Examples indicating the role of memory and memory-aids may be cited :

☐ Musicians of the older order used to devote a full night every week merely to reel off the skeleton-compositions of *raag*s in their repertoire. This was known as *aavrutti* (lit. repetition).

☐ Another practice was to recite a musical composition as if it was 'prose'. Thus changing the original musical context, the song-text was temporarily isolated and could therefore become an item of concentrated attention, so helpful in memorization.

☐ Almost as a rule, *sthaayi* and *antaraa* the two main halves of *cheez*s today, are made to rhyme. Sometimes even the word-groups at the end of both these parts are kept the same, as end-rhymes are an aid to memory.

7. *Ritualism*

Rituality is consciously employed in the practice, teaching or making of Hindustani music. The aim is to achieve maximum and efficient concentration of both physical and psychological forces active at various levels of the human psyche. Some of the ritualistic features occurring regularly in musical behaviour are indicated below:

i) Gestures and movements are heavily stylized.

ii) Definite external conditions (in fact special environments) are insisted upon.

iii) Whether in practice, teaching or music-making, rules about time-music associations are laid down and adhered to.

iv) By singing or performing for the *guru* or a particular deity, etc. a special type of psychological equipoise or co-ordination is sought to be achieved.

v) Though rarely, specific items of musical behaviour are also associated with *mantra*s, *mudraa*s or *aasanaa*s.

vi) Ceremonial goal-setting and an equally ceremonial task-completion are ritually executed. These seem to follow sacramental models.

Some of the well-established ritualistic features in musical behaviour are *gandaa-bandhan, chillaa, aavrutti, Saraswati-poojaa, guru-pournimaa*.

One side-observation may be made here. Musical ritualism is not religion-based though its peripheral factors might exhibit a bias of a particular religion.

8. *Prestige of the* naada-*principle*

If anything can be singled out as 'the most relevant material' of music, it is sound. Hence the hierarchical prestige of sound is unequivocally described. *Naada* (that is, sound) is often described as *naadabrahma* (that is, *brahma*—the supreme being). Almost as a corollary, music is also set forth as *naada-vidyaa*, that is, the study of sound. Texts of musical compositions very often express the musical problem faced by any musician in a metaphorical manner. According to them the problem faced by a musician is : how to cross the ocean of sound! The same concern is shown in a less figurative manner in other compositions which enumerate the stages in which pure sound is processed in order to transform it into Hindustani music. For example, one of the *khayaal* compositions refers to the following successive stages: infinite sound, sweet sound, musically useful sound, *graama*, note (*swara*), *taan*.

Yet another proof of the reputation which the principle of sound enjoys is obtained in the numerous terms used to describe subtle varieties of sounds. It becomes essential to differentiate between sound-tints because recipients of a particular culture are not content with primary levels of experience as well as the accompanying verbalization. As a general rule, every language-culture seeks to strike a balance between terminology and the related experience. The basic strategy aims at avoiding both the extremes—excessive terminology and inadequate verbalization. Terminological surfeit is the result of an overreliance on the bookish tradition of learning while deficiency of verbalization follows in the wake of unjustifiable lack of analytical activity. It must be admitted that since the thirteenth century or thereabouts, musical thinking in India has erred on the latter count.

However, there are sufficient terms in currency today to hold that Hindustani musicians do exhibit discrimination through the terms connected with the *naadatatva*. For example, terms like *avaari*, *zaar*, *band*, *khulaa*, *jhankaar*, *laakadi*, etc., suggest a close scrutiny of the *naada*-phenomenon and perception of its subtler shades.

A clear echo of the qualitative discrimination of the sounds heard in day-to-day life is also evident in the traditional eight-fold division of sound. In brief, the eight divisions are:

1. *Ghosh:* Sound one hears while one's ears are plugged with fingers.
2. *Raav:* Sound produced from a broken metal pot.
3. *Swana:* Sound produced by a bamboo with a hole in it.
4. *Shabda:* Any articulation that produces a noticeable sound.

5. *Sphuta:* A sound that results from an activity which diffe-
rentiates phonemes, morphemes, sentences, etc.

6. *Dhwani:* Sound caused by the vina-string tuned in the fifth.

7. *Jhankaar:* Sound produced by strumming of the above mentioned string.

8. *Jhankrit :* Shrill and blasting sound.

The famous sonar distinctions of the metaphysical category,
aahata and *anaahata,* are not relevant here.

Even today, timbre is the least studied of the sound-dimensions.
Under the circumstances, the finer distinctions discussed above
appear impressive. Moreover they support the observation that
sound *per se* is a cherished principle. It was carefully examined so
as to yield finer distinctions.

9. Multiplicity of communicators

Comparatively speaking, this seems to be a feature that is fast
vanishing from the Hindustani musical soundscape.

Communicators in general are carriers of tradition: they discharge
two main functions. They bring about a complete evolution of a
specialized expression and effect a division of labour aimed at the
transmission of the totality of experience.

The melodic nature of Hindustani music plays an important role
in this respect. Due to its melodic nature Hindustani music tends
to emphasize only one of the two musical strands (that is, the tonal
and the rhythmic) in a particular performance. However the strand
which is not in central operation continues to be active in providing a reference-frame. For instance, in a vocal solo, the
tablaa-player supplies a steady reference-frame of *taala* while in
the *tablaa*-solo, the *sarangi* or the harmonium player does the same
on a melodic plane. What is pertinent here is that in earlier days
the task was delegated to a separate agent: he was called *taalpaani.*
The independent assignation and designation bring out the multiplicity of communicators referred to. In the changing situation
more and more overlaps are experienced in this respect. (For instance, a vocalist tends today to accompany himself on instruments
like *swaramandal.*)

A yet more obvious illustration of the phenomenon under discussion is available in early Indian history. Functions like reciting geneology, narrating stories, singing praise of kings or patrons
were assigned to separate individuals and the persons concerned
specialized in their respective musical modes. The following

instances are revealing:

Vaitaalik: A singer of verses appropriate to the time of the day and one who also uses appropriate *raag*s, etc.

Bandi: A singer of praise of a family.

Naandimangal paathak: A reciter of verses pleasing to the king and auspicious for him.

Soot: A singer of verses who sings in the early morning and at bedtime.

Maagadhik: A singer of praises of persons staying with the king.

In this context, it will be easily remembered that till the recent past Hindustani musicians used to specialize in *dhrupad*, *khayaal* and *thumri*. It was assumed that to be a specialist in any of these forms meant restricting one's main (if not entire) musical activity to that particular genre. Of course this did not mean that musicians were prohibited from learning and practicing more than one form. It only meant that they had to undergo the rigorous training in each of the genres before they could claim authority to render them.

To recapitulate, we started by examining the chief characteristics of the oral tradition in the general Indian context and proceeded further to relate them to particular features of Hindustani music. However, the larger object was to make a plea as to the continued relevance of the oral tradition as a mode of communication. It is suggested here that in this respect it is still not obsolete. On account of its capacity to draw our attention to the content instead of remaining satisfied with organized information, the oral tradition proves socially significant. Under the circumstances, once we are convinced of its relevance it is imperative to effect suitable changes in educational methods and apparatus. The Indian educational system is being subjected to unnecessary tensions because there has been a blind reliance on print-culture. If the oral tradition is granted its proper place and role, it may answer our quest for quality in education.

NOTES

1. Srivastava, Sahab Lal, *Folk Culture and Oral Tradition*, Abhinav Publications, New Delhi, 1974, p. 9.
2. Vansina, *Oral Tradition : A Study in Historical Methodology*, Penguin University Books, 1973, p. xiii.
3. Preminger, Alexander S., *Princeton Encyclopedia of Poetry and Poetics*; Princeton, 1974, p. 591.

4. Winternitz, M. *A History of Indian Literature*, University of Calcutta, 1962, p. 29.
5. *Ancient Indian Education, Brahmanical and Buddhist*, Motilal Banarsidas, New Delhi, 1969, p. 211.
6. Joshi, V.K., *Hindu Dharmashastra*, Prachin Bharatiya Vidyeche Punardarshan, Vedashastrottejak Sabha, Pune, 1978, p. 254.
7. Tandon, Prakash, *Beyond Punjab*, Hind Pocket Books Ltd., New Delhi, 1971, p. 126.
    A remarkable feature of the old generation of traders was their deep sense of financial integrity. With never anything committed to paper, they trusted each other for unlimited amounts; their word was a guarantee. They seldom chose bankruptcy as the easy way out; and if they were forced to accept it, sons and grandsons have been known to honour the debts.
8. Kane, P.V., *Sahitya Darpan*, self, Bombay 1923, p. CXLI.
9. Bhat, G.K, *Bharata Natya Manjari*, Bhandarkar Oriental Research Institute, Pune, 1975, p. 250-53.
10. Private communication from Mr. Javed Akhtar, Programme Executive, Urdu Vibhag, AIR, Bombay:
    While tracing the history of the various facets of Urdu poetry it should be remembered that the tradition of Urdu poetry as such dates from the end of the sixteenth century in case of Deccani Urdu and from 1730 onwards in the case of Urdu shaped in the North.
    In the context of your query, it is interesting to note that poetry is also known as *bayaan* (description)—a word that denotes someone speaking to someone. The listener is known as *same* and he is expected to register his responses to poetry in accordance with certain norms of general behaviour and with the aid of accepted phraseology.
    Urdu poetry was not read. It was recited and the model still persists. The recitation-mode remained constant irrespective of the form of poetry involved. Poetic forms like *nazm*, *ghazal*, *rubayi*, *quaseedaa*, *rikhtaa*, *marsiyaa*, *musaddas*, *mukhammas*, *vasokhtaa*, *masnavi*, etc., are relevant in this context. These forms are chiefly classified by using the criteria of theme and the number of stanza-lines (and not by applying the criterion of metre). For example, *quaseedaa* is an eulogy to a king, *marsiyaa* is a song of grief, *masnavi* is a longish poem in couplets and *mukhammas* contains five-line stanzas. However, as far as the recitation mode is concerned, the way it was carried out in princely courts should serve as a good model for explaining the tradition.
    Court-sponsored poetry-recitations followed procedures and protocol firmly founded. The ruling prince usually occupied the chair. Some elderly person, preferably a poet, used to compere the entire programme. The seating arrangement was in Indian style, i.e., the audience sat on the carpeted floor and only the prince occupied a high seat—the *masnad*, usually green in colour. The prince's favourite poets or poet-laureate and such others ranged on his right and all the rest on the left. The poets recited in order of their seniority as well as in accordance of their general social status. Younger poets or those who had started composing poems lately were asked to recite first. The *shamaa* (flame, lamp)

was placed before the poet who was invited to recite. Though this last custom has vanished today for the obvious 'electrical' reason, many other norms like seating arrangement, order of recitation are still observed.

In the court-*mushaairaas* appreciation or disapproval used to be less vocal because court-manners and the presence of the king forbade loudness in general. Yet, verses that found favour were cheered and request for repetition, etc., was loudly made and readily honoured. The established terminology for the sort of participation suggested is briefly listed below:

Wah, wah = excellent
Mukarrar = encore
Khoob, bahut khoob = good, very good
Aapne to haq adaa kiyaa = you have done justice
Apne to shaairi ki hai = you have really composed (poetry)

The *shair* (poet) says before reciting his poems, *matlaa arz hai* (the burden of the song is submitted). Other poets and the gathering then respond by saying, *irshaad* (please recite). Similarly before reciting the last verse the poet says '*akhri sher samaa-at farmaeiye*' (please pay attention to the last verse) and the audience responds with the word *irshaad*. The last line of the verse (which consists of the *nom de plume)* is repeated by the audience and this act is called *misraa uthaanaa* (to take up the ending couplet).

The last well-known *court-mushaaira* of the traditional model took place in Delhi under the patronage of the ageing, last Moghal king Bahadurshah on the twentieth of July 1845. The king himself was a poet and his *nom de plume* was Zafar.

11. Private communication from Mrs. Saroj Chandola, Assistant Station Director, Doordarshan, Bombay:

Hindi *kavi sammelan* has evolved from a long tradition. Even in the early historical period poets and *chaarans* were patronized by kings and recitation of stray *dohaas* on erotic and ethical themes was a regular feature of court-life. The *chaarans, bhaats*, etc., also recited narrative poems describing the valour of kings, etc. These compositions were known as *raaso*-compositions.

Like *raaso, aalhaa*-compositions also belong to the recitation-tradition and they at least date back to c. 1212 *samvat*.

Aalhaa-recitation is in existence to date and it follows definite norms in the associated behaviour-pattern and presentation. Usually the *aalhaas* are sung in village-squares on winter nights. People gather there after their meals and form a circle. Dressed in white *dhoti*, shirt and *pagadi* the main singer sings and accompanies himself on a *daphali*. He moves around a lot and especially in the area where the village-elders are seated (facing eastwards). Once in a while he moves along the circle formed by the audience.

During the medieval age, recitation traditions flourished in the courts. For example, poets Gang, Abdul Rahim *Khankhaanaa* and Birbal are on record as having recited in Akbar's court. During the period 1375-1700, *bhakti* cult prospered and this too acted as a fillip to the oral tradition in poetry.

In kingly courts, poets used to stand on the right of the throne and on a lower level while reciting. *Ashtechhaap* poets of the *bhakti*-cult used to sing and perform *keertans* in temples. They performed with their backs to the audience and faced the idol. Saint-poets like Soordaas, Nanddaas, etc., used to sing in this manner. The audience used to participate and especially used to join in chorus for the burden of the song.

The period from 1700-1900 is known as *reetikaal* in Hindi literary history. The court variety of the patronage continued with the usual consequences in respect of style, theme, etc.

From 1900 onwards, Hindi poetry entered the modern age and the foundation of the modern *kavi sammelan* was laid. The legendary Bharatendu (Samvat 1907-41) used to hold them in Kashi on the occasion of the famous *Budhawaa Mangal* festival celebrated on the last Tuesday of the Hindu calendar year. The *sammelans* were arranged on decorated boats and barges floating on the waters of Ganga river.

A more modern version of the *kavi sammelan* was made possible owing to the political, social and cultural renaissance which took place in the first quarter of the present century. These *sammelans* were arranged with a missionary motive of popularizing Hindi language and literature. It is natural that universities and other cultural bodies showed initiative in organizing and shaping the *sammelans*. For example, Ratnakar Rasik Mandal, Deen Sukavi Mandal of Kashi arranged many *sammelans* successfully.

In such *sammelans*, the poets sit on the stage in a semi-circle in the Indian style, i.e., on the floor (of course covered with mattresses, etc.). White *chaddar*, called *chaandani*, is spread and cushions, etc., are also arranged. In the centre sits the senior-most, local and presiding poet flanked by other local poets on the one side and by the invited outsiders on the other side. Poets sit in order of their seniority with the younger poets occupying the outer edges of the semicircle. The presiding poet introduces each of the participants who then come forward on the stage and recite while standing up—only the presiding poet recites from his seat and while sitting. Additionally, the presiding poet recites only after the organizer duly invites him to bless the gathering with his compositions. The organizer himself recites before the president presents his compositions.

The audience sits facing the poets, on a lower level but never too far from the dais. In the early days of the *sammelan*-tradition the audience was, more often than not, quite well read and hence there was not much of 'platform-poetry' in those days. To recite subtler poetry was not a performing risk! The listeners used to send suggestions for recommended compositions on chits through volunteers specially kept roving for carrying them to the poets—and the recommendations were mostly respected.

From Bachan (b. 1907) starts the prominence of the musical element in recitation. With pronounced voice-modulation and nasality designed to sound sweeter, he used simple but varied tunes. Listeners often rightly guessed the second half of the line, etc., and used to declaim it along with the poet. Poets used to signal the repetition of their lines by appending a *to* (so) and this became an established convention of practical importance.

From 1935 onwards, the audience became more vocal in its appreciation and participation and various verbal and non-verbal signals were used to make the audience-response manifest.

Some of these responses are listed below:

Ek baar phir = once more

Ek au,r or *aur sunenge* = once more, we will listen to more, suggesting that the poet should not discontinue.

'*Jay Shankar*' and '*Bam bam bhole*' = Both are laudatory references to Lord Shiva (Shankar). These were thought of as corresponding to *subhanallah* of the Urdu *mushaira* tradition. That they did not catch on, once more brings out the secularity of the performing tradition.

Total silence, animal cries, imitation, mock weeping aloud.

Nahi sunenge = we will not listen

Baith jaaiye = sit down

Vaapas jaaiye = go back

Collective chanting of *raamdhun* will drown any other sound!

Torches with red-paper covers = disapproval

Torches with green-paper covers = approval

12. Tandon, Prakash, *Punjabi Century*, Hind Pocket Books Ltd., New Delhi, 1961, p. 71 (with reference to story-telling).

It was customary to sit in a ring in front of the story-teller, who before starting would appoint some one in the audience an *angaaraa bharnewaalaa* whose duty it was to keep the story-teller company by making suitable interjections like *yer* and then what happened, and so the prince said. As children we always competed for this task.

13. Jha, Vashistha Narayan, Shikshaa, Pratishakhya aani Dhvanivichar, *Praachin Bhaaratiya Vidyeche Punardarshan*, op.cit., pp. 77-93.

14. Stutley, Margaret and James, *A Dictionary of Hinduism, Its Mythology, Folklore and Development, 1500 B.C.-A.D. 1500*, Allied Publishers Pvt. Ltd., Bombay, 1977. pp. 180-81.

15. Dattil, *Dattilam*, (Hindi translation), Sangit Karyaalay, Hathras, 1960. p, 9, verse 3.

16. Ingale, K.G., *Gokhale Gharaaneki Gaayki*, self, Ichalkaranji, 1935, pp. 63-73.

3

Popular culture and music in India

Few concepts have attracted Indian cultural thinkers in recent years as the concept of popular culture.

One of the reasons might be that on account of its inherent inter-disciplinary nature the content of the concept borders on the amorphous. The very fact of a poorly defined content offers opportunities to interpretative freedom with an unrivalled scope.

However, in the context of music, the concept of popular culture becomes really challenging. This is so because our increased understanding of the performing arts (as distinguished from the fine and composite arts) has almost compelled us to degroove our cultural criticism and primarily achieve its disentanglement from literature-heavy conceptual structures. The task is only seemingly easy because one of the chief features of popular culture is print-dominance, and in its wake follows the bias of literature.

Added to these conceptual problems we also have to contend with the taxing claims of Indian musical situation. With its two systems of art-music, at least fifteen sets of folk-musics—tribal groups remaining largely unexplored—the sheer variety assumes a forbidding magnitude. Popular culture or its influences have touched the afore-mentioned musical expressions in varying degrees and this makes it difficult to generalize.

India is today an amalgam of simultaneous processes, operative in all areas of corporate life. For example, as a nation India is near industrialized. In more and more walks of life India is making a steady movement towards secularization. Indications of political polarization too are not missing, and *examined culturally, India is poised for a serious confrontation with the occidental.*

Hence, even a cursory exploration of a phenomenon claimed to be a symptom of modernity is bound to reward us with insights into paces of cultural development relevant not only to India but to the Third World taken as a whole. It is on this background that popular culture can be defined afresh.

Popular culture is a surface-behaviour of cultural forces discernible in a society which is only partially responsive to aesthetic stimuli. The said responses are partial mainly because of three factors: impact of mass-media, repercussions of change in patronage and an interrupted or intermittent operation of commercial and religious pressures.

In India, popular culture needs serious study because its cumulative manifestations have been instrumental in highlighting a number of conflicts: between the oral and the print-culture, between tendencies of assimilation and confrontation with alien cultures, and finally between the tendency to accentuate or to play down the contradictions existing between the theory and the practice of music. Pending adequate area-studies and sufficient field-work, it is inescapable to start the discussion by examining the impact popular culture has on the established categories of music in India, namely, art-music, folk-music and popular-music. Tribal music needs to be left out because data on this category is woefully negligible.

Art-music

According to the accepted usage in India the term 'classical' will signify art-music. However, the chronological and the art-historical overtones of the term 'classical' are likely to overshadow the aesthetico-musicological shades; hence it is deemed advisable to replace the term 'classical' by the term 'art-music'. By using it in this manner we do not imply that the other varieties of musical expression are to be treated as automatically aesthetic failures. It is only suggested that art-music is the type of music which is the least functional, avowedly the least commercial and intentionwise the most artistic of all the music-varieties. For all practical purposes Indian art-music is equated with *raag*-music. Some of the principal ways in which art-music is affected by popular culture are discussed here.

Time shrinkage

A very noticeable effect has been the shortening of the time musicians now require to unfold their musical ideas as well as for their presentation. A similar shortening is also detected in what the listeners accept as the legitimate, allowable duration desired by the artists to successfully realize their musical designs.

It is commonly known that both theoretically and customarily, concerts of Indian music and the individual items performed therein, are of indefinite duration due to the employment of improvisation and such other similar procedures. The traditional whole-night concerts and single *raag*-presentations of long duration (e.g., more than one hour, etc.) are frequently cited as instances of stretchability and indefiniteness in Indian music. It can however be argued that these features indicate how music used to be in the near past. The contemporary concert-duration has shrunk to less than three hours. There are of course festivals which still boast of all-night music, but the attendance is either poor or selective, selective also in the sense that listeners select the artist they would like to hear. For other artists the listeners are not available or they turn out to be inattentive, passive receivers. It is worth noting that Indian musicians touring the West and performing for western audiences have effected further curtailment in the concert-duration which seems to have stabilized around ninety minutes.

A similar time-shrinkage is also seen in the broadcasting of music. From its inception in India in 1927, broadcasting has been a major mass medium that has propagated art-music. It is reported that the art-musicians of the early era used to complain about the short duration allowed for their performances. However, apart from the National Programme of Music (and items of similar nature) all music-programmes broadcast from the All India Radio (A.I.R.) are today confined to a thirty-minute span. Musicians and listeners seem to have adapted themselves to the time-shrinkage. In fact, the adaptation is so smooth that the occasional grumblings heard in this respect need to be treated as voices from the past. How is one to explain the docile acceptance of the time shrinkage?

In this context it is necessary to note that temporality is an absolute prerequisite for music. Not only that music takes place in time but music is realized as music mainly because it manipulates the time-dimension. The fact that clock-time shrinkage has become possible in case of Indian music can only mean either of two things: time-shrinkage has not affected Indian art-music; or, alternatively, it has affected it so deeply that profound qualitative changes are brought about. If we accept the first position, the conventional music-presentations appear full of superfluities. Acceptance of the second possibility means that a radical alteration has taken place in Indian music. By any standard, the time-shrinkage that has taken place is drastic: it has affected all aspects like the repertoire, presentation-method and the overall aim of music-making.

However, the effect of time-shrinkage on art-music could be better explained only after we take note of a little movement to the contrary in another music-related mass-medium—the gramophone. The medium arrived in India in 1898; by 1921 recordings of art-music came into circulation in a large way. As is known, the duration of the discs has been continuously on the increase. Today with the unlimited use of magnetic tapes and casettes, there seems to be no difficulty in recording items of fuller lengths. Yet, in spite of the technical possibility and practical feasibility of recording extended musical expression, the actual recorded durations are being stabilized around the average span of thirty to forty minutes per single item. In other words, irrespective of some movement in the opposite direction, the overall tendency towards the phenomenon of time-shrinkage is confirmed.

The causal explanation of the time-shrinkage and the accompanying change in the character of Indian music is not far to seek. Along with other factors that have characterized modern life, the collective impact of the mass media has led to a predominance of the element of composing in Indian music. The term 'to compose' must be rightly understood in this connection. In the present context it means predetermined detailed and a prior decision *vis-a-vis* the content of music presented in a performance. Interpreted in this manner, composing is in direct contrast with improvisation—an element which is specially associated with Indian art-music. Art-musicians involved in the modern situation are anxious about the success they are able to achieve by emerging as 'effective' musicians in the limited time-span assigned to them— whether in broadcasting, telecasting, recording, or while participating in music-conferences, etc. This has compelled them to lay aside the traditional mode of elaborating their music. The traditional mode of musical elaboration requires that the successive musical

patterns and the corresponding musical mood-responses be conceived, executed and received respectively *while* the artist is engaged
in the process of music-making.

What is happening today is quite a different story. In place of
the fascinating process of 'composing while performing' the present-
day musician tends to take up and pursue only those musical
structures and strategies which have secured him an 'effect' in the
past. Thus he ends up by presenting music which is largely pre-
composed rather than improvised. Today we get from a musician
a cool and deliberate arrangement of effects instead of a free play
of interesting, interacting musical forces initially generated by the
artist but which gather their own momentum as music proceeds.
The traditional music-expression could be truthfully characterized
as a 'concert'—a coming together of musical ideas. Now its place
is being usurped by a 'recital'—a rendering of what is previously
learnt by heart. Memory rather than creativity is being exhibited.

Contemporary Indian musicians are prone to try to eliminate
the uncertainties of effect, congenitally bound with music allowed
to grow naturally in the traditional mode of musical elaboration.
He tends to rely more and more on sure-fire strategies that possess
proven capacity to elicit laudatory response from the audience.
The copious use of *tihaais* by Indian musicians today is very
symptomatic. *Tihaais* are rhythmic triplets which, by their very
nature, indicate calculation, pre-setting and definiteness of an expected effect on the audience. Their abundant use suggests an attitude rather than an ability.

The contemporary accent on fast tempo is also explained in the
same manner. Fast-moving *taan*-patterns in vocal music, *jhaalaa*-
playing on instruments like *sitaar, sarod, saarangi*, etc., *relaa-com-
positions in tablaa* are all very popular. Firstly, because a faster
tempo necessarily means a shortening of duration—and this
confirms the tendency towards time-shrinkage. But the more important second reason is that the faster tempo communicates a
quicker as well as an easily discernible movement towards
climactic phases of any musical progression. Fast-tempo renderings serve as unambiguous suggestions of identifiable climaxes
and function as signals possessing inbuilt answering responses.
In a way, they carry out duties of rhetorical questions in music
and seem to contain definite indications of proper and legitimate
listener-responses accepted as such. In this way listeners are

guided to socially acceptable group-behaviour. As a result, belonging to a music-oriented group becomes easier. This is the rationale
behind the enthusiastic welcome accorded to the *tihaai*s and the
fast tempo.

In sum, art-music is no longer allowed to become and remain
tantalizingly suggestive—a state of being which requires an extremely alert and a decidedly qualitative contribution from the
listeners.   With its closely woven, pre-composed texture and the
predictable ideational structure, contemporary art-music makes
lesser demands on the listeners though it succeeds in eliciting definite and predetermined responses from the audience.

The novel and repetition

Following closely on the heels of time-shrinkage are the existing
contradictory pulls of the novel and the repetitions that Indian
art-music is subjected to.

The most prominent victim of the tug-of-war has been the
raag-repertoire.   Due to his deep anxiety to succeed, the contemporary musician either holds fast to the *raag*s, he has effectively
handled before or repeats those he has already recorded on discs,
etc.   Hence, even though one reads about the mathematically
possible thirty-five thousand and odd *raag*s or hears about a
more practicable repertoire of a mature musician (which consists
of about two hundred *raag*s)—not more than fifty seem to be in
actual circulation! *Resorting to pre-composed music has certainly
weakened the risk-taking abilities of the Indian musicians.* The
artists prefer repeating the established and the accepted to the new
and the potentially creative.   Instead of looking at every performance as an invitation to innovate they regard it as a fateful
occasion endangering their reputation.   Igor Stravinsky once
ruefully commented that people are happy to recognize than to
cognize! Indian musicians seem to have taken to the comment too
seriously!

The interesting paradox however is that Indian musicians are
also known to luxuriate in an unrestrained indulgence in presenting 'mixed' *raag*s and new *taal*s structured on fraction-based
intricacies. The number of vocalists who compose their own *cheez*s
is also multiplying.

Viewed superficially, the situation seems to be full of contradictions. However, a little examination reveals that the situation

is otherwise. The opposite and coexisting pulls in connection with the repertoire are only logical consequences of explainable interaction of musical forces. As pointed out earlier, a majority of *raag*s are repeatedly presented by a number of musicians because their individual musical images have been formed by a consistent inclusion of certain *raag*s in their respective repertoires. The consequence is that a section of the total *raag*-corpus is virtually preempted as far as other artists are concerned. These latter artists are therefore forced to move out and seek new *raag*s, etc., in order to create and then to ensure consolidation of their own musical identities. It is obvious that the easiest way out is to present *raag*s and *taal*s which are describable as rare or exotic! Thus, too many try to win by sheer novelty while a few clutch hard to the accepted and the achieved through sheer repetition!

The specialist and the omnific

The contradictory pulls on the art-musician's repertoire are also reflected in his attitudes towards musical forms. Traditionally nurtured Indian musicians used to specialize in one musical form in view of the varying requirements of different musical forms vis-a-vis aptitude, voice, training etc. Versatility was not frowned upon but, at the same time, specialization was not interpreted as a lack of musical richness. Thus a *khayàl*-singer who did not sing *thumri* was not ranked low on that account. In fact, narrower repertoire was understood to be an attempt at concentration which finally led to a more discriminating channelizing of the individual's musical resources.

The contemporary picture is quite different. Musicians of today are more inclined to diversify; unfortunately it can hardly be claimed that the diversification is backed by genuine aesthetic urges and the requisite competence. The truth of the matter is that musicians try to handle a variety of forms with a desire to enhance chances of satisfying a larger number of people actuated by differing musical needs.

It is a sad reflection on the musical reality that a musician's inclination towards variety can no longer be easily construed as a prompting of his inner artistic voice struggling to find a proper format conducive to his musical ideas. Musical forms are used today for their supposed efficacy in arousing stock-responses in a

large, undifferentiated audience exposed to music. It is only on
rare occasions that musicians are able to justify their deviation
from the earlier patterns of musical specialization. Most of the
time they fail to produce proofs in support of their attempts to
arrogate to themselves powers of unlimited creation.

At this stage it is expedient to relate effects of popular culture
discussed here to the definition of popular culture formulated in
the beginning.

The time-shrinkage to which art-music is subjected to, is attributable to many factors. In some measure the general pace of
communication is responsible for time-shrinkage. The fast pace
of communication in general has considerably compressed clock-
time and this has its effects on the arts which in themselves are
special communications. Apart from the generally increased life-
pace, the impact of mass-media has also contributed to the
time-shrinkage as well as to the artist's tendency to prefer pre-
composed music to the improvised variety. Media-audiences are
heterogeneous and their patronage is indiscriminate in quality.
Feedback received from such an audience has compelled the
media-administrators to allow non-aesthetic and neo-commercial
pressures to play a greater role than is really justified and
desirable in the shaping of media-attitudes towards art-music.

Print-culture too has made its share felt in the process. Today
song texts, i.e., *cheez*s are often made available in print; and
as a consequence, both musicians and the listeners are more criti-
cally aware of the semantic (if not the poetic) dimension of the
compositions. An interesting corroboration of the influence of
print-culture on art-music is seen in the fact that composers of
art-songs are no longer content to remain anonymous or under-
publicized. The underlying demand seems to be that an *art-
song be treated as an equal of lyric in literature*, a stage-song in
music-drama and a song-number in films!

The detailed documentation and availability of an exhaustively
compiled *raag*-grammar is also to the credit of print-culture. A
greater section of musicians and music-lovers today insist on
conformity to the written characteristics of art-music. The natural
gap between the practice and the theory of music has become more
glaring on account of the permeating influence of print-culture.
It is print-culture which gives teeth to the puritanical adherence
to grammar demanded by the scholastic tradition as contrasted

with the more accommodative stance of the performing tradition. The latter relies on oral culture which positively discourages definitive versions of music. Today the isolated splendour of the art-musician and the grand aesthetic abstraction of art-music are confronted with serious challenges. The diversity of pressures acting on art-music have considerably eroded the freedoms usually associated with a strongly non-representational art. Art-musician has to face the music literally! He has to join in the general fray of cultural forces.

However, this does not mean that everything that popular culture has done to art-music is to be decried. Some favourable impact-points can also be mentioned. For example, on account of the underlying motive to pre-compose in order to succeed, the Indian art-musicians have succeeded in getting rid of repetition within a performance. His general approach to music has become more purposeful in respect of design and execution. Irrespective of the musical form involved, musical renderings have certainly become more compact. Another equally welcome side-effect is the curtailment of the warming-up period and mood-initiation procedures which every musician needs to follow. These are no longer thrust on the audiences. The picture of an audience patiently waiting for an artist to warm up his voice or instrument and to get into the right mood has undergone a radical change. Like a Shakesperean play, today a musician takes a direct plunge in his music. Things have to start happening right from the beginning and the artist's attempt is to avoid all tentative gropings and false starts. The cumulative effect has been to make the beginnings and the ends of music easily perceivable; consequently musical structures are more surely erected and easily detected. (In this regard, ethnomusicologists can heave a sigh of relief!) Ostensibly it can also be maintained that the musicians themselves have become more conscious of the concept of form. They are more deliberate and formal in employing musical vocabulary, ideas and forces.

The popular culture has also scored another gain for art-music by bringing about a better appreciation of the timbre-music relationship. Before the advent of the public address systems, audio equipment and the acoustically treated auditoria, musicians used to lavish attention only on two physical dimensions of musical sound: pitch and volume. The third parameter, that of timbre, was almost neglected. Since the arrival of the microphone, 'close-ups' of sounds have become a reality. Musicians have been freed from the elementary worries of being heard over the surrounding noise-level or remaining audible throughout a performance. Thus they are able to devote more attention to the texture of the sound. In this respect film-music (which forms a very significant component of popular culture) has given a significant lead to art-music. It is barely forty years since Ananda Coomaraswamy averred that a concern for the quality of voice is likely to distract listeners from appreciation of the musical content. He had further argued that Indian musician's indifference to voice-quality is justifiable to that extent! Today this argument will not be put forward seriously. Though vocalists with good voices are as yet a rare commodity, none will be found to deny the relevance of a good, that is, a sweet-sounding voice. This is what the regard for the third dimension has achieved. Instrumental music is no exception. Instruments are considered in a new light. Their alteration and modifications are attempted. Contact-mikes and amplifiers are employed and *the accent on timbre is unmistakable.*

The salutary effect of film-music on art-music is also discernible in one more aspect. Art-musicians are becoming more solicitous about the meanings of the song-texts. Traditional compositions in art-music are too cliche-ridden to be of poetic or literary value. On the other hand, film-music as a genre has heavily depended on digestible, perceivable meanings and poetic content of the same communicable variety. It has also ensured that the music-items are conveyed in a manner which makes an impact. The advantages of this approach have not been lost on art-musicians. They now try to attend to the 'poetic' or the 'literary' dimension of their *cheezs*. This is amply reflected in compositions of some of the major musicians of the new generation, like Pandit Kumaar Gandharva. Indian vocalists are also more emotive in their enunciation of words. This too is an indication of the awareness created by the unprecedented following film-music has managed to get and retain.

Folk-music
Compared to art-music, the folk category of music has been less affected by popular culture in India. The chief reason for the reduced intensity of effect is that this type of music does not have an urban base. India has the vastness of a sub-continent: as yet

its rural areas are not effectively opened up by modern means of transport. It is also to be remembered that most of the rural population in India continues to be semi-or non- literate even today. Further, the linguistic diversity of rural India also contributes to its comparative insulation from the print-based urban and metropolitan features of popular culture. For all practical purposes, only broadcasting, films (and to a very negligible extent, television) have registered some impact on folk-music.

'Produced' folk-music

As a result of a very conscious policy decision, broadcasting has made a noticeable impact on folk-music. Soon after Independence, the A.I.R. authorities felt the need of attracting greater rural audiences to its programmes. Hence various stations of the All India Radio were directed to encourage programmes based on regional music(s). In fact, music-producers on the staff were instructed to use the idiom of folk-music and compose new songs suitable for broadcasting. This effort to manufacture a special type of music and feed it to the listeners received further support when the A.I.R. started a separate service of variety entertainment programmes and made it available throughout the nation. Instituted in 1957, the service was aptly named Vividh Bharati—a fitting tribute to the multi-coloured character of Indian culture. Examined music-wise these efforts seem to have created a musical genre that is heterogeneous by nature and disturbing to the spirit of folk-music. This deliberately created 'folkish' music results in a music which is separated from its natural, psychological and collective matrix. Shorn of its ritualistic and religious adjuncts and spontaneity in expression this music becomes a forced exercise in cultural engineering. It cannot prove appealing to the 'folk' because they have the prototype itself with them. The processed folk-music also fails to attract the musically sophisticated and urbanized listener who is hardly enamoured by the doctrine of authenticity of tunes.

Musically speaking, most of the folk-music is bound to be boring; its power resides chiefly in its collective projection which is by definition ruled out from the broadcast programmes. When folk-music is torn out of the surrounding socket of the communal psyche and the ritualistic aspects, etc., it cannot hope to retain its pull unless it is musically attractive. As a result, the doctrine of authenticity of tunes cannot rescue the produced 'folk' music from its ineffectiveness. In sum, the specially and abundantly turned out folk-music of the A.I.R. alienates both the folk and the urbanized listeners from itself (and perhaps from each other at a more subtle level).

Urban models for folk-music

The combination of A.I.R. and the films have led to another debatable effect of popular culture on folk-music. Indian film-makers have always believed in churning out synthetic versions of all folk-manifestations including musical ones. The music-compositions which they turn out are vulgarly saturated with sound, studded with cliche-embellishment, and embedded in grossly imitative orchestration. Their only redeeming feature is a highly polished presentation. Film-music is ideally equipped for encroaching on the privacy of the individual because it is in a position to provide cheap, instantaneous and readymade entertainment. Its aggressive posture is further strengthened because the far-reaching network of the radio and television channels is also available to it. Both these media are loaded with film-music which therefore becomes an ubiquitous phenomenon of incantatory influences. Nothing could have succeeded in making it so offensive culturally than its universality! As a consequence film-music has virtually started dictating programme-models and musical content to the folk-musicians themselves! The latter now tend to imitate folkish film-music because they see it so firmly entrenched in the governmental agencies, avidly and approvingly reproduced by the urbanites and lavishly rewarded by all! In music too, bad coins drive out good coins out of circulation.

The neo-professionals

A side-effect is becoming discernible gradually but surely. From among the folk-musicians themselves, a new class of professionals is cropping up. Musicians of this class periodically come to the urban centres. For their urban patrons they perform in marriage ceremonies, birthday-parties and similar social occasions. They get well-paid (by village standards) and go back richer to their native places. In all probability they cannot be expected to accept the village reality in the same, pre-urban-visit manner. In place of the earlier professionalism, signs of commercialism are seen

clearly. Folk-music is only one strand of the total fabric of life in
a village-based society. Forcing the pace of change of any single
isolated strand or turning it into a commodity is bound to prove
disconcerting and destabilizing. It does not bode well for a society
that needs a smoother change-over in its essential core: the
village-life. In addition, the latter has so far always opted for the
strategy of assimilation as opposed to that of confrontation. Indian
ethos has accomplished the act of assimilation (and not merely
of accommodation) because forces that attracted the assimilative
processes have not been so far thrust upon it at an artificially
stimulated pace.

History instructs us that alien people or other agents serving as
carriers of a different cultural content have ultimately become
components of Indian society. This picture was radically reframed
when the British became more substantially imperialistic (from
about 1857 onwards). The point is that every planned attempt
of bringing about a cultural transformation must therefore be
combined with a clear understanding of the national temperament.
The produced folk-music of the A.I.R. or the commercial film-
music that overflows everywhere or the new professional folk-
musicians described above, are all *symptoms of a cultural drift*. To
a great extent, cultural forces are controllable and they can be
channellized provided we take hard decisions about our identity.

Displacement of folk-music
Social legislation, print-culture and urbanization of the performing
arts (and of music and drama in particular) have combined to
produce another subtler impact.

Folk-music today provides a good feeding ground for the
nostalgia of the city dwellers who are progressively and increasingly cut-off from their village roots. The city dwellers now find
it particularly difficult to keep a continued though occasional contact with their village-bases which have been the customary
centres of family rituals, religious festivals, etc. Progressive agricultural legislation has discouraged absentee-landlordism as well as
the subsistence relationship of the agricultural labourer with the
village land. In the past, petty landlords used to have a village
seat to supplement their city earnings with the land-produce.
Whatever the other consequences that flowed from this pattern,
this style certainly allowed them to keep a living contact with

village life. In a similar fashion, labourers engaged by such landlords also developed close links with the same land. The situation has now radically changed. The cumulative effect of legislation based on the 'land to the tiller'-principle has been to sever the connections of the above class of people with the village. This has developed in them a nostalgia about life in villages in general. This generalized nostalgia seeks an outlet in the urbanized presentations of performing arts. It is not surprising that such presentations are debilitatingly and cloyingly sentimental and cliche-ridden. Though it is true that cultural exiles always try to transplant the original cultural vision, it is also true that they rarely succeed. There is one more telling instance of the urban nostalgia. State-sponsored shows of folk-arts of the similar incubated variety have also become a regular feature of the city scene. In such shows, items are selected/pruned/modified by the organizing authorities to suit the requirements of the event which is, to all purposes, a staged administrative venture. It is unavoidable that the musical content of such manifestations gets altered. Yet another newly found (and therefore more zealous!) patron of the folk-presentations is the tourism industry.

In such shows the performing arts suffer more than fine arts, because unlike the visually oriented expressions, music, dance and drama are more directly and essentially affected by changes in locale, audience, and other performing conditions. When folk-music becomes only an item to be ticked off by the organizers after a session, it can hardly be expected to be itself.

The city-dweller's nostalgia for the folk-expression in a way raises an important question: can city-dwellers have their own root-culture? There is an affirmative answer. Such a culture becomes available to those who are total products of the urban areas, not merely city-dwellers. Even if this answer is not accepted, *displaced and processed folk-presentations are surely not the right culture-generating agencies.*

Popular music

In a way, discussing popular music while examining popular culture vis-a-vis music might appear pleonastic because popular music is itself an offshoot of the particular culture-category under scrutiny. The redundancy can however be avoided by adopting a level different from the one employed while dealing with relationships bet-

ween popular culture and art-music, etc. Hence, it is to be remembered that to argue about the effects of popular culture on popular
music is in actuality to consider the existing relation between
a parent concept and a derived one. However, the difference in
approach-levels does not diminish the utility of the discussion
because Indian popular music has as yet not fully realized the
potentialities afforded to it by the multifaceted phenomenon of
popular culture. In fact Indian popular music draws sustenance
from its matrix in such a haphazard fashion that it harms the
sustainer itself! The truth is that popular music fails to exploit the
resources of popular culture which in turn remains impoverished.
As both have to play a mutually supporting role, their failure to
attain their respective statures presents a serious problem of
cultural imbalance. To be co-extensive with popular culture in
scope and efficacy, popular music in India must do justice to the
aspects of media-use, topicality and mass-appeal. A brief discussion of the three features may prove useful.

Media-dominance
In case of mass-media, the chief damage done to the entire communication process is due to the reversal of the 'user-used' roles
in the Indian situation. Firstly, due to various reasons, the print-
based media are underdeveloped in India. Secondly, there hardly
exists any genuine competition among the other media. As a result
the films and the radio have become dominant in that order. Under
the circumstances, the user (i.e., music in the present case) is dicta-
ted to and controlled by the used (i.e., film and the radio in this
case). In addition, broadcasting and television are government
monopolies in India. The consequences are two-fold: there is no
competition and the media can afford to be less responsive or indif-
ferent to the audiences. In the absence of competition the media
lack the motivation to do better and as they are in a position to
ignore the audience-responses, the disapproval or rejection of the
media-messages by the audiences deprive the media of the urge to
examine themselves. As a result both the media fail to do justice
to the variety, topicality and the finished quality of the popular
variety of music. Further, Indian broadcasting and telecasting
governmental agencies are also backed by censorship powers that
are usually exercised with a literary bias which is blind to the
power of music to wrest authority from the accompanying word.

In reality, popular culture is expected to be sensitive to the evanescent but real needs of a society at a particular point of time. As even the passing and the temporary have a place in cultural development taken as a whole, the popular strata of cultural life of a community are extremely important. *To confine culture only to the eternal is to put it in stocks.* This is the reason why accepting the legitimacy of the temporary and recognizing its utility is a sure and heartening sign of moving with the times. Indian broadcasting and telecasting can hardly be accused of keeping pace with the times! If one remembers that till recently there was only one gramophone company in India, the crushing power of the monotony of musical soundscape can be easily felt. In this way the media dominate and create a situation where popular music is forced into narrow and repetitious grooves.

Media-dominance is also characterized by the overshadowing of broadcasting and telecasting by films, as suggested earlier. Both go *the filmy-way* in their own productions and also dole out film-music in large chunks. Both radio and the television do not seem to be keen on having their own individual modes of cultural expression. The result is a type of cultural regimentation. The experience thus conveyed is so narrow in its reach that it kills the appetite of the receiving audience for anything larger and different.

Lacking the topical touch

Due to its very nature, an important and an everpresent asset of popular culture is its kinship with the fashionable and the modern. It is in the interests of any society to have a popular stratum to its culture because it is the popular sensibility which attends to the immediate cultural needs of the society. Once having accommodated the immediate with the help of the popular sensibility, a society gets breathing time to sift the original from the novel and the significant from the attractive. It must be noted that it is popular culture that bears the brunt of the untried new, tests it by allowing a temporary acceptance and consequently keeps the whole structure of the societal responses in a state of shock-absorbing flexibility. It is clear that everything new that happens in a society may not be culturally significant. But it is also true that the conservative resistance in any society cannot always be trusted to respond to the new according to its merits. The collective mind works slowly and often rigidly over a small span of time

and the long-term adverse effects of this type are sought to be
prevented by the alert and quick reflexes of popular culture.
It is on this background that the topicality of popular music has
a positive function to perform which can hardly be delegated to
any other genre of music. Without disturbing the steady rhythm
of the deeper cultural dynamics, popular music picks up the
more surfacial musical pulses which also possess a more immediate
and widespread appeal. Topical is the need of the hour and the
property of having many faces enables music to fulfil the need.
Political slogans, electioneering songs, spontaneous collective
chants at sports meets, etc., provide opportunities for the incidental, occasional, momentary formulation of music or musical sounds.
Regional variation, peculiar intonations of various language-
speakers, all form an important part of the genre under discussion.
Even the semi-musical phonating exemplified in exclamations in
various parts of the country are to be considered here. The topical
in popular music essentially makes it allusive and occasional.
Understood in this manner, only the advertisement-jingles display
the quality of allusiveness to some extent. It is a pity that the
topicality-touch should be so scarce in Indian popular music.

Mass-appeal
One thing that popular music has definitely achieved is mass-
appeal. Film-music (with the help of broadcasting) has reached
almost all nooks and corners of the country.

The author, however, feels that the present references to 'appeal'
need not be restricted to the fact of reaching a large number
of people. Appeal is a quality, not a mere statistical quantity.

It is a noteworthy fact that in the existing state of Indian
media-operation, there is no free play of competitive forces
vying with each other to provide better services. It is therefore
difficult to conclude that passive exposure to the fare provided
can be construed as endorsement or approval of its quality. With
no alternative available to users it is unfair to interpret the
tolerence of the *culturally cornered people* as their voting in
favour of the quality of music they are inundated with. Therefore
the existence of mass-appeal cannot perhaps be deduced in India.

Further, the conception of appeal also connotes reception of
music with an inclination to recreate or hum it. Even though
routines like humming, etc., are aesthetically poor, they are 'real'

substitutes to participation in music-making. Of late the tendency is to play film-music (or any music for that matter) on the hi-fi systems and not to hum or create it oneself. In the present, non-aesthetic context even an approximate reproduction is akin to creation if it is prompted by an intention to create. In addition, *the loud level at which music is played also suggests an added dehumanization of music.* Used in this way, *music is reduced to an atmospheric agent* which is expected to envelop the hearer by sound or to isolate him from the outside sounds which are not under his control. One more popular way of making music is also worth noting. Groups of singers are formed to give renderings of 'hit' film-songs. These are called 'orchestras' and are largely attended. All these are instances of vicarious music-making and all of them underline a trend: a desire to enjoy without participation. In case of such music, mass-appeal is hardly the term to be used; it is only mass-consumption.

In sum, popular culture in India seems to be in a state of weak formulation. Media—the main vehicles of popular culture—are themselves lop-sided in development because the full media-range is not in operation; also because the *existing media are explored in an unimaginative manner.* Patronage enjoyed by music is changing gradually and popular culture is playing its part in the process. It is also true that culture-leaders and media-operators are hampered in working out their ideas on account of interference from political and governmental agencies which display *no grasp of the overall cultural perspective.* In this manner popular culture is not able to function properly. These remarks apply in toto to popular music which forms a significant part of the popular expression taken as a whole.

4

Indian film-music :
changing compulsions

India ranks second in the list of film-producing countries. In the popularity ratings of film-personalities, music-composers (or music directors as they are generally known) enjoy star-status, next only to the film-stars themselves. These and similar other observations only confirm the tremendous hold that film-music has over the film-viewing public as well as other music-exposed sections of Indian society taken as a whole. How does one explain this extraordinary attraction of the Indian film music?

Almost all the major composers have their own distinct clienteles (and sometimes musical identities also). Through innumerable interviews, etc., they have frequently aired their assessment of their own successes, relating them to their intentions and motives.

Their views may be a fruitful starting point for discussion. Even in an ethnomusicological situation an informant is regarded as valuable. In the final analysis, however, the motivation-search turns out to be a false start. Firstly, intentions and similar personality-manifestations are insufficient indicators of the total reality in aesthetic matters. True or real intentions can hardly be known or surmised correctly. Secondly, even if we do manage to get a clear idea of these motives they prove to be poor pointers to the ultimate quality which reaches the people. A great number of agencies operate before the composer's musical idea assumes concrete shape in a song, etc.

Under the circumstances the shaping forces of Indian film-music are to be best viewed as a series of changing compulsions. These compulsions function at various points and in varied proportions.

The final film-music product is fashioned by all of them. A true and extensive study of film-music can be taken up only if the study-perspective includes all the compulsion-points, namely: music-director's personal capacities/incapacities, the producer's, director's, actor's contributions, the script and its linguistic quality, the distribution system and the target audience, the musical hinterland of the music-director, the play-back voices, etc. In contrast to art-music, folk-music or primitive music, film-music reveals itself as being a result of industry-processes: its analysis therefore requires a methodology which is complex and to an extent extra-aesthetic. An attempt is made here to emphasize the aspect of the filmic and the musical content of film-music, and to that extent it is an aesthetic inquiry. However, a larger awareness of other factors referred to earlier should not be lost sight of.

Even a cursory glance at history reveals that Indian film-music has been confined largely to being a song—at least in the earlier stages of the art. Within a year from the advent of the talkies, we had *Indrasabha* (1932) with its 71 songs! A little later, when the ever-enterprising Wadias produced *a film without a song* (*Navjawan*, 1937), the viewers were so disgruntled that the producers had to screen a trailer seeking to explain the unexpected absence of the song-cushions! In fact it was not till K.A. Abbas's *Munna* (1954) that a songless film could be produced without apologies. A question thus becomes inevitable: why was the song so important? The question is relevant even in the contemporary situation.

Barnouw and Krishnaswamy (1963) have argued chiefly in favour of the following two reasons to explain the song-dominance:

(1) In its dependence on 'song' the Indian film was exploiting the readymade receptivity of the audience, created and conditioned by the regional theatre which had newly emerged in the nineteenth century. The presentations of this theatre were replete with songs. Films were thus only following a strategy of imitating the successful in order to succeed.

(2) For all purposes, the Indian film was a continuation of the tradition popularized and perfected by the musical folk-dramas of various regions (for example, *tamashaa*, *jaatraa*, *keertan*, etc.). In turn, the folk-dramas were carriers of the heritage so thoroughly systematized in ancient Sanskrit dramaturgy.

However, to show the origins of the intensive use of songs is not enough to explain song-dominance. In Bombay, the base of the nascent film-industry, the tradition of prose-plays was also well-entrenched. In fact, Marathi prose-play which began its career in 1861 overshadowed its musical counterpart (the music-play) since 1920. The point is that the real causes of song-dominance are to be detected in the filmic-content itself.

It was mythology which provided the chief source of thematic content till the late thirties. This was so in both the film produc-ing centres in the country, Bombay and Calcutta. The very first Bengal-produced talkie was *Chandidas*; the first Bombay-based talkie to make an impact was *Raja Harischandra*. In fact the first five years of the articulate cinema turned out no less than three *Tukarams* and five *Harischandras*! It is an anthropological truth that in all cultures, music is invariably employed to estab-lish links with the supernatural, the element which enables mythology to have a firm base. It can therefore be plausibly suggested that the Indian cinematic impulse was congenitally bound with music. In addition to this, Indian music is itself characterized by the primacy of vocal music. The song-syllogism is therefore complete:

Mythology and supernatural were the staple of Indian films;

Indian films therefore needed music intrinsically; (Indian music is primarily vocal)

Therefore, Indian films depended on songs.

Secondly, it is also necessary to remember that due to its very nature (being a mass-medium) films aimed at an all-India audi-ence. Phalke, the father of Indian films, used to have Hindi and English explanatory titles to his silent films as far back as 1913. An interesting parallel is from the field of music-drama, another Maharashtra-based entertainment medium. Vishnudas Bhave who was the first to give Marathi music-drama a modern footing in 1843, came to Bombay in 1853. Apart from his presentations in Marathi he staged a play in Hindi (*Raajaa Gopichand*, 1853), though his chief efforts were confined to Marathi. The strategy was repeated in later years by other ace dramatic troupes further-ing the cause of Marathi drama: whenever they wanted to have a pan-Indian audience, they staged plays in Hindi. It so trans-pires that therefore the regional theatres were language-based while the films aspired to be culture-based. Music and mythology

are known for being expressive agents that possess an in-built
cultural appeal. Consequently they enjoy trans-regional effectiveness. Indian films were motivated to secure a pan-India clientele:
hence music became the chief component in their make-up. The
song-dominance of the early films in India is to be viewed in this
perspective.

Another important aspect of song-dominance is the 'classical'
(art-music) base of early Indian film-music. It was the nature
of musical traditions current in India which was responsible for
the art-music weightage. Due to various historical factors the
sub-continental expanse of India is divided musically in two
large segments: Hindustan and the South. The former has
nurtured the *Hindustaani* tradition of art-music and the latter
has developed the musical system known as *Carnatic*. It means
that irrespective of the immense multiplicity of the linguistic and
the literary sub-traditions, art-music(s) and mythology remain
the two features which can provide common cultural hinterland of
their own, both to the North and the South. As Indian films
were born and brought up in Bombay and Calcutta, centres
located in the Hindustani-music sector, the deductions are
obvious. Because of its extra-regional aspirations and predilection for song (which followed from the all-pervasive oral tradition
in India), Indian film-music fell back on the Hindustani art-
music—the dominant system in the areas which were the primary
seats of early Indian films. The recourse to art-music of the
areas was inevitable since the regional musical traditions possessed only a limited appeal at least till the effective operations of
the mass-media increased the reach of the regional music(s) to a
great extent.

Supporting evidence is available in the success story of the
Marathi music-drama which flourished as an urbanized entertainment from 1843 to 1931. Marathi music-plays, especially those
staged by the Gandharva Naatak Mandali attracted non-Marathi
audiences in considerable numbers from 1920 onwards. The main
attraction was Balgandharva's music which was steeped in
khayaal, *thumri* and other varieties of *Hindustaani* music. A number of plays he staged were also mythologicals. It is clear that the
art-music-mythology combination was an answer to the language-
barrier and a positive aid in securing mass-appeal.

At a deeper aesthetic level the readymade moulds of art-music and mythology also proved a help in patterning the new cinematic experience—in conception as well as in its reception. Thus patterned, the filmic experience became more sharply defined and durable. *Music and mythology performed a sort of cementing act* which held together units of the audio-visual experience which otherwise lacked the familiar live-touch of actors, musicians, dancers, etc., on stage.

In this context, a subtle distinction needs to be made between 'song' as it is understood today and the songs of the early films. In reality, compositions of the early films can be called songs in the true sense of the term, only with difficulty. More often than not, they were merely verses set to tune. For instance, the film *Indrasabhaa* mentioned earlier is reported to have been structured as a verse-play. The composition-units were verses only in the sense that they were deviations from prose and from the plain narration-tone associated with it. Therefore they were less positively inclined to possess musical quality, which is after all the hall-mark of a song. The rationale behind these 'songs which were less than songs' must be clearly understood. In cultures permeated with the oral tradition it is a common procedure to move away from prose-tone repeatedly, unobtrusively and imperceptibly in order to shift to metrical movement and yet to keep away from a fullscale song-structure, and finally to return to prose-tone. The recurring deviations from the prose-tone are aimed at avoiding monotony and the firm non-use of the song proper is to ensure that the semantic content, the meaning, does not get obscured due to the long shadows cast by musical tunes.

Indian film-music followed the same strategy but introduced a slight change at the second step. Instead of dry metricality it opted for simple but perceivable rhythms and equally simple but cleanly felt tonal contours. In this way it managed to rise above a metrical recitation though it could not give us a song. The deliberate, logical exercise of a delicate and efficient choice continued till the hold of the oral tradition weakened with the advent of the literary cinema. It was at this juncture that song-spaces were created in the dialogues and naturalistic causation was laboriously sought after to utilize 'singable' material. Of course it is true that oral traditions too are fond of carving out occasions, excuses for music/song but yet their exercise is less deliberate and less insistent. The oral tradition has a different motivation for what it does to build up a particular kind of prose-music relationship.

To state briefly, the motivation is provided by a very important principle operative in oral tradition: the principle of speech-song continuum. It means that vocalization-speech-verse-song-music are treated as degrees in a continuous activity of content-projection instead of separate categories. The early film-makers followed the same rationale. This is the reason why there is a repeated back and forth movement between prose and intoned verse in the early film-music. It is a pity that this verse-in-tune phase of the early Indian film-music is often regarded as the root-cause or a prototype of the present-day 'plot and song' dichotomy in film-music. It is also argued that contemporary film-music is only carrying on the tradition of the early films. Nothing can be farther from the truth, because song is a much-processed version of a literary intent while the verse-in-tune is only a crystallization of the narrative function with a musical overlay. It is a logical howler to lump together the two fundamentally different manifestations through an unwarranted attribution of an artificial art-intent to a simpler but authentic sensibility.

Can one describe the compulsions operating behind the early Indian film-music as aesthetic? The author feels that the answer is in the affirmative because in the phase discussed, the main aim and the effect was to reach and hold the audience which itself was new to the fare. The attempt did not have a valuational bias. This is the reason why so many of the examples of early film-music are musically so unexciting. They had no aesthetic function to discharge vis-a-vis music. Their underlying compulsions were those of initial communication, which though fundamental, are not aesthetic. However one need not be apologetic because in denying them the aesthetic grade we are not rejecting their claim to filmic efficacy and excellence. Though it must be realized that in the early stages the Indian film failed to grasp its own composite nature for lack of conceptual awareness. As a consequence, for its very fundamental need of establishing the initial communication, it turned to the model used by the performing arts, that is, drama, music and dance. The model of these arts (intrinsic to them) laid down the first norm: to establish contact before trying to communicate the content. Due to their very nature the aesthetique of the performing arts is intertwined with communication-features like audience-response, audience-participation and improvisation. This is not so in the case of films which are made for hypothetical audiences temporally and spatially distanced from the filmic creation. The cinematicians sensed the special, non-performing and composite nature of the cinematic sensibility, only later. The late arrival of background music on the filmic scene or a comparable delay in the introduction of sound-effects in the films is causally connected with this late awareness of the composite character of the art by its Indian practitioners.

The idea of background music in itself presupposes a conscious, methodical splitting of the unit of experience into its components, thus making them amenable to the manipulations of the art-intent. Aestheticising always aims at ultimate fusion preceded by a fission of creative forces. Whenever aestheticizing takes place, the experiential units which have been originally conceived and operated in an integrated manner have to undergo successive processes of dismantling and reassembling. Conception and utilization of background music or sound-effects are a creation of this characteristic deliberate procedure. A similar cool and aesthetic act was to be performed later to make the emergence and entrenchment of play-back singing an indivisible feature of Indian film-music.

To make the distinction between the communicational and the aesthetic compulsions clearer, a few characteristics of the latter can be briefly discussed.

Firstly, the aesthetic compulsion is seen in the frequent recourse to the criterion of correspondence reflected in the choice of music for a particular filmic situation. According to this criterion, music which is selected or composed for a particular event is supposed to reflect the nature of the event or the mood of the character. In other words, the correspondence-aesthetique consisted of discovering music that matched the filmic fact. The situation, its structure, its pace and other features are thus employed, so to say, for a musical take-off. Such music is expected to enhance the effect of the filmic event correlated with it. Interpreted in this manner, the relationship of the two components, music and film, bases itself on the principle of similarity. It is not necessary to state that 'the correspondence aesthetique' is not the only one which can function or that the principle of similarity is the only possible way to build a relationship between the filmic and the musical. But that does not invalidate the claims made on their behalf.

It is instructive to see how this 'correspondence' was established in Indian films. Two devices were chiefly employed for the purpose. The first was acoustic and the other can be called musicological. The acoustic way of achieving correspondence was equated with the use of 'appropriate' sounds or musical instruments, etc. This was such a consciously designed aesthetic device that the booklet containing the dialogues and lyrics of *Kunku* (1937, Prabhat) also listed all the sound-effects composed for the film! The second device was comparatively less innovative as it relied on the readymade musicological combinations of *raag* and *rasa* in composing the score. For example, *bhairavi: karuna rasaa, adaanaa: veer rasa, darbaari kaanadaa: shaantarasaa, khamaaj: shringaar rasa* and other equations were strictly followed. It is not surprising that this typology held a great sway over the composer's imagination, because the line-up of music-composers at both the Pune and Calcutta centres included persons who were basically trained as professional art-musicians. For instance, the roll-call included Govindrao Tembe, Keshavrao Bhole, Master Krishnarao, Punkaj Mullick, R.C. Boral, Saraswati Devi *et al*. (The lone lady was in fact a degree-holder in music from Maurice College of Music, Lucknow.) It can be suggested that till the late forties, film-composers were art-musicians turned composers; hence the musicological typology of mood-music relationship came to them naturally. Their faith in the predetermined correspondences between musical stimulants and audience-effects was in reality designed to trigger-off stock responses. The device might therefore rank lowly on the aesthetic scale, yet its legitimacy cannot be denied. After all, associations have a place in the cultural armoury; till such time as the films remained culture-centred on a rather obvious level, the use of association-clusters was a foregone conclusion in music too.

However, composers were able to shake-off the musicological tyranny due to another feature of the aesthetic compulsion: the criterion of naturalism (and not naturalness) which was gradually acquiring a stronger grip over the directorial vision in general. The directorial vision expressed its naturalism in choosing non-urban themes, characters and accompanying dialects, etc. It is obvious that the music-directors who composed for such ventures had to leave aside the well-established categories of art-music. In a way the situation could be aptly described as 'a literary compulsion behind film-music' because the filmic conception of the non-urban was itself modelled after the stylized version of the non-urban realized in the literature of that period. The literary sensibility of the time was loyal to the creed of naturalism and the canon of realism was yet to become a force. The upshot was the depiction of the so-called non-urban which was in fact a stylized, sentimental and urban version of the rural, inevitably lacking the authentic ring. As yet, the filmic sensibility was looking at the world around through literary glasses, which were unfortunately clouded. However, if examined musically, even the semi-authentic and literature-biased loyalty to naturalism proved helpful to the extent that it brought about a radical change in the range of music employed in films. This necessarily led to the loosening of the hold otherwise enjoyed by art-music. The fact that even an artificial and made-up literary sensibility should prove a liberating force need not surprise us: because, our entire filmic sensibility and the changes that have come over it, were literature-based till very recent times. Whether it is humanism in social thinking, nationalism in politics or aestheticism in art—all have sought their initial inspiration in literature. As a consequence the quality of contemporary literature and the current obsession it suffers from, have often proved to be obstacles in the realization of the individual and independent sensibilities of other arts in all cultural periods. Instead of responding to their own inner promptings and the needs of their own relevant aesthetic areas, composers have therefore tended too often, to eat their musical revolutions from the hands of their literary colleagues! Indian filmic language too suffered through this dominance of literature and the literary. As late as 1940 Phalke admonished the Madras film-world for being too wordy and also for forgetting that the filmic art is essentially a photo-play. The bane of literature-dominance has been so ruinous that it is time that all non-literary artists momentarily turn literary and legitimately exclaim: 'Thus literature does make cowards of us all!' It is indeed ironical that in a country which could boast of a rich oral tradition, over-indulgence towards the written word should bring about an extreme atrophy of arts and that the 'literary' thraldom should go unchallenged. However, it must be admitted that film-music could secure a brief respite from art-music because it followed the artificial literary mode.

Correspondence-quest, acoustic and musicological basis of the sound-effect syndrome, literature-based interpretation of naturalism and the consequent freedom from art-music can thus be listed as the main features of the aesthetic compulsion. Apart from these, some others can also be included in a more detailed discussion of the subject. The new awareness of timbre, a sense of movement-oriented musical punctuation, conscious exploration of the speech-music continuum and the fuller use of musical time could figure in such an attempt. In addition, some of the sophisticated applications of recording and play-back techniques, etc., also deserve consideration in the contemporary context. The present essay is however aimed more at directing attention towards the conceptual frame-work involved. It is in this perspective that we turn to the third type of compulsion that shaped Indian film-music. This is the category of the musical compulsions.

In this context it is possible to start with a generalization: the tendency after the forties has been to make every individual composition musically attractive so that people should retain it in memory *as a song*. The chief desire is to compose an item possessing its own melodic draw. Hence it could be received, reproduced and remembered in isolation, that is, irrespective of the presence of the filmic setting in which it was intended to appear. In this manner, the composition is expected to be a musically self-sufficient unit. The advent of mass-media (e.g., stage-song-discs from 1921, cheaper Japanese phonograph machines from 1928, broadcasting from 1931) considerably accelerated the process of severing the internal bindings of film-music and enabled it to become a free agent in the category technically described as popular music. As a consequence, the entire stance of the composer has undergone substantial changes. He is no longer satisfied with a complementary role. He desires and has managed to win an independent status because repeated, isolated and organized exposure to his music has successfully induced the people to take a specific and independent interest in his creations. In this manner, the composer and the film-director have become joint operators in a common business-cum-art venture, instead of being associates in a unified filmic exploration of a composite sensibility.

It is safe to say that during the same period (that is, the post-forties) the film-director was supplanted by the film-producer. The musical fare of the period predominantly consists of catchy tunes, accompanying fillings of large orchestras, a frequent and almost blatantly plagiaristic use of 'foreign' musical idioms, etc. In the era of the silent films, receivers of cinematic creations constituted an 'audience'; a little later the audiences were replaced by the 'people'. Since the forties the people have been supplanted by the 'public'! No elaborate conceptual analysis is needed to convey that the above characterization tries to suggest a progressive heterogeneous character of the receiver. The successive stages in which the receiver went on becoming more and more amorphous are reflected in the three terms. It is symptomatic that an abundant use of meaningless words in songs, frequent use of non-musical intonations, employment of near-prose stresses or rhythms based on them, deployment of deafening and over-whelming percussion instruments and screechingly high-pitched singing have all become pervasive musical features during the period. Music has become so liberated from the constraints imposed on it by virtue of being a component, that it has ceased to be film-music. It has become a joint presentation of film and music, each making an excuse of the other to hang together. The cumulative effect has been to make the contemporary Indian film-music less culture-bound. It is worth noting that the Indian service of the B.B.C. could use a choral theme from a Bombay Talkies production, *Janmabhoomi* (1936) as the signature tune. This could happen because Indian film-music could then become a tonal and cultural symbol. A comparable situation is difficult to imagine today. Indian film-music has started reaping all the advantages of being a success-formula in circulation. It is produced on a mass-scale; it is quick to act; it is easily available and remains the same in all the corners of the country. The compulsion that made such music possible has no doubt given us music of greater abandon, more tonal colour, variety and finish. But it has in the bargain also become transient, rootless and artificial.

5

Music and music-films

Why is it necessary to take a special look at films on music and musicians? The answer is that such films create a peculiar aesthetic and conceptual situation. In such films music is related to the cinematic art in two ways. Firstly, music is present and operative as in any other film. That is, at one level or the other it functions as a component of a total filmic whole. Secondly, music also becomes a subject or a theme in such films. It therefore becomes a controlling and channelizing centre. All the creative forces converge at music and operate from it. This is frequently in addition to its former role of being a constituent. The whole structuring therefore becomes very intricate. As a consequence, the weightages enjoyed by the various combining factors or the interacting forces vary to a great extent and a consideration of crucial importance becomes necessary: there cannot be a common set of criteria readily available to judge the artistic merit of films in general and of films on music and musicians. Or, to put it more correctly, it is necessary to have an additional set of criteria to judge films on music and musicians. The situation is, aesthetically speaking, challenging and may need more than an adroit handling of art-concepts.

In music-films, music itself becomes a theme. What is a theme? We are aware that the term is used widely in almost all arts; it is also frequently regarded as synonymous with the term 'subject'. However, it is preferable to treat the latter as having a wider scope. Thus a subject can have many themes in it. Coming back to the particular context it is seen that when music becomes a subject of a film, the theme can be a musical form, or an instrument or a personality. The list of such themes can of course be a long one but at any rate, music-film means a film which enables us to have musical experience apart from other concomitants like the literary or the visual experience, etc. This needs to be stressed because the tendency to interpret terms like 'theme' and 'subject' with a literary bias is very pronounced. The reason is that on an abstract conceptual plane there are close parallels between thematic developments in music and literature. For instance, statement, reiteration and elaboration of a theme; use of the associated or the contextual emotive or intellectual features in elaboration; organization of the thematic material aimed at facilitating emergence of a definite basic structure or pattern; employment of techniques suitable to allow the theme itself to decide the course, the pace and the movement involved, are some of the characteristics common to thematic development in both literary and musical progressions.

It is however to be noted that these similarities are mostly confined to the structural aspect. Beyond this point the ways and means of literary development differ from those considered desirable for music-film as the latter should follow the contours of music in its attempts. If music-films follow literary methods they will convey literary-visual messages rather than communicating musical experiences. It is of course possible to maintain that as all music-films are not designed to transmit musical experience the literature-biased devices of the thematic development need not be completely set aside. They can therefore be used with great advantage in educational, documentary, biographical and informative music-films. Perhaps it is better to clarify what these categories mean. In the present context 'educational' means a venture which involves actual teaching. The 'documentary' music-film records and stores evidence for future use. A 'biographical' music-film narrates or constructs a person's life, partially or totally. 'Informative' music-film is an objectively passed-on totality of facts with or without explicit or implicit value-judgement.

It is instructive to note the devices used by music-films which do not aim at communicating musical experience. Educational music-films rely on narration; the documentary type use commentary and persuasion; the biographical music-films depend on chronology and historical perspective, while the informative ones concentrate on an uninvolved statement and neutral presentation of facts. It is hardly necessary to explain what is meant by the term narrative, etc. It may however be helpful to know why these devices are categorized as 'literary'. They are classified thus, because they tend to be conducive to the type of experience passed on to us through creative and critical literary expression. On the other hand, they do not lead to musical experience. In conclusion, music-films should try to evolve a way of combining musical characteristics with film-logic instead of falling back on literary-visual allusions to music and resorting to organizational principles capable of providing only literary experience.

The devices, identified as literary because they are content-oriented, allow the linguistic meaning to assume an important role. Words their combinations according to certain rules, the roots and derived meanings of the words, the affective aspect based on word-meanings, concepts of style and similar items follow. Particular ways of literary expression and the consequential emergence of literary forms or genres become a reality *because* words have meanings. In this manner, content conditions the expression and the devices referred to earlier come into operation.

A question now arises: why is it that literary devices prove incapable of providing musical experience? The answer lies in the intrinsic distinction between literary and musical experiences. In the absence of a clear understanding of the distinction we are likely to use wrong (irrelevant) devices and end up with unexpected and frustrating results. It is necessary to realize that the meaningfulness accompanying the linguistic expression invariably relies on succession of meaningful units, unilinearity of progression in the presentation of these units and the equivalence between meaningful units and the content relevant at any particular moment of time. The printed word which is the most common and widely received literary expression suffices to bear out the existence of these qualities as typical of literature and literary experience.

In this way, the trinity of succession, unilinearity and unit-content equivalence, distinguish literary experience from its musical counterpart. In a manner, the trinity can be traced to a yet more fundamental distinction between the two arts of music and literature. Of the two, the former is a performing art and the latter a non-performing, composite art. The distinction assumes significance because certain consequences flowing from the distinction are related to the kind of 'time' each art recognizes and the use 'time' is put to in their respective manifestations. Stating it briefly, musical time can be characterized as one that makes for a simultaneous rather than a successive experience. In reality, musical time demolishes chronology, succession and unilinearity through simultaneity, multiphony and circularity. Total disregard of the day-to-day clock-time eliminates the chronological aspect; effective use of more than one note, etc., at a time, does away with the aspect of succession; and finally, the recurring time-patterns, etc., with their roles unchanged, removes unilinearity from the line of action. *Musical time has a continuous presence.* When Poe, Pater and other aestheticians eulogized music and suggested that 'All arts aspire to the state of music', they were only alluding to the simultaneity of musical experience and the aesthetic value of an achievement imparting it.

It is to be noticed with advantage that most of the creative writers who are keen on extending the dimensions of literary experience, have assiduously directed their efforts at attaining the simultaneity of musical expression. The stream of consciousness method, the episodic plot-construction, the twin-story arrangement, the use of symbols and synesthetic imagery are some of the major ways in which literature has tried to aspire to the state of music by manipulating the dimension of time. Recourse to such methods was found essential because the inherent qualities of literary time would not otherwise be able to explore the simultaneity on its own. It is therefore logical to follow in the footsteps of music vis-a-vis time-manipulation if we wish to enjoy the aesthetic gains associated with it. Approximation to musical experience is therefore a frequent operational strategy employed by creative writers.

The ground covered so far leads to the conclusion that literary devices which assume their particular character on account of the inherent disposition towards literary time cannot conceivably lead to musical experience.

Under the circumstances what should the music-films do? A little consideration will make it clear that to evolve and to use methods as well as devices possessing qualities of musical time, is the aesthetic nostrum that could be administered. A further thought also makes it obvious that the cinematic art need not overexert itself in this respect in order to renounce its literary crutches. This is because flash-back, juxtaposition, montage and similar devices are already in cinematic circulation. What is lacking is a firm conceptual awareness and a resolve that there is a special affinity between such devices and the musical experience. If film-logic is judiciously combined with the cinematic representation of musical time, the resulting framework will surely prove salutary for the communication of musical (and not the visual-literary) experience which music-films try to provide. It is therefore imperative that music-films should place greater trust in auditory imagery; they should also seek their thematic development in the permeating usage of sequence instead of relying on chronology and finally depend on the employment of juxtaposition instead of succession. Ultimately it is music which should get a 'role'—proper and functional in this intricate situation.

To say that music should be allowed to play a proper role in a music-film is to put forward a plea that proper music be used in a music-film. The tautology is only apparent because a music-film is an instance of *music commenting on music* with a view to communicate musical experience. What is the proper music in a music-film? The question boils down to a yet more basic question: what is the nature of relationship of the arts of cinema and music when they come together? Both music and cinema are independent arts possessing their own characteristic expressive powers. It is therefore inevitable that their coming together should require a careful balancing of creative forces and a skilful use of their respective strengths and weaknesses. It is on this background that we have to examine the inter-art relationship and arrive at a conceptual decision about the nature and function of film-music. This in turn will clarify the role of music in a music-film.

There are two major theoretical positions that deserve consideration. They are: the Organic Unity Theory and the Limited Autonomy Theory. From these two, many decisions of a conceptual nature follow and condition the type and extent of music used in films.

The main premise of the Organic Unity Theory (henceforth referred to as the O.U. theory) is that film is a composite art and as such can use music only as one of the integral components. It may of course become more or less predominent depending on the type of film concerned. Nevertheless, it remains a component. A component is only a part of the whole and hence less than the whole, both quantitatively and qualitatively. Further, being a component, music merges with the film. While in the process of merging it cannot remain the same, nor does it remain a separate entity. In tone, texture, feeling, pace, etc., it becomes one with the film. In fact its effective existence is owing to its merging with the film. As a consequence if it is taken out of the whole in which it has merged, music loses its identity. Film-music has a contextual value and in respect of significance it is not self-sufficient.

A very important contention of the O.U. theory is that the merging of music in the total film-structure reinforces the artistic endeavour. The musical structure gets its particular form on account of the totality of the film-structure with which it maintains a definite identifying relationship. The relationship between film-structure and musical construction is chiefly characterized by the phenomenon of correspondence. The correspondence phenomenon connotes similarity in matters of design, rhythmic structure and associational clusters. In a way the construct of film-music reflects the relevant part of the film structure.

Correspondence however does not exclude the use of contrasted expression. This is logical because contrast is only an inverse correspondence. Correspondence means that in matters of tonal design, rhythmic stresses, durational aspects, variations of pace, the shape that music assumes is determined by the film-structure. The affective aspect is also not left out in this scheme. What the film-structure wants to achieve in respect of emotional impact, etc., is to be reinforced by music. Music is to use its own powers or explore them in such a way as to successfully match the intent, direction and method followed by the non-musical, filmic part of the whole.

What needs special attention is the insistence of the O.U. theory that a 'music-emotion' correspondence is in existence and it is to be selected and subsequently matched with the 'emotion-filmic unit' correspondence. The O.U. theory takes for granted that musical units can be gay, sad, disturbed, etc., in their own right and by themselves, and further, it believes that a subsequent act of matching them with the relevant film-units with similar associational hinterland is possible. The final product is therefore a quantitative doubling of forces leading to a qualitative reinforcement of emotional effects.

A little reflection makes it obvious that all the argument outlined above becomes tenable because of the underlying faith of the O.U. theory that *music has meaning*. According to it, there exists a definite equation between music and something which stands outside music (and for which music stands). Just as there is a linguistic unit which becomes a literary unit on account of its capacity to have a definite dictionary meaning accompanied by a suggestive aura; similarly a musical piece or phrase carries a definite emotional content in addition to the nebulous but equally real suggestive aura. The Indian musicological categorization of music according to the *navarasa* scheme is a very pertinent instance of this way of thinking. It is evident that the literary or the content-oriented concept of meaning is here transferred to the art of music.

The Limited Autonomy Theory (henceforth referred to as the L.A. theory) takes a diametrically opposite position.

To start with, it holds that music is an entity by itself even as film-music. It has an independent identity and hence it possesses its own laws of organization and expression. The inclusion of music in the total artistic endeavour is effective because music is important *as music*. Therefore music is on a different and higher level than that of a component. To be aesthetically valid, this music has to fulfil the basic condition of being music and in addition to this it has to be appropriate in the filmic context. Film-music is no doubt 'in' a film. It is also true that without this excuse it could not have come into existence at all. All the same it retains its separate identity and it is felt as such. The miracle is possible only because it does not allow a merger with the total endeavour. It is conceived, expressed and received in a way that negates the rationale behind the terms like merger, fusion, unification.

Why does film-music resist merger, etc.? It does so because the reinforcement and intensification of the intended aesthetic effect in a composite art-expression like film is possible only if simultaneous or synchronized and parallel musical structures are erected while keeping in view the overall structures and their respective contours, etc. At times, the parallelism is achieved through onomatopoeic expression. A very important feature of the onomatopoeic parallelism is that the concerned structure is not restricted to the use of sounds customarily treated as musical. They are undoubtedly musical as far as their organization, conception and intention are concerned but if their basic material is examined, they are found to have a much wider acoustic base than is usually obtained. Such music might not be sweet or melodious in the established sense of the term but it is distinguished by its appropriateness. That is, it is music with a relevance. That makes it successful in the task of reinforcement of the general thrust of the art-work in question.

A subtle conceptual shift will be noticed here. The 'relevant music' we are describing reinforces not through correspondence but through approximate equivalence. These obtained equivalences are emotional, that is, they are related to the affective aspect of music. They are approximate because there is no one-to-one and intrinsic relation of affirmation between a particular content-situation and the musical unit in question. Further, they are emotional in the sense that they base their operations on a firm cultural belief that due to various musical and extra-musical associations, different musical and non-musical sounds are psychologically connected with affective life and content: situations like birth, growth, initiation, separation, marriage, death, etc. The 'relevant music' also believes that expression and reception of one member of the pair leads to the arousal and the experiencing of the other member. It is obvious that these approximate affective equivalences differ from culture to culture and therefore can hardly be described as intrinsic to music.

It is on this background that the L.A. theory holds music to be significant but not meaningful. In other words, it takes up the position that even though music has the capacity to give valuable experience it lacks the property of pinpointed reference to emotional or intellectual experiences of established connotations and denotations. The autonomy-slant of the L.A. theory is detected in its suggestion that music-experience can enrich the total experience in question *only* if music is allowed to follow its own logic in matters of internal organization and inter-structural balancing of elements. At the most, music takes a cue from the filmic or the dramatic or the choreographic situation when these composite art-forms create categories like music-film, opera, ballet, etc. Thus the autonomy (reflected in the freedom to follow the musical impulse) is 'limited' as the original opening for the musical impulse is provided by non-musical expressions and also because music is to that extent subservient to the overall filmic, dramatic, choreographic purpose.

The L.A. theory, it must be noted here, gets additional support from the Indian film-situation in which song numbers predominate. No song can become a 'song' unless it succeeds in creating its own micro-universe and stand out in musical relief. To desire the merging of a 'song' is to ask for an aesthetic impossibility. Song is too integrated an entity to allow the slightest dismembering. On the other hand, some kind of loosening of individual structures is a precondition for all mergers, fusions and similar processes. A song protrudes and therefore intensifies. It is a completed and closely woven structure which gives a firm foundation to the parallelism discussed above. Nothing vindicates the L.A. theory so strongly as do the songs.

To sum up, we started by tracing the reasons of the special problems posed by music-films. It was argued that music-films cannot give musical experience they seek to provide *if* they insist on following the content-oriented literary devices of narration, etc. A suggestion was made that the root-problem is the incorrect conceptual understanding of the relationship between two arts belonging to two differing categories. Discussing the two major theoretical positions regarding music-film relationship a conclusion was arrived at that the structuring of a music-film must follow the lines of music itself if the filmic venture is to communicate musical and not visual-literary experience. A brief mention was made of the Indian situation in which it is the song which exemplifies the film-music co-appearance.

6

Music and autonomy :
a conceptual examination

The concept of autonomy is widely discussed today due to various socio-political and historical reasons. An understanding of the concept will help in striking a balance between the increasing social and state controls on the individual and the individual's growing demand for more freedom to achieve self-determined goals.

Before attacking the central issues, certain preliminary statements need to be made:

Firstly, even if the possibility of a general, all-embracing discipline of aesthetics is accepted, music will continue to enjoy a limited aesthetic autonomy. This would also be true of other arts. Autonomy here means what its root-meaning suggests: self-rule or self-law, that is, the freedom to make one's own rules and regulations.

Secondly, like many other issues, the autonomy-issue encounters special difficulties vis-a-vis music because the latter happens to be a performing art. *Music needs performance to realize itself as an art-activity.* The concept of performance acts as a limiting condition and to that extent musical autonomy is limited.

Finally, there are in fact two varieties of autonomy associated with music: the first can be called the internal and the second can be classed as the external. External, as against internal, means located outside the system. Within a single culture it is logically expected that the two autonomies are co-terminus, though arriving at the same point from opposite directions. However, this ideal is hardly ever realized. The two are often out of step with each other. In fact, there is a time-lag before they attain a balance.

The two types of autonomies provide a suitable starting point for discussion.

What do we mean by the concept of internal autonomy? Internal autonomy is the elaborational freedom allowed to the individual artist within the relevant musical framework. It can also be described as the scope afforded by a culture for structural rearrangements of elements which succeed in creating an organic musical whole.

On some occasions this freedom or self-rule can be made explicit in terms of musicology (understood in a narrower sense as the grammar of musical practices in a particular culture). The two basic modes of organizing the tonal material of music, the melody and the harmony, can be mentioned in this respect. For instance, at one time the western musical system regarded musical intervals of the third and the sixth unacceptable as members of the harmonic structure. They were felt to be dissonant and were therefore denied entry into the tonal nuclei. Later in history they were, however, admitted into the fold. The point is that the later recognition of their musical legitimacy signified more scope in theme-selection or elaboration. In a similar fashion, Indian *raag*-grammar at one time did not authorize the consecutive use of the *komal* and the *shuddha* varieties of the same note. In fact the very idea of the *raag* itself constitutes an example of grammatical constraints self-imposed by a musical culture to create narrower frameworks which could function autonomously. In this context an autonomous functioning is to be equated with a continued operation of a closed system which allows freedom within itself and simultaneously precludes entry and use of non-conforming extraneous elements. Therefore in every elaboration of a *raag*, the individual artist has a choice —but the choice is to be exercised strictly within a pre-determined framework. The autonomy is here virtually confined to carrying out permutations and combinations of the given musical items or units. Even when the elaboration is of a non-*raag* progression, the musical idiom of the genre or the stylistic conventions of the particular *gharaanaa* involved act as controlling factors. The internal self-rule described here also extends to other matters like voice-modulation, word-pronunciation, tempo-variation, allowable body-movements and facial gestures, solo-choral distributions of the musical parts and finally, the place and importance of the audience-response in actual performance.

Another instance of the self-regulated internal musical functioning can be observed in the hierarchical existence or system of the various musical forms. One of the chief distinguishing features of musical forms is that each form presupposes a definite apportionment of the different musical elements. Ingredients like importance accorded to words, weightage given to *aalaaps*, stress on rhythm, etc., combine in varying proportions in various musical forms: in this manner a whole hierarchy comes into being. Each form allows manipulation of the basic musical elements—though within a certain range. *Gharaanaas* in Hindustani music too exemplify similar autonomous working—each *gharaanaa* being a microcosm within a larger musical macrocosm. *Gharaanaa* is a statement of a closed and coherent point of view which allows reinterpretation of interrelationships of musical elements and also of the derived details. Whether in the matter of musical forms or in respect of the *gharaanaas*, the autonomous musical functioning reveals a valuational bias as opposed to the technical bias present in the musicological variety. In other words, the former concerns itself with the quality of experience and the relevant criteria useful to make an aesthetic judgement. On the other hand the musicological bias concerns itself with rules and regulations laid down in order to preserve the correctness of music. However, both the aesthetic and the musicological orientations are instances of the internal variety of musical autonomy.

In a way the problem was so far simple because in dealing with *raag* or the non-*raag* music of the Hindustani type, we continued to treat material that was intrinsically related to or belonged to a system acting as a larger reference-frame. For example, in the present context the material belonged to the melodic and Hindustani frame-works. But what will be the position of the smallest musical phrase or a single, isolated musical note? Both these are virtually speaking, reference-neutral. Therefore, will a phrase of this kind allow the building-up of any variety and any number of phrases to be associated with it? Or, will a single, isolated note mean an unrestricted musical elaboration? In such circumstances it may appear that the available self-rule may not be subject to any restraint whatsoever.

The counter-arguments are very strong. Firstly, there is no dearth of theoreticians who argue that even a single note has a direction, a rhythmic weight and a nuclear proclivity, etc. Hence it is argued that the autonomy is not as unlimited as it appears.

In fact there could be a clearer statement of this position which raises a crucial question: can a note really appear in isolation and by itself? When a single, isolated note is put forward as an expressive agent, is it not an example of a hidden melodic phrase with its expressive power concentrated in one of its members? In such a case a single note acts as a spokesman of a melody and thus there are perhaps no single notes in music. The restated position about a single note is that it has within it an implied but definite line of subsequent musical elaboration. It is in actuality a musical phrase with some components less 'vocal'. In this manner the problem of a single-note gets transformed into a problem of a single phrase appearing outside the larger frameworks like melody or *raag*, etc. In such circumstances does a phrase enjoy limitless autonomy?

In my opinion it is at this stage that the centre of discussion moves out of the domain of internal autonomy. The point is that a minimal musical unit like a single phrase has the maximum ambiguity. It has therefore the lowest reference potential and this is accompanied by the consequent absence of rules, etc. Here the aspect of meaningfulness in music looms large and we cross into the region of the external autonomy of music. Absence of the internal self-rule does not mean absence of any rule because such a freedom will in fact be a negation of freedom, as in its wake follows an explicit annihilation of form.

What is external musical autonomy? It is the freedom to incorporate and manipulate new musical material which, if viewed in itself, belongs to an alien cultural group and musical ethos. The new musical material is of course subjected to the scrutiny of the established cultural (and not musical) norms before it is accepted. This variety of autonomy is described as external for two reasons: firstly, the material subjected to the scrutiny is outside the extent of the examining culture, and secondly, the criteria employed to determine the musical legitimacy of the items are cultural and not musical. In this manner the emanating centres of self-rule enjoy an externalized status vis-a-vis total culture as well as the musical sub-culture respectively.

For example, though both the Indian and the Chinese systems of music are melodic in a broad sense, the Indian musicians or their system will not accept the Chinese musical intervals. Nearer home, *Hindustaani raag*-elaboration cannot employ *gamak* in the

Carnatic manner unless as a special effect. The very fact that a *Carnatic gamak* can achieve a special effect in *Hindustaani* music proves that it cannot form a part of the accepted vocabulary of the latter. More importantly, the reluctance of the *Hindustani* musician to imitate the Chinese or the *Carnatic* musical thinking is not because he lacks the necessary initiative or on account of his musical puritanism. His reluctance is due to the fact that the freedom to go out, to deviate, is conditioned by the internal autonomy and the desire to accommodate alien features into the musical family is limited by cultural conditioning. The ultimate authority is wielded by the concern to remain meaningful musically.

It is the operations of the external autonomy which deny entry to outside musical elements unless their claims pass the initial test of cultural acceptability. Unless the verdict of the external autonomy is in their favour, certain musical items, phrases, structures may not be recognized or categorized as art-structures at all. Hence musical expression of alien cultures may appear to us as significant and yet (musically) meaningless. *Every culture determines what it can regard and accept as music* and external autonomy applies the filter through which new material has to pass. Once a decision in this respect is arrived at, internal autonomy takes over and applies its musical criteria. The external autonomy employs relevance as the chief criterion. This criterion is aesthetically neutral. On the other hand the internal autonomy uses the criteria of correctness (musicological) and valuableness (aesthetic). On this background it may be stated that music as a phenomenon possesses two categories of meanings: cultural and musical. The external autonomy is concerned with the cultural meaning and the internal autonomy with the musical meaning. If certain acoustic concretisations are accepted by a culture as music, the same will be said to possess cultural meaning and if they are recognized by the group concerned to have value or quality in musical activities taken as a whole, the concretisations will be judged to be musically meaningful.

The latter musical meaning has a further connotational aspect. For example, the statements which affirm *rasa*-music correspondences or music-colour-relationships or propositions like 'music *x* is gay' or 'music *y* is sad', bring out the connotational aspect of the musical meaning. Musical meaning of this type is determined ethno-culturally and not by structural or formal features. This is the reason why similar or the same sound-patterns 'mean' differently to different cultures. The larger the musical unit and more the number of items included in it, the greater is the possibility that it will have a more easily determined and discerned connotational meaning. To have a connotational meaning is tantamount to having looser external autonomy. The reasons are not far to seek. As the connotational meaning depends heavily on the association-analogy syndrome, alien sound-material will find it harder to penetrate into the corpus of musical frameworks already accepted as musically meaningful. Compared to the external autonomy, controls of the connotational aspects operate less rigidly in the internally autonomous material. Even so, the more the connotational meaning, the lesser the intra-structure freedom to carry out the intentions to invent and execute patterns.

By now it must have become clear why the minimal musical unit is associated with musical meaning on the one hand and with external autonomy on the other hand. It is so because this unit has the maximum autonomy but also the minimum of meaning. It is interesting to note that the universals of music which have met with the maximum of approval are all instances of minimal musical units. They are those musical relationships which are actualized through the operation of:

1. The Principle of Tonality,
2. The Principle of Absolute Consonance,
3. The Principle of the Cycle of the Fifths.

Musical units realized through the operation of the above principles achieve an immediate impact, that is, they are accepted as effective musical signals without the mediation of any other cultural concept. Irrespective of the culture of origin, or the system of origin, the manifestations of these three principles are accepted as musically significant though they are not granted the status of connotationally meaningful musical expressions. Thus the expanse or the elaborateness of the individual musical unit and the existence of musical meaning go hand in hand while the degree of the minimality of the musical unit and greater autonomy prove to have closer intrinsic links.

The external musical autonomy has one more important characteristic which needs mention. It is related to the fundamental aesthetic truth that sound as a raw material of music has no representational content. As the onomatopoetic element in music is negligible, it can be stated as a general rule that musical sounds *per se* do not stand for anything else located outside. This is the reason why routine human life and its various manifestations cannot find place in the composing or performing of music. *Music does not reflect the ordinary and the concrete concerns of life because it cannot do so.* As a consequence musical golden ages very frequently coincide with a general, material or economic decline. To the extent that they admit representational content, other arts are conditioned by external events. On account of its non-representational content and the unique quality of its raw material, music can pursue a course of development that might be contrary to the overall cultural tendencies. Therefore a Nero could strum lyre-strings while Rome was in flames!

In sum, it seems that music as a whole enjoys a greater degree of autonomy. On the other hand a close acquaintance with the systems of art-music reveal that they are less autonomous than they appear to be. Further, if the inter-cultural aspect is examined, the autonomy enjoyed by the art of music shrinks considerably. It is also clear that the problem of musical autonomy is multi-faceted. For example, the implications of the concept of autonomy change in their nature and extent when music is allied with other arts. The tenor of the treatment also undergoes radical changes when socio-economic concepts like commitment, progress and modernity are brought into the fray. As discussed here, the problem is stated in a slightly abstracted manner in order to make an unambiguous preliminary consideration.

7

Music and modernism

There are some terms which seem to possess an enduring prestige. More often than not, such a prestige indicates presence of qualities which enjoy an inherent capacity to answer certain needs of the collective cultural mind. Such terms can be called cultural terms. They mirror the living, contemporary aspect of social life and thus acquire a hold over thinkers as well as laymen. Modernism is one such term.

The word-history of the term carries a useful hint of the basic cause of its perennial attraction. Modernism or modernity, etc., lead us back to '*modernus*', meaning 'just now'! Even the contemporary usage keeps the original meaning. Today too, the terms signify a desire 'to be with the present'. What is thought provoking is the fact that the desire to keep pace with the times is not a new phenomenon. All evidence suggests that modernity and its characteristics have a tendency to recur. Every student of cultural history comes to note that cultural modernity *had been here before*. The wider the spectrum before us, the stronger the feeling that creative minds had been 'modern' before our times.

However, the distinction between modernism and modernity cannot be overlooked. Firstly because they are overlapping concepts; secondly because very often they are confused with each other. Modernity is a wider term encompassing within it the areas of science, religion, art, etc. Compared to it, modernism is a narrower manifestation which moves to establish a clearer, coherent and almost a philosophic relationship with a particular, well-defined life-area. Of necessity, an *ism* tries to construe happenings in a particular walk of life at a particular period. When a number of minds feel a property or a group of properties to have achieved the status of a *zeitgeist*, an *ism* is born. Focussing our concern on arts, we can state that when a group of qualities is discernible in creation, reception and appraisal of an art-activity, the event exemplifies the advent of an *ism*. It is in this context that the relationship of modernism and music is sought to be examined here.

Musical modernism : the two aspects

It has been suggested earlier that the patent question raised in relation to modernism is whether the concerned art is keeping pace with the general life-style in a given period. It should therefore lead one to conclude that the concept has two aspects: the temporal and the content-oriented. In this way terms like contemporary, period-piece, futuristic, etc., reflect the temporal aspect. On the other hand, use of terms like new, neo, traditional, revolutionary, etc., refer to the content aspect. When modernism is averred of music, both these aspects are expected to be duly reflected in it. In other words, when a piece of music is accepted as 'modern' it means that it is accepted as 'belonging to the present' and also because it displays a capacity to cater to certain musical needs which would not otherwise have been satisfied by the existing music.

This general position cannot however be easily assumed because of a complicating factor. It must be remembered that music can hardly be confined to art-music alone. In all sophisticated societies, four musical streams flow side by side to complete the soundscape. No instance of modernism can hold good in case of these varieties in equal measure. For example, primitive music proves to be a test-case. The very reason for its existence is its inseparableness from the totality of life. Primitive music is so intertwined with the life-style in question that it can hardly be dissociated from the latter in respect of its promptings, reception, expression, etc. As a result, 'modernism' and primitive music can hardly be brought together in an affirmative relationship. Modernism can be predicated in case of only those phenomena which allow non-coincidence of life-style and music-style. In other words, the presence or occurrence of modernism needs an inherent cultural possibility of dissociation of sensibilities on the temporal axis. Primitive culture is too homogeneous to allow it; hence there cannot be a modern primitive music. Thus understood, modernism turns out to be a relational concept. Nothing can be modern by itself. To be modern is to repattern temporal relationships of cultural manifestations of a social group. It is evident that primitive life excludes such a possibility.

Folk-music is in a slightly different position. A considerable portion of folk-music is secular. As a result it does not totally eliminate the possibility of a partial change. However, the changes can only be partial because the characteristic of functionality has its own constraints on folk-music. In this manner, though modernism *is* possible in the case of folk-music, the proportion of the potential or possible change is too inadequate to merit a discussion while considering the problem of musical modernism.

There remain therefore the three major categories of music: urban, popular and the art. Of the three, the urban variety is entirely shaped by the needs of urban societies. Political songs, *mela*-songs, *bhajans* recited in the crowded metropolitan trains, band-music of the marriage bands, etc., are instances of musical structures that possess in-built mechanisms responsive to the needs of the time. And as far as popular music is concerned the very category chiefly consists of music which is propagated and often manufactured by the mass-media including broadcasting, television, films, recorded music and the like. Popular music, as a musical category, is a product of the total social, economic and cultural processes initiated and carried out by the mass-media. It can therefore be expected to be modernist on account of intrinsic compulsions.

The third major category—that of art-music—needs a separate discussion. Art-music suffers the least from the direct pressures of day-to-day life. Its basic motivation too exhibits the touch of materialism to the minimum. In short, modernism which it can boast of, is bound to be a direct result of aesthetic compulsions. In order to get an idea of musical modernism if we decide to apply the convenient yardstick of examining the nature and proportion of changes that take place, we note that art-music exemplifies two types of changes: some introduced during a performance and some other that occur in the tradition taken as a whole. During actual performances the logic of the internal and intended organization of the musical components undergoes continuous changes. Quite often, the approach that leads to such changes are in reality due to atavistic tendencies. Thus, a reappearance of tendencies apparently belonging to the past makes its impact felt as an instance of modernism. On the other hand on occasions, the changes are prognostic in character (though they are realized to be so only later!) In sum, modernism in art-music is a complicated affair. The complications are multiplied further when various forms of music are brought into the picture. The forms differ in the extent of modernism they display. It is next to impossible to bring in graphic exactitude to describe modernism vis-a-vis various forms of music. As art-music is not our central inquiry, it is not even necessary to do so. Therefore, on the background of the foregoing remarks, it is now proposed to deal with the characteristics of modernism likely to hold true in respect of musical activity considered as a whole.

1. The urban base
The very first characteristic of musical modernism is its urban base (and not merely an urban foundation.) It is of course true that the three musical categories of urban, popular and art-music can reach human groups living in non-urban areas but they cannot germinate in non-urban centres. It is not necessary for us to define what is 'urban'. By collecting and collating data on population, available communications, location of administrative centres, distribution of educational institutions, the above question has been answered. Without having any technical knowledge of any kind even a layman is able to distinguish among seats of human culture, as for example, habitation, hamlet, village, township, city, metropolitan city, etc. The point is that from among such, modernism depends on urban places for its gestation, flowering and evaluation. Modernism is therefore an urban manifestation.

2. Deviation : the mainstay of modernism
Musical modernism invariably expresses itself as a deviation from the established tradition or occasionally even as a break with it. Sometimes it is also possible that the deviation is actuated by extra-musical events or ideas. However, in the final analysis the deviation has to meet definite musical needs in order to justify its continued consideration as a characteristic of musical modernism.

Nevertheless, the deviation that marks the onset of modernism proves to be a continuation of a larger tradition—a fact realized when the situation is appraised in its totality. In other words, events or ideas that appear revolutionary during a particular period or at a particular point of time, later impress us merely as consolidations or continuations of larger continuities perceived when a perspective (covering a longer period) is obtained. Retrospections are virtual denials of revolution though the initial impact of modernism is often felt as being radical deviations or revolutions. The phenomenon is detected with such a regularity that it compels inclusion as an inherent facet of musical modernism.

However, why does this happen? A closer examination of a longer period reveals that events, ideas sporting a revolutionary label are found to have 'similar' precedents. What appears to be new, radical, deviationist or revolutionary, etc., turns out to be a convincing example of recurrence. Once having lost their revolutionary character, the only alternatives that remain open in respect of such events are either to interpret them as evolutionary or to classify them as changes with open possibilities. *Per se* this is of course not displeasing. However it means that the concept of revolution suffers an attenuation of ideological splendour However there seems to be no escape from the fact that continuity is the essence of the cultural movement.

3. Grammatical deviation: highway to modernism

It could be easily maintained that the easiest and perhaps the commonest way in which modernism takes its first effective step is by resorting to grammatical deviation. In fact, even if the basic motivation is aesthetic, the initial impact of modernist music is a deviation registered in respect of the established musicological rules. For example, very frequently it is found that a musically modernist situation is created because the established norms about acceptable sounds, their sequence, accompanying rhythms, etc., are set aside.

Reference to grammar brings in its wake a reference to the criterion of correctness or purity. Usually the first and the strongest exception taken to modernism is on the ground that it fosters incorrect and impure music. The precise nature of this criticism should be properly understood because it has the widest circulation.

Grammar means an automatic invoking of the sanction of the scholastic tradition in art. Art-activity always presents two streams of tradition: the performing tradition and the scholastic tradition. It is the second which is strongly represented by the written grammatical code. It is commonly perceived that the scholastic tradition diverges from and lags behind the performing tradition. Just as literary expression and tradition remain ahead of the grammatical tradition in language, similarly, modern music is always found to register a deviation from the written, grammatical tradition. As only the codified portion of the art-activity is reduced to *writing*, deviation from the written is inevitable. The fact that art-practices and their codifications are not co-orbital, is absolutely unregrettable because it goes to prove that performers in general are less weighed down by the grammatical constraints. At the same time, it also signifies the importance of avoiding a hasty codification of new, untested art practices. It is on this background that every generation needs its own musical Manu, as also its own deviators.

The point is that both the grammarians and the performers can stake their claims to musical modernism through deviation— though with a difference. The difference is that in order to judge a grammarian's deviation, one has to refer to the scholastic tradition, while to do so in the case of a performer one goes back to both the traditions. Under the circumstances, it appears that a performer has more opportunities to be a modernist because he enjoys the option of deviating from two continuities unlike the grammarian whose choice is restricted to only one tradition.

4. Performance-oriented characteristics

Features of modernism discussed so far have been of a general nature in the sense that they possess validity vis-a-vis other arts too. Of immediate interest however, are characteristics with a direct bearing on the performance of music.

a) New relationships in internal organization

No music can be composed out of silences alone. Sound as a physical phenomenon remains the basic raw-material of music. Further, as a physical manifestation music will always be subject to the acoustic laws that govern the behaviour of sound as such. In sum, music has to live with sound though changes can be introduced in the internal organization of the acoustic and musical components. For instance, the mutual relations of notes, rhythms and tempi can be changed. Selecting the fundamental strategy of tonal organisation opens up immense possibilities of melodic and/ or harmonic 'thinking' in music. In addition, words too establish varying relationships with all the other fundamental elements of music. In these ways new intra-structural musical relationships can come into being. The contextual changes thus effected have a direct bearing on the aesthetic significance of the pieces.

b) New musical instruments

Musicians in quest of new timbers are naturally interested in inducting new musical instruments. However, extra-musical considerations also provide impetus in this search. Deliberate manufacture and use of new musical instruments have often sounded a note of musical modernism. Attempts at using the same instruments in a different manner or with changed playing techniques are also responsible in bringing about changes in the existing soundscape. Sometimes all other factors are kept constant while the context of employing the instrument is turned into a variable. Females taking to instruments conventionally restricted to male players is also a modernist 'gimmic'—which may or may not affect the performance in substance.

c) Changing cartography of musical forms

A very important indication of musical modernism is the shifting of boundaries that divide the existing musical forms. More often than not, a strong battle-cry is raised in defence of maintaining 'purity' of the forms whenever their contours are sought to be altered.

Whenever the limits that demarcate the subdivisions of the total musical territory are blurred or shifted, an interesting consequence is noticed: new 'mixed' art-forms come into vogue. Two or more existing art-forms are combined and new genres come into being —in the process, throwing fresh challenges to creative, receptive as well as critical sensibilities. The artistic excellence of such forms cannot of course be guaranteed. However they are expected to be at least 'different'. Novelty, and not originality, may happen to be their main characteristic. Nevertheless it allows them to lay claim to modernism.

d) Composite art-forms

Composite art-forms tell a story different from the one traced by the mixed art-forms. In their case two or more arts (and not art forms) interact to create the composite art-forms. Thus drama and music come together to give us opera, music-drama, musicals, etc., dance and music combine to yield ballet; photography and literature join to create films. The point to be remembered in this context is that each of the combining arts is a full-fledged, independent and adequate aesthetic expression; hence the generation of composite art-forms which they lead to, proves to be an exciting event. The three main combining categories of art relevant in the context are fine arts, performing arts and the literary arts. The aesthetic outcome depends on the nature and the varying ascendencies enjoyed by the combining arts participating in the creative adventure. It can be broadly stated that those developmental phases in which arts are inclined to come together seem to alternate with periods in which arts tend to move away from each other. Tracing such movements back to known antiquity, it is revealed that in those times two or more arts were generally found in a common or a combined expression. Individual arts began charting their separate courses in later ages and succeeded, after a time, in creating their own smaller autonomies. Once again, after a lapse of time they started coming together severally to create composite art-forms mentioned here; this third phase has universally been acclaimed as a modernist symptom.

Composite art-forms too cannot claim aesthetic excellence just by virtue of their having combined. However, there are more possibilities of their being so because the combining items themselves are proven depositories of aesthetic values.

e) Closer literary orientation

Examination of the performance-related characteristics of musical modernism also reveals that modernist music exhibits a closer alignment with literature. (In this context literature excludes oral literature.) The reason is that due to various aesthetic and non-aesthetic reasons modernism accentuates the function of the written and writing in general. This is not to suggest that all musical forms come under the influence of literature in an equal measure. Generally speaking, greater awareness of literary meaning, increased solicitude about pronunciation, greater variety in the poetic forms included in the overall musical repertoire and such other features become noticeable in the musical activity considered as a whole. It can in fact be safely argued that a high regard for language as such (and not only the 'literature' part of it) is asso-

ciated with musical modernism. The newly felt respect for the
language-literature pair does not remain confined to performance.
It spreads over to conception, preservation and criticism of music.
The way criticism is affected by it, is briefly described at a later
point.

f) The Janus-faced artist

Protagonists of musical modernism are found to possess two
musical faces! At least from one end the intriguing phenomenon
is related to performance. The artist-protagonists in question are
Janus-faced in the sense that they are bred and brought up in the
authentic older tradition and yet they manage to grow out of it.
For example, in India they are exemplified by musicians whose
pedigree is traced through the time-honoured *guru-shishya* school-
ing in learning, teaching, performing practices, etc. However
they take valuational decisions which ultimately lead to deviations
so essential to bring them and their music in the modern stream.
Their's is a case of a desired musical apostacy which results into a
cultural enrichment. These Janus-faced musicians are able to
intuit the nature of the necessary deviations and follow up the
intuitions with actual practice coupled with an evangelic fervour.
Apart from the artistic courage and the aesthetic convictions they
possess, such artists also seem to be endowed with qualities of
charismatic leadership. To that extent they hardly conform to
the image of artists as ivory-tower personalities. It is significant to
note that such artists though often born in villages or backward
areas, soon move out to settle down in urban areas. In view
of the urban connection of musical modernism, this can hardly be
described as an unimportant coincidence.

g) Changes in critical stance

The pervasive influence of musical modernism does not fail to
affect exercises of the critical faculty.

In the first instance, as the cartography of the musical forms
has already undergone changes, the critical criteria or the canons
of evaluation are also compelled to register a parallel change.
Ideally speaking, the critics are expected to keep criticism coextensive with the efforts of the creative artists; hence a change in the
existing corpus of the criteria is inevitable.

It is noticed that such a change results into the adoption of the
multiple criteria method. Modernist criticism tends to regard each
work of art as a multi-faced and complex phenomenon: as such, it

reveals the need for the application of the multi-criteria method. A closer examination further shows that the criteria are drawn from diverse disciplines like linguistics, anthropology, psychology—thus bringing into the field of operation, sets of interdisciplinary criteria that open up a number of new approaches. Under the circumstances, even the 'older' criteria acquire new contexts. To that extent modern criticism can become subtler.

Secondly, the entire critical usage displays a new flexibility and there is a symptomatic abundance of new critical isms. The monolithic evaluative theoretical structures based on *rasa, dhvani* or imitation doctrines, etc., no more enjoy their undisputed predominance. Instead, the critical scene is now peopled with a plethora of visions or insights vying with each other for a comprehensive validity. It is likely that some of the new isms themselves might develop into rigid conceptual frameworks after some time and thus lose in the name of action. But the very fact that there *can* be a new flowering of isms is itself an indication of a more liberal critical climate and the subsequent flexibility of thought-structures.

Thirdly, modern musical criticism shows a better consciousness of other arts as arts. This can be interpreted as a significant benefit accruing from its overall accommodativeness.

5. Socio-economic features

So far, we have been dealing with features which were patently performance-related. However, there are others which may not display such a direct connection. These may be categorized as socio-economic.

The very first change that takes place is in the patronage given to music. Modernism can be easily equated with a discernible heterogeneity of audience. Demands made on the artists by a heterogeneous audience are bound to be more general, varied as well as numerous. As an antidote to the adverse effects spilling over from this generality of the audience, many devices are employed to organize the audience. For example, with the onset of musical modernism, music-clubs or music-circles are formed, public concerts are organized by sale of tickets and felicitation programmes and such other music-situations come in vogue. All such attempts are indications of the desire to reorganize the heterogeneous audience and to ensure a homogeneous audience (with its musical expectations enjoying a neater focus).

From this point of view the modernist patronage could be described as the result of a simultaneously carried out bi-directional movement. On the one hand patronage of a single individual (like that of a king, feudal lord, etc.) becomes less prevalent; instead a social patronage takes its place. At the same time the social patronage is accepted only after a group is subjected to a reorganization designed to ensure that the artist and the audience are tuned to each other. Music is a performing art; as such it is shaped by the audience-participation to a great extent. Hence the change in patronage assumes significance. A modernist audience means patronage which has undergone changes due to factors like urbanization, mass-media-culture, etc.

Another modernist feature of the socio-economic category is the musician's growing internationalism. The modernist artist moves out far and wide in search of new patronage. Of course, it is true that even the earlier musicians used to travel widely and visit places beyond the national borders to seek new and more munificent patronage. There is however a qualitative distinction between the two quests. The modern artist moves out to a patronage that is essentially provided by a culturally alien group. He is therefore required to operate in a radically changed situation. In a very large measure the non-Indian patronage of the various national musics (e.g., Indian) is a patronage offered to music dubbed as an 'ethnic' music—a term suggestive of unhappy concepts of cultural hierarchies and unable to do justice to highly sophisticated music-systems. The contemporary modernist has to improvise, adapt, modify or even dilute the musical content in response to the new 'foreign' patronage. Even the mode of presentation does not remain unaffected. Further, once an artist turns into an internationalist in this manner, his presentations before the home-audiences undergo a gradual but sure transformation.

It is not easy to judge the desirability or otherwise of being an international artist in the sense discussed above. Many valuational decisions become necessary while facing the unique problems raised by situations involving cross-cultural communication. The mature approach needed to meet the challenge is obviously a rare commodity.

Musical modernism is also found to register a rise in the social prestige of musicians in general. This is so chiefly because musicians are no more treated as mere skilled entertainers or craftsmen.

They are accorded a status of an important cultural component. Modernism favours an educational philosophy which
regards music as a discipline on par with others generally included
in the category of humanities. It is also seen that a modernist
musician might come from a family or a caste not conventionally
given to the pursuit of the arts in general and music in particular. This latter feature also indicates a rise in prestige.

On account of the enhancement of his social status, a modern
musician tends to adopt changed techniques of creating and maintaining his own social image. Self-advertisement and propaganda,
interviews, news-conferences, delegations, committees and such
other paraphernelia of the modern social communication
are now regularly exploited by musicians. To that extent, he has
been forced to curb his individuality and conform to an image
which is acceptable to modern society. He now organizes himself
in a way that is conducive to *project* an acceptable image.

Perhaps the least recognized characteristic of musical modernism is the introduction of a new ritualism. Musical modernism is
generally associated with a better academic education of the
artist; hence it is probably true to say that ritualism manifest in
initiation-acts, *guru*-worship, first-performance ceremonies, etc.,
is regarded as dispensable. It is however not 'correct to say that
ritualism is completely eliminated. The fact is that the earlier
rites are replaced by new secular or a-religious or semi-religious
rituals. (A proof of this observation will be found in the study
and practice methods, preservation techniques as well as reception
of music by listeners, etc.). In this context a ritual is to be understood as any purposeful act or activity regularly enacted or carried
out by an individual to attain a psycho-physical state of equilib-
rium in order to ensure or enhance the effectiveness of study, practice, performance or reception of music. The stresses and the
strains of modern life call for a quicker and closer coordination of
the faculties involved in an act of performance; hence a rise of
new ritualism is inevitable. It is not rare to find similarity or
connection between a modern ritual and religious practices of a
bygone era. In fact such a phenomenon can often be interpreted
as a reappearance. It only proves that by definition, ritualism
need not be equated with superstition.

It is obvious that while one is considering characteristics of
musical modernism in a wider perspective, two disturbing prob-

lems remain. Firstly, can every act of change claim to be modern? And secondly, is the concept of modernism related to that of progress?

Every change cannot be classified as a manifestation of the modernist temper, nor can every act of change lay claim to modernity. Every change by itself satisfies one pre-condition of modernism, that is keeping pace with the times. This takes care of the temporal aspect of modernism. However, the content-aspect remains. Those events or changes which fail to pass the test set up by the second pre-condition (i.e., the content-aspect) are only accepted as fashions or popular modes. In this manner every change can validly stake a claim to modernity on account of having exhibited a temporal consonance but it has to bide time in order to gain full recognition. The full status of being modern can only be accorded to it after the content-aspect too displays a similar consonance. It is obvious that the temporal consonance is easier to realize and is usually detected early. The existence or the absence of the content-consonance is confirmed or can be confirmed only after a time-lag. Admitting a slightly paradoxical situation it is to be stated that a full modernist status can only be judged to be so in retrospect!

Turning to the second question, that is of the relation between the concepts of progress and modernism, it must be understood that the former concept does not belong to the field of art and aesthetics. Its proper field is to be found in politico-economic thought. In its ultimate and abstract state, the concept of progress is related to the concept of the Good. In asking a question like 'is work progressive?' we are going beyond aesthetics. It is not suggested that the question has no validity. It is however argued that it should be raised in different disciplines and in a different manner. A progressive work of art might thus be an inferior work of art. On the other hand, a work that passes the tests set up by both the aspects of modernism will turn out to be a great work of art.

To sum up, musical modernism has a function to perform. It provides an ideal and effective answer to stagnation in musical activity considered as a whole. Whatever might be the principles on which cultural development operates, modernism must have a place in it. In total disregard of our likes and dislikes, all changes are entitled to parade as both modern and artistic, at least in the initial stages and they will be inclined to do so. Resorting once again to a paradox, it could be said that the *timelessness of a work of art is only proved by the test of time!* It is only the deeper intuitions of artists and critics that possess the power to proclaim the timelessness of art without relying on the test of time.

8

Keertana :
an effective communication

With his usual perspicacity Lokmanya Tilak detected the communicative efficacy of the *keertana* and declared on one occasion that he would have chosen to be a *keertankaar* if he had not become a journalist. It is no wonder that the form flourishes in Maharashtra, Gujarat, Andhra Pradesh, Northern India, Bengal and in other regions of India. The reasons for the favour it has found are not far to seek. Firstly, it appeals to the solo as well as to the communal or the collective elements simultaneously. Secondly, it is multifaceted in the sense that it has speech, song, dance, mime and narration; therefore like a good dramatic piece it has something for every stratum of Indian society. The bases for its hold over the people are therefore comprehensive.

Whatever may be the type of *keertan* and whichever may be its parent religious sect, the *keertan* trains its sights outside itself, on the audience. Like a performer, a *keertankaar* describes his *keertan* as having *rang* (lit. 'colour') or failing to have it. Even if a *keertankaar* stages a veritable one-man show (and to that extent he can boast to be self-sufficient) his need for an audience is as real as that of a performing artist in music, dance or drama. Not only does he need the presence of an audience but he also yearns for that unique and final self-surrender of the audience to his effective communication. It is obvious that the process of communication as well as the concept itself changes in nature and scope, etc., from art to art and from one discipline to another. However, communication as it is realized in performing arts displays some common features like audience-response, improvisation, resorting to devices that have come to fruition in the oral tradition, etc. *Keertana* in India is to be examined on this background. Our chief concern therefore is to consider questions such as: what happens in a *keertana*, examined as an act of communication? How does a *keertana* formulate and execute its strategy of dealing with an audience? Indian aestheticians do not seem to have paid attention to *keertana* as a form. Nor has our 'bookish' art-criticism taken note of its achievements. Just as our music-thinkers have turned a deaf ear to outdoor music-forms like *powaadaa*, band-music, etc., they have also ignored *keertana*. In the absence of a critical follow up, *keertana* is categorized as 'mixed' or 'composite' in nature. This almost amounts to a critical dismissal! *Keertana* really deserves an alert and keen evaluative consideration by the aestheticians in general, music-thinkers in particular, and in fact by all performers.

The *keertana* has a number of components. *Keertana* has a narration. Ostensibly any event can be narrated. However an isolated and bare event in itself is consistently frowned upon by *keertankaar*s. They tend to provide every event with the perspective of a story at one level or another. (The levels the *keertankaar*s utilize can be of realistic accounting, mythological presentation, eye-witness narration, etc.) Treated in this manner an event always becomes a construed fact for the *keertankaar*. All events are hence provided with contexts. There are many ways of supplying these contexts. A context can be temporal. Thus a *keertankaar* invariably tends to point out an earlier event or series of events as antecedent to the event he is focussing on. This is the reason why a *keertana* so repeatedly harks back to chronological, mythological or the mythical past. A *keertankaar* is found to employ verbal formulae like 'Once upon a time it so happened, O ye lords!' In a large measure these formulae are instances of stylistic moulds used by a performer who wishes to channelize the imagination of his audience in an effective manner. In the present instance it is also to be noted that the indeterminate temporal frame suggested by the verbal formulae is an evocatioɴ which becomes doubly effective because there is no chronological pinning down that would have restricted its appeal.

Apart from the temporal setting provided, the narration and the speech are also distinguished by a repeated induction of the drone in the background. The drone continues to provide support for an intoned prose delivery. What is the purpose of intoning a part of the sentence or a group of sentences (forming a part of the narration taken as a whole) on a particular note—preferably the one used as a fundamental by the *keertankaar* in question?

One reason might be the concern felt by the *keertankaar* for continuity. He prefers to avoid abruptness. A *keertankaar* sings frequently and it is perhaps advisable not to have too noticeable and sudden change in pitch-levels that may occur while switching from narration to a song, etc. This however cannot be the whole truth because even those portions not adjacent to the song, etc., are found to have the intoned character. A more satisfactory answer seems to be indicated by the content-quality of the intoned prose. The import of some portions of the prose-narration is of such intellectual and emotional quality that it needs a special emphasis aimed at impressing the minds of the audience. This is the reason why a special method of 'intoned narration or delivery' is employed deliberately and repeatedly. Though the normal speech activity *does* use many pitch-levels in day to day life, it does not possess definite pitches. To intone is to exploit the definite and the discernible pitch-levels. In a manner of speaking, the intoned delivery carves purple passages out of the total narration hoping that they may thus acquire a special hold over the listeners' memory.

Next in consideration follows the stylized tonal moulds like *gajar*, *ovee*, etc. In this manner there emerges a hierarchy of musical orientation, as we have a prose narration, intoned and emphasized narration, and then *gajar*, *ovee*, etc., (the latter characterized by being set in tunes consisting of very few and unvarying group of notes). The changing proportion of musicality of these three items is important while examining the musicality of the *keertana* as a whole—because the phases of non-music, suggested music and minimal music are all represented here. Further, it is also possible to establish some correlationship between the nature of the narrative-content and the proportion of the prevailing musicality. It could be seen that all explanatory content relies on prose-narration; the supporting evidence or the linking of various points in the arguments is presented through the intoned prose and finally, the conclusions arrived at, or the moral lessons derived from or the theoretical positions following from the entire endeavour are expressed through the minimal musical moulds of *ovee, abhang, gajar*, etc. In other words, the points of emphases and the phases of musicality are deliberately matched in a *keertana*.

Perhaps at this point it is also necessary to have a look at the type of *aangik abhinaya* employed in accompaniment to the verbal, tonal stereotypes of delivery. The prose-phases are almost neutral in respect of the *aangik abhinaya*. The intoned prose is accompanied by gestures of emphasis. As far as the stylized tonal moulds are concerned the accompanying *abhinaya* is considerably exaggerated. The body-movements, facial gestures are all keyed up in order to suggest a prophetic intensity and sureness. The total bearing is of a charged personality intent on making an impact and a clear didactic thrust.

As any *keertana* is a prominent example of the speech-music continuum so characteristic of the performing traditions, it is inevitable that the diction-aspect be ,also examined. In the present context diction is to be understood as style taken along with delivery. To a certain extent the diction is obviously conditioned by the content. In its turn the content is largely determined by the overall aim of discussing problems of a metaphysical nature. In a *keertana* though a story is narrated, an anecdote is dramatized or an entertaining aphorism is related, coming back to the metaphysical, ethical or the didactic text is never far out of sight. Thus a closer examination reveals that themes at the centre have always an abstract import. The quest of the Supreme Being, the nature of God, the indestructibility of soul and such other themes form the core of the *keertankaar*'s thematic repertoire. It is clear that these themes are so general that they are bound to confront every human being at one time or the other with more or less intensity. At the same time, the themes do not have an immediate or a topical relevance. As a consequence, *keertana* achieves a remarkable double success. In spite of its abstract content it reaches the common multitude and does so without being topical. Given such a generality and a calculated imprecision or vagueness, the employed vocabulary tends to be suggestive rather than pin-pointed and the listener gets a continuous reassuring feeling of comprehensibility. It must be remembered that as *keertana* has a long, centuries-old tradition, its language has now attained a certain level of acceptable familiarity. In fact many of the proverbs, metaphorical expressions or thought-cliché have always percolated to the common man through *keertana* and other agencies of the oral tradition. This too helps in increasing the level of their intelligibility. However, the prime credit of the particular success in communication goes to the fact that *keertana* being a performance-activity is more social than individual in its essence. It is the social or the collective orientation that has in fact led the *keertana* to avoid the concrete, the personal and the topical. Instead, it has opted for the metaphysical/abstract, the collective and the suggestive. Consequently it becomes easily recognizable and real for the 'man in society'.

Further, the peculiar impact has been made possible through the role of the saint-poets of India. At this stage it is sufficient to mention that all over India the voice of the saints is characterized by three features: simplicity, musicality and prophetic confidence or assurance. *Keertana* employs poetry of the saints as its main structural support. The immediate impression of the total *keertana* communication is therefore of having found something durable, trustworthy and great enough to induce a submergence of the ego. *Keertana* has the power, the tone of authority to convey the effectiveness of the panacea it swears by. However temporary or transitory the effect may be, the message is efficiently communicated.

An important item, so far not discussed while examining the musicality of the *keertana* performance, is the musical instruments traditionally employed. They are *taal, mridang* and the *veena*. Later, the pedal-harmonium and the *tablaa* have appeared on the scene. Sometimes *manjiri, zaanz* or *chiplyaa* are also to be seen and heard. The *taal* and *zaanz* are played by the accompanists. These have an a-tonal, clear and strong sound and provide an ideal rhythmic accompaniment. *Manjiri* and *chiplyaa* do the same but have a smaller reach. Only the last, that is, the *chiplyaa*-pair has a wooden frame and hence altogether they supply a metallic, abrupt and percussive accompaniment—which unambiguously establishes the rhythmic-patterns. On the other hand, the *mridang* has its right face neatly tonal and the left in a resonating a-tonal bass. Hence, though it is a rhythm instrument which produces patterns of isolable percussive strokes, it could also provide the listeners with a sustained, hypnotic sonority. It is a logical choice for being the chief *taal-vaadya* as opposed to *taal, chiplyaa,* etc.—which are to be appropriately described as *laya vaadya*s. It is the *mridang* which supplies the resonating, gradually fading-out rhythmic lines while the *taal,* etc. take care of transmitting the main beats of the rhythmic patterns, forcefully and surely. The entire outdoor or partially covered acoustic space is thus effectively filled by these instruments (consisting symptomatically of only one membranophone). What remains to be considered is the *veenaa,* an instrument that could aptly be described as the pocket-edition of *taanpuraa* which is used to provide the drone in Indian art-music. Being a string-instrument, the *veenaa* produces a more musical though weaker sound barely sufficient to provide the *keertankaar* with the necessary tonal base. It is as well that the *veenaa*-drone is not carried to the audience in general. Its constant availability as a reference would have made stricter musical demands on the *keertankaar* whose motto usually does not include a high degree of musical fidelity. As a general rule the *keertankaar*'s music is of a less subtler variety and a deliberate introduction of a stricter and truer touchstone of musicality might have proved to be a distracting force. A very late introduction on the *keertan*-scene of the pedal-harmonium and the *tablaa* corroborate the observation. The use of these instruments is a positive indication of the deliberate, artistic evolution of the *keertana* which, while reaching that stage, surely registered a deviation from the traditional format. Of this however more is to be discussed at a later stage.

Like many other performance-acts *keertana* evolved its own tradition and in the process found solution to the many problems faced by performers in general. In fact this is what determines its distinctive form. Unless this aspect is attended to, its nature and role can hardly be evaluated adequately. Our aesthetic and critical thinking has so far helplessly relied on literature to such an extent that it had found no criteria to judge forms like the *keertana*. The tendency is to ignore forms which have evolved from the corpus of the already established art-forms—in spite of the fact that the forms do fully display elements of art, results of an aesthetic awareness and evolution. Till the defect is rectified both our aesthetics and critical activity are bound to remain anaemic.

II

It was argued in the preceding section that *keertana* should be discussed as a process of communication and further that it needs to be examined as a performing phenomenon. It therefore requires a conceptual framework different from the one so far applied. The dividing lines between various sub-traditions of the *keertana* were therefore deliberately kept out. Having identified the *keertana* as a communicational, performing and composite art, it is now necessary to take a closer look at the *keertana*-varieties like *Naaradiya*, *Vaarkari*, *Eknaathi*, etc. This shows that the sub-traditions consist of varied proportions of *keertana*-components like singing, dancing, *abhinaya*, story-telling, etc. Further, it is also seen that in spite of having certain common features, the motive forces which have acted to propel them through the centuries have also led to certain developmental features overlooked so far.

The word *keertana* has two seemingly unrelated meanings: i) narrating, story-telling, praising; ii) temple. As it happens frequently, both the meanings taken together give us a better idea of the total semantic hinterland. In most parts of India, *keertana* is today equated with devotional story-telling, heavily interlaced with music and employing dance and *abhinaya* to some extent. *Keertana* is much in vogue in northern India, Bengal, Gujarat, Andhra Pradesh, Karnataka, Maharashtra and with more or less intensity in other parts of the country. It is true that there are regional variations of format and occasionally different terms are also used to denote the *keertana* (e.g., it is known as *kalaakshepam* in Andhra Pradesh and *Harikathaa* in Tamilnadu), yet the commonly understood core-meaning cannot be missed.

There are sound reasons for the term to have a common core-meaning. Firstly, because all the *keertana* subtraditions have their genesis in the *bhakti*-cult in India. Though it is true that as an idea the *bhakti* phenomenon goes back to ancient times, it gathered a unique intensity and purposeful following during the medieval period and became a movement. In fact it swept all over the country from the seventh century onwards and continued apace till about the end of the seventeenth century. In contemporary India, the *bhakti* movement has attained the status of an established school of religious thought.

Secondly, the main protagonists of the movement throughout

the country were the saint-poets. They were highly spiritual poets who achieved an uncommon blend of music and literature to shape and express their devotional drive. All over the country their works provided the *keertana* with a firm foundation. In fact, the capacity of the *keertana* to reach deep and wide in the societal mind can be directly attributed to its heavy reliance on the poetry of the saints. The grip of this poetry on the masses could in turn be traced to the saint-poets' skilful use of music.

The third reason for the common (and countrywide) core-connotation of the term is to be sought in the progressive though gradual crystallization of the multiple channels of the oral tradition in religio-ethical communication taken as a whole. The process of crystallization was strongly precipitated by the *bhakti*-movement. Thus *pravachana, puraana, bhajan,* and *keertana* all acquired settled and individual formats of their own. These genres enjoy varied proportions of musical, narrative, didactic, mimetic as well as choreographic content. In addition, the regional variations became more and more prominent through the course of centuries and thus were brought about interesting changes in structure, content and presentation aspects. A study of the constants and the variables in the *keertana* traditions thus becomes a fascinating study in cultural dynamics. The present attempt is devoted to an examination of the *keertana* tradition in Maharashtra.

Perhaps a little explanation is necessary as to the reason why music-thinkers should deem it desirable to take a serious look at the *keertana*. A very basic reason is that *keertana* is so permeated with music that it has inevitably functioned as an effective carrier or propagator of music, and that too for centuries. In other words, the *keertana* has led the way to greater musical literacy on account of its long tradition, mass-appeal and selective as well as reiterated use of musical moulds which in reality form a bulwark in art-music against an enveloping formlessness. In this respect items like *raag, taal, aalaap, tihaai,* etc., easily come to mind. *Keertana* therefore *causes a deep sinking-in of musical ideas* through an effective act of non-verbal communication. Admittedly, *keertana* was not originally intended or designed to spread the gospel of music, but it achieved the distinction of doing so (without of course neglecting to spread the spell of God!) Nevertheless the undeclared, successful dissemination of musical ideas compels attention of all music-educators and music-thinkers. No consideration of a musical tradition can be complete unless it takes into account the contributions made by the indirect channels like that of *keertana,* prosody, etc. It was surely not a coincidence that an action-oriented music-educator like Pandit Vishnu Digambar came forward to sponsor the fourth and the fifth *keertana* conferences held in Bombay (1920) and Nasik (1921).

The all-pervasive musical influence of the *keertana* is also borne out by the nature of the Marathi tradition of stage-music. In itself a powerful percolator of musical ideas, Marathi stage-music was heavily dependent on the musical idiom of the *keertana* in the early golden era of stage-music (1880-1920). Historians unanimously agree that being a new form it was a wise choice for stage-music to borrow from and refine an already established musical language. To strive to win acceptance through the accepted was an efficient cultural strategy and it certainly proved effective. In Maharashtra (and perhaps in other regions too) looking a little below the musical surface leads one to the *keertana*-idiom.

It is at this juncture that the various sub-traditions established in Maharashtra need to be noted to help define, neatly, the scope of the discussion.   In this respect the following presentation could be of use:

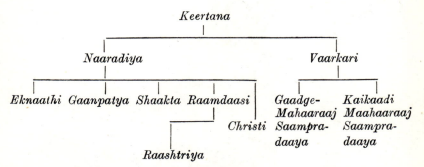

Not all of these need separate discussion as many follow the basic formats developed either by the *Naaradiya* or by the *Vaarkari* sub-tradition. These sub-traditions evolved at various chronological points which cannot be too precisely traced. Hence in questions of chronological priority one has to tread warily.

For example a verse from *Padmapuraana* (400 A.D.) is usually quoted to prove the ancientness of the *Naaradiya* subtradition. In reality however it only proves that the current emphasis on

Pandit Dhundamaharaj Deglurkar
Varkari kirtankar

music in the *keertana* has its predecessors. In translation the verse reads:

> Pralhaad kept the rhythm, Uddhav played the gongs in quick tempo, Naarada played the *veenaa* while Arjun was rendering the *Raag-raaginis* with skill. Indra played on *mridang*, Sanatkumar raised the *jaijaikaar* and Shukracharya, the son of Vyas, was the emotionally charged singer of high-quality compositions in God's praise.[1]

Perhaps it is instructive to juxtapose this ancient description of the *keertana* with another definition of a more recent origin. Dhundamaharaj Deglurkar, a revered *keertankaar* of the *vaarkari* sect has defined *keertana* in a very comprehensive manner. A translation (with slight rephrasing) runs as follows:

> *Keertana* is a narration of the praise of the Supreme being or of his respected devotees. The narration is presented with the help of music and poetry in an assembly of auditors and includes a mixture of repetition/recitation of their (God's and his devotee's) names (*naamkeertan*), of the praise of their attributes (*gunakeertan*), as also the praise of their great deeds (*leela keertan*). The aim of the *keertana* is to impress on the minds of the listener (through explanation) those ideas and thoughts that are likely to prove beneficial in their personal and social life.[2]

Though Deglurkarbuwa firmly belongs to the *vaarkari* sub-tradition, his definition obviously tries to accommodate all major sub-traditions of *keertana*, even those that chiefly flourish outside Maharashtra. Thus what he alludes to as *leela keertana* may cover the traditions prevalent in Gujarat and Northern India. These varieties are devoted mainly to describe Baalkrishna's exploits and are replete with story-telling as well as music. On the other hand the reference to *gunakeertan* may apply to the *Naaradiya* sub-tradition in which description of the attributes of the deity or its devotees provides the foundation. Finally, what Dhundamaharaj describes as *naamkeertan* may accommodate the *vaarkari* sub-tradition in which repeating God's name is regarded as indispensable— though the performance of the *vaarkari* variety includes a didactic portion which is called *nirupana*. The term *naamkeertana* also applies to those gatherings solely organized for a weeklong, uninterrupted chanting of God's name. These are usually described as *naam sankeertana*.

It is really not necessary to stress the chronological priority of
one sub-tradition over another, since performing traditions are
characterized by continuity. It is advisable to describe the structures of the *keertana* sub-traditions as of today and then proceed to
other issues.

Keertana : the vaarkari sub-tradition

The *keertana* performance begins with a *bhajan* in which ten to
twenty *taal*-players stand flanking a *veenaa*-player and accompany
him. The *mridang*-player is to the left of the *veena*-player and at
some distance from him. The *bhajan* text is usually '*Jai jai
Raamkrishna Hari*'. The *veena*-player leads the *bhajan* and often
executes a few step-movements, backwards and forwards. After
the *bhajan*, *abhang*s that describe the Vitthal-idol are taken up.
They are aptly called '*roopaache abhang*' and the first one is
'*Sundara te dhyaan ubhe vitevari*'.

It is then that the main *keertankaar* stands up. (All the while
he has been sitting nearby on a mattress called a *gaadi*.) He
now takes a position in the middle and also receives the *veenaa*
from the *veenaa*-player who recedes in the background. Once
more a *bhajan* is taken up and rendered in chorus. This time the
bhajan can be '*Raamkrishna Haari*' or '*Jnyaneshwar Maauli*'. This
bhajan is followed by *naman* (salutation) presented with the
abhang '*Roop paahata lochani*' to be succeeded by the *bhajan*
(*Raamkrishna Haari*). The *bhajan* brings to the end the first phase
of the *vaarkari keertana*.

The second phase opens with the singing of the *abhang* which is
selected by the *buwaa* (as the main *keertankaar* is known popularly)
for the philosophico-ethico-didactic elaboration he is to embark
upon, a little later. The singing of the *abhang* is succeeded by the
bhajan '*Vitthal Rakhumaai*' in turn to be followed by re-rendering
of the first two lines of the *abhang*. Once again the *Vitthal-bhajan*
echoes through. The *veenaa* is passed on to the original *veenaa*-
player by the *buwaa*—and they bow to each other while the take-
over takes place. The elaboration of the philosophical-metaphysical
idea contained in the *abhang* begins. This is called *nirupan*. Before
the *nirupan* the *buwa* executes one more interesting act: he ties the
uparane tightly around the waist, almost a literal tightening of the
belt! *Nirupana* (sometimes referred to as *pratipaadan*) literally
means investigation and definition. The thematic elaboration or

the semantic explanation is aptly called *bhaavaarth* because it is much more than an act of literal construing. It lays bare the essence of the *abhang*-text in simple language. Thus comes to an end the second phase.

The beginning of the third phase is marked by the garlanding of the *buwaa* and the application of the *bukkaa*-powder to his forehead. The *buwaa* immediately uses the same garland to garland the *veenaa*-player. The *taal*-players once again sing the first two lines of the *abhang*-text. At this point the *buwaa* uses the *abhang*-text to deviate slightly from its direct meaning and goes on to discuss the eternal issues: how the reiteration of the God-name gives peace of mind; how to break the cycle of recurrent births and deaths; who can become a saint? Why are the *gurus* necessary? *et al*. The deviations are of course marked by repeated approximations to the *abhang*-text. In fact once the *buwaa* has judged the deviated content to have reached a certain adequacy, he links it firmly with the original text: this skilful coming back is rounded off by a collective singing of the *bhajan* '*Jnyaaneshwar Maauli Tukaaraam*'. While the *bhajan* is being sung collectively, a very impressive to and fro swaying movement is executed by all the *taal*-players. Once again the last line of the *abhang*-text (which usually contains the *mudraa*, i.e., the name of the poet) is sung in a fitting *raag* of conclusion, like *bhairavi*. The *veenaa*-player comes forward, thus indicating that the *buwaa* is no longer the centre of the activity. Follows *Vitthal-bhajan* and then the *aaratis* of Vitthal, Jnyaaneshwar and Tukaaraam are sung in succession. (It is to be noted however that the singing of the *aaratis* is *not* accompanied by the actual act of *ovaalne*.) After the *aarati* the *abhang*-group described as '*pasaaydaanaache abhang*' is rendered and the *keertan* ends—after a duration of about two to three hours.

Historical comments

Sant Namdeo (1270-1350) is regarded as the originator of the above-described sub-tradition. We are told that Namdeo used to take *darshan* of the Vithobaa-idol in the famous Pandharpoor temple. After the *darshan* he used to move to the sandy banks of the Chandrabhaagaa river without turning his back to the Vithobaa-idol and the *keertana* was performed in the open air. Obviously this format could not be adopted at other places in toto. The present format (with the *taal*-players, etc.) is credited to the inventive adaptability of Pandit Vishnubuwa Jog (1867-1920).[3] Alternatively the name of Pandit Bhausaheb Katkar Maharaj (1813-1878) is also mentioned as the originator of the present *vaarkari* format.[4]

As far as the musical essentials are concerned, there seems to be a consensus that *veenaa*, *pakhaawaj* and *taal* are the instruments traditionally employed. *Dhumaali* is the only rhythmic cycle used. The position in respect of *raags* used is much more ambiguous. However an indirect clue is available. Like all other saint poets Namdeo toured all over the country and was received well. The sacred book of the Sikhs in the Punjab, the *Granthsaaheb* includes sixty-one compositions of Namdeo and the written records show that eighteen *raags* were employed to set them to tune.

One more important feature relates to the 'texts' used for the *Nirupan*. The text is always chosen from the corpus provided by the works of Dnyandeo (b. 1275), Namdeo (1270-1350), Eknath (1548-1599), Tukaram (1598-1649) and Niloba. Various reasons are put forward to explain the exclusion of other saints. The strongest is that the deliberate narrowing down is conducive to an intensive study of the selected works.

Other features

The *buwaa* is attired in white. He wears a white *dhoti*, a full-sleeved shirt, silk or cotton *phetaa* around the head, white *uparane*, vertically applied *gandh* or *ashtagandh* on the forehead, *bukkaa* between the eyebrows, sandlewood *mudraa* on the temple and finally the tulsi-garland around the neck—a 'complete' professional image indeed!

The Eknaathi keertana

The way this sub-tradition has been nurtured and nursed into prominence provides an interesting case of fusion. *Sant* Eknath followed the tenets of the *vaarkari* sect and in fact he was responsible for rejuvenating the tradition by force of his personality, conduct and writings. It was he who rediscovered after a lapse of 300 years Dnyaneshwar's seminal work and brought it into the *main stream* of the sect. It is no wonder that his work is included in the *vaarkari* text-corpus.

By all accounts, however, his own style of *keertana* was inclined towards the *Naaradeeyaa* rather than the *vaarkari* style of presentation. There are three main arguments to support the position.

1) Eknath himself stated that a *keertana* should consist of narrating of the '*sagun* life-stories of God'. This is quite the opposite of the *vaarkari nirupan* and comes very near to the strategy of the *Naaradeeyaa* sub-tradition to have a regular recourse to story-telling, i.e., *aakhyaan*.[5]

2) Unlike the *vaarkari keertana*, Eknath relied more on the element of dramatizing as well as on liberally employing the sublimated erotic. The former he achieved through his *bhaaruds* and the latter he realized through the use of the perennially attractive *gaulan*-songs. In sum, artistry and not didacticism came into ascendency in Eknath's *keertanas*.

3) Even today those who declare themselves to be the followers of Eknath perform their *keertanas* in the *Naaradeeyaa* way.

4) Finally the dress of the *Eknaathi keertankaar* proclaims his *Naaradeeyaa* ancestry. He wears a *pagadi*, a long sleeved shirt as well as an *uparane* with a narrow silk border.

The Raamdaasi keertan

Like *Sant* Eknath, *Sant* Raamdaas (1608-1681) stamped the prevailing *Naaradeeyaa keertan* with his own personality and with the politico-religious fervour that all his actions carried. Himself a performer, he instructed his disciples to follow suit, recommended the *keertana* as a great act of devotion and with his usual thoroughness described in detail the format to be employed.[6]

Some of the important features that he has described lead to the following significant deductions:

a) The sub-tradition which Raamdaas strengthened, carried on the effort of the *Eknaathi keertan* to be entertaining, interesting and didactic.

b) In order to achieve this aim, the sub-tradition unambiguously recommended resorting to other effective communicative channels like dancing, singing, humour, the erotic poesy and accent on prosodic variety. The aesthetic and the artistic were clearly brought to the foreground.

c) It is also deducible that Raamdaas's era saw the beginning of royal patronage for *keertan*. Raamdaas was Shivaji's *guru* and the latter was a generous patron to the *muths* established by the former. The disciples in charge of the affairs of the *muths* were encouraged to organize festivals and celebrations in which *keertans* formed a

Dr. Dattopant Patwardhan
Rashtriya kirtankar

Pandit Kavishvarbuwa
Naradiya kirtankar

major item. In sum, the time was not far off when a court-*keertankaar* as such was to be appointed.

d) Apart from avoiding the austere didacticism of the *vaarkari* format, the *Raamdaasi keertan*, like its predecessor the *Eknaathi*, relied very prominently on the folk-heritage in matters of instruments, metres and diversification of source-material. This was clearly aimed at reaching wider audiences. Given the continued wanderings of the *Raamdaasis*, their wider *repertoire* could certainly be counted as a force that led to a greater spread of musical literacy.

Other features

Very often a *Raamdaasi keertankaar* sports long hair and a beard, wears an ochre-coloured *kafni* and wraps around the shoulders an *uparane* of a similar colour. Occasionally, wearing a *phetaa* is also found acceptable.

The structuring of a *Raamdaasi keertan* is very much similar to that of the *Naaradiya keertan*. The *Raamdaasi keertankaar* begins with the chanting of the *naman 'Jai jai Raam Krishna Haari'* and proceeds to sing a *pad* in praise of the patron-saint *Raamdaas* (viz., Ramdas *maauli*).

Then an *abhang* is taken up for the *poorvaranga* followed by the *uttarranga* with a story. After the *uttarranga* an incident from *Sant* Ramdas's life is narrated before the *keertan* comes to an end.

The *keertankaar* is accompanied by two *zanz*-players as well as by *tablaa* and harmonium-players.

As it will become clear, the total format is modelled on the *Naaradeeya keertan*, discussed below.

The Naaradeeya keertan

Like an absent hero of a hero-centred drama, the *Naaradeeya* sub-tradition seems to be always present in the background in every discussion of *keertan*-traditions in general. This is specifically so in Maharashtra where it has acquired such a comprehensive form that other sub-traditions could be discussed with greater facility when reference is made to *Naaradeeya* sub-tradition. Its salient features are briefly described below.

Naman or mangalaacharana

The *buwaa* (as the *keertankaar* is usually known) commences with successive invocations to Ganesh, Saraswati, his own family-deity and the deity of his home-town. His *guru*-tradition is also included in the invocation.

The pad of jaijaikaar

Singing (and not mere chanting) of the *pad 'Jai jai Raam Krishna Haari'* comes next. Very aptly one version of the *pad* refers to sages Shuka and Vyaasa—the ancient originators of the *Naaradeeya* sub-tradition. The praise of the *guru* follows. Most of the *keertankaars* then initiate the chanting of a *bhajan* in which the audience is encouraged to join.

The poorvaranga : abhang or pad

The true beginning of the *keertan* is its *poorvarang*—the first half of the *keertan*—performance in which the religio-philosophical-didactic exposition of a chosen theme is presented on the basis of the text of an *abhang* or a *pad*. Saint-poets from other regions of India are also pressed into service in selecting the text. For example, works of Soordaas, Meera, Tulsidaas, Narsi Mehta and others are often used.

The *abhang* or the *pad* is properly set to tune in *raag* and *taal* and some musical elaboration is also included. While the thematic elaboration is in progress, the *buwaa* repeatedly brings in the *abhang*, etc., but usually takes care to render it in faster tempi and very often he sings a *taraanaa* in the same *raag*. The *abhang* is repeated but not always in full—sometimes a partial repetition too is judged to be sufficient to impress on the audience the didactic message.

The thematic elaboration is characterized by the *buwaa*'s *bahu-shrutta* (lit. wide or comprehensive listening), that is, *buwaa*'s ready and witty references to supporting quotations, aphorisms, similes and illustrative examples, etc., from Sanskrit, Marathi and other literatures. The Sanskrit learning is exemplified by his drawing on the *vedas*, *smritis*, *puraanas* and other ancient and early texts as well as by *buwaa*'s use of other branches of learning of *nyaaya*, *vyakrarana*, *vedanta*, etc.

References to the Marathi literature includes the saint poets and the *pant*-poets whose longer narrative works as well as short *pad*, etc., are repeatedly utilized. In fact, the *buwaa* throws a very wide net in this phase—even at the risk of appearing pedantic. The audience is allowed to feel the full weight of his learning in *poorvaranga*. According to the established norms of the oral tradition, a lot of course depends on improvisation, elocution, variety of sources touched upon and the diversity of associations aroused. In other words the *buwaa* leaves no stone unturned in the *poorvaranga* in order to establish the thesis he wants to propound and which he has already suggested in the *abhang* or the *pad* chosen by him as the 'text'. (Sometimes the *buwaa* may select his own composition as the *poorvarang* 'text', but this is very rare.)

Though the *buwaa* assumes the role of a teacher in the *poorvaranga* and hence becomes didactic and propagandist, he does not forget the primary task to remain interesting. Hence he resorts to repeated deviations and diversions. Of course he comes back to the original *abhang*, etc.: that marks the end of the *poorvaranga*.

Bhajan

The conclusion of the *poorvaranga* is followed by *bhajan* singing in which the audience joins.

Uttarranga

The latter half of the *Naaradeeya keertan* is known as the *uttarranga*: its beginning is signalled by the organizer's bringing in *bukka* and a garland. *Bukka* is first applied to the dignitaries present (seated usually in the front) and then to the *buwaa*. The *buwaa* in turn applies it to the person who brings it and scatters it in all directions. The *buwaa* is also garlanded.

The *bhajan*, collectively rendered, goes on in a rising tempo and the *gajar* is also performed. (Significantly, the *Naaradeeya gajar* is not confined to any one sectarian deity.)

After the *gajar*, a *pad* is taken up for a right royal musical rendering—hence all musical features like *aalaap*, *taan*, *tihaai*, etc. come to the forefront in this section. In fact, quite frequently a composition from the art-music *repertoire* is selected. If the *buwaa* himself is not a well-equipped musician, the harmonium-player is asked to sing the composition. It is clear that the aim is to ensure a high musical quality in the rendering.

Aakhyaan

The most important feature of the *uttaranga* is the dramatic narration of a selected story that matches the text of the *poorvaranga* in the moral lessons derived and the messages preached. Before plunging into the one-man show that is presented to the audience in the *aakhyaan*, the *buwaa* takes care to tie his *uparane* around his waist.

The narration is replete with dialogues, singing, *gajar*, body-movements, gestures and mime—in short everything that can make the performance successful in a dignified manner.

The stories are often selected from the great epics or from the *puranas* or even from the lore of the saint-stories. The abundant use of Moropant and the other *pandit* or the *pant-kavis* is a distinguishing feature. The musico-dramatic story-telling is a veritable challenge to the *buwaa's* artistry just as the *poorvaranga* is a challenge to his learning.

The mool-pad

However entertaining and artistically satisfying the *aakhyaan* may be, it is to be linked to the original text so as to underscore the moral of the text. Hence elements common to both the text and the *aakhyaan* are repeatedly pointed out, and, to emphasise the similarity, the original text is sung once again though in a different *raag* and in a slightly faster tempo in the final stages of the *uttarranga*. The skilful leading back to the *mool-pad* is rightly viewed as a feature of successful artistry.

Pasaaydaan

The last important item is invoking God and sing the *aaratis* in which the listeners are expected to join. A *tabak* is taken round for the audience to deposit its money contributions. The *keertan* ends with a *saashtaang namaskaar* offered by the *buwaa* to the deity.

Historical comments

Apart from the ancient phase of its development, *Naaradeeya* subtradition underwent its first major transformation in *Sant* Eknath's time (1548-1599). The chief effect was to take it further away from the unalloyed didacticism and the slightly mechanical *naam samkeertan*.

In all probability the next stage was reached during *Sant* Raamdaas's days (1608-1681), when the sub-tradition obtained a generous court-patronage. Raamdaas's description also proves that the format was further expanded to accommodate numerous items from the folk-traditions of music and literature. Raamdaas's didacticism was less metaphysical and more down to earth. In his artistry too, the verve and the vigour came to the forefront, rather than the delicate touches of sophistication.

The third developmental phase was reached during the period of the later Peshwa rule (the 18th century). Historically speaking the following features of the sub-tradition in vogue during the period are noteworthy:

a) This stage saw the sub-tradition relying very heavily on the *bhakta-kavi*s or the *pant-kavi*s (e.g., Shridhar 1658-1729, Madhva-munishwar 1680-1734, Amritrai 1698-1753, Mahipatibuwa Tahrabadkar 1715-1790, Moropant 1724-1794).

b) Prominent *shaahirs* steeped in the *tamaashaa*-lore turned to the *keertana* in their later years. They were accepted and also acknowledged as highly successful practitioners of the form. Anant Phandi (1744-1819), Raam Joshi (1758-1813) are prominent examples.

c) During the reign of Bajirao II, Antaji Manakeshwar was appointed as the court-*keertankar*.

d) Sometime during the same period, forms of pronounced aesthetic orientation (e.g., *baithakichi laavani*) were also coming to fruition. Hindustani art-music and musicians were receiving increasing patronage and appreciation in Maharashtra. These features too adorned the setting in which *Naaradeeya* sub-tradition was coming to a fuller stature.

The most recent developmental phase could be said to have been the post-1818 period. Generally known as the British period, it registered certain important changes:

i) Many prominent *keertankaar*s made a name for their extraordinary prowess in singing. Some names are listed below:

Vithoba Anna Daptardar (1803-1873): he is reported to have studied art-music under the guidance of a *sanyaasi*.

Govindbuwa Hoshing: he had a unique voice that ranged over three octaves. He won high praise from Ustad Haddukhan and Hassukhan—the two legendary high-priests of the Gwalher *Gharaana* of Hindustani art-music.

Gangadharbuwa Kashikar: he was proficient in *dhrupad-dhamaar*, *khayaal*, *thumri* and *tappaa* and was well-trained in the *Gwalher* music.

Narayanbuwa Gogte-Phaltankar: he was a contemporary of the great Marathi dramatist-actor Annasaheb Kirloskar. Known for his voice and attractive singing, Gogtebuwaa could by his singing tempt the audiences attending a theatre performance to leave the theatre in order to listen to his own singing!

Pilubuwa Phaltankar: he was known for his mastery over the *laavani*-idiom of singing.

Vishnubuwa Lalit: operating in the coastal areas of Maharashtra, he was so proficient in the intricacies of *taal*s that even well-known *pakhaawaj*-players were scared of him!

Moreshwarbuwa (Joshi) (d. 1912): he was the first in the four-generation lineage of *keertankaars* and was known for his knowledge of *dhrupad-dhamaar* singing (*Gwalher gharaana*).

Krishnabuwa Kavishwar (b. 1914) comes from a family of *keertankaars* and is known for his proficiency in singing *taraanaa*, *dhrupad* and other forms of art-music.

Haribuwa Karhadkar: he was extremely popular as a singer and possessed a very sweet and high-pitched voice.

ii) Sometime around the 1880s, the *keertankaars* started using the pedal-harmonium for accompaniment. The event is of great musical importance as it indicated on the part of the *keertankaars* an awareness of greater and better musical potentialities.

iii) The tradition has it that Govindbuwaa Hoshing was responsible during the period for bestowing the present *poorvaranga-uttarranga* structure on the *Naaradeeya* sub-tradition. The broad bifurcation of the overtly didactic and the overtly entertaining, along with the skilful joinings and the reference-back is so unique in the context of the entire *keertan*-tradition of India, that Hoshingbuwaa could be said to have brought about an aesthetic revolution. His style is known as *Tarakaashram sampradaaya* because the *buwaa* had established a *muth* in Kashi and named it *Tarakaashram*.

iv) A number of achievements of an aesthetic or an artistic nature have been noted in the performances of many *keertankaars* during this period.

Gangadharbuwa Kashikar (apart from being proficient in Hindustani art-music) was well-known for his skilled presentation of simultaneous, coupled *akhyaan*s (two or more). He is also said to have presented each *aakhyaan* in different languages on such occasions. He won popularity in the Punjab and Nepal too. It is evident that a high degree of sophistication and constructional craftsmanship was involved in such renderings.

Another instance is of Rajarambuwa Nisal of Sangamner. He was famous for his ability to interpret and expand his themes in a variety of ways. Once in a festival *keertan*-series he is reported to have presented five *poorvarang*s on the word Raama (as God's name) and five more on the word *maraa* (literally—'die'.) The latter is the inversion of the former!

Ganeshshastri Modak was a blind *keertankaar*. He was so well known for his ability to explain the obscure passages from Moropant and other poets that post-graduate students, etc., used to attend his *keertan* to take notes! Ramkrishnabuwa Dhole of Bombay too was respected for his mastery over the *Aryaabharat* of Moropant and students of literature made a beeline for him.

Pilubuwa Vadujkar was known as an extremely effective and popular performer. He used to pre-set, completely, his prose-verse portions to ensure effect. Murlidharbuwa Nijampurkar, another proven crowd-drawer, too was noted for his well-rehearsed, sure-success performances.

v) Princely patronage given to the *Naaradeeya* sub-tradition did not remain an isolated case during the period under discussion.

For example, Govindrao Hoshing was regarded as *guru* by Jivaji Maharaj of *Gwalher* and the latter once worshipped the former with gems! The Holkar prince too respected him.

Another instance is of the learned Ramchandrabuwa Kashikar who always received invitations from various princes including that of Nepal. Yet another polyglot *keertankaar* performing in Marathi, Hindi, Sanskrit and Gujarati was Shridharshastri Deshpande: he received patronage from the Tanjore as well as Nepal princes.

vi) The *Naaradeeya keertankaar* was in demand to such an extent that he could receive 'attractive' remuneration for his performance (unlike the *vaarkari* counterpart). For example, Ganeshshastri Modak (Nasik) used to get one and a quarter tola of gold for each performance. As mentioned earlier, Hoshingbuwaa was worshipped with gems. Ramchandrabuwaa Kashikar reportedly received a thousand rupees per performance at the Nepal court. Shridharshastri Deshpande often received golden bracelets along with cash emoluments. The vocation was equally valued as entertainment as it was respected for its role of dedication.

vii) A significant indication of the well-rounded growth of the sub-tradition is the written-literature (of the manual type) produced by the practitioners themselves. The organizing of the *keertan* conferences is also to be noted as an indication of a pervasive awareness of the cultural importance of the *keertana* phenomenon. Of similar import is the founding of institutions for the training of aspiring *keertankaars* and for fostering the growth of the vocation in general. Some early attempts on these lines are listed below:

Institutions
1. Shri Harikeertanottejak Sabha, Pune, estd. 1883.

2. Bhadrakaali Mandir Keertana Sansthaa, Nasik, estd. 1898.
3. Keertan Paathshaala, Pune (1927).
4. Akhil Bharateeya Keertan Sansthaa, Dadar, estd. 1940.

Keertan sammelans
1. Nagpur, 1912, presided over by Dadasaheb Khaparde.
2. Nagpur, 1918, presided over by B.G. alias Lokmanya Tilak.

Books
1. *Kirtanaacharyaakam*, Sanskrit, Bhagwat V.G., Kashi.
2. *Keertan: kalaa aani shaastra*, Kolhatkar V.S.

Other features

Traditionally the *buwaa* wears a red *pugree*, white *dhoti* and shirt
(full-sleeved) and an *uparane*. He plays the *manjiri*-pair with his
left hand, thus keeping the right hand free for expressive gestures,
etc.

    Keertans are mostly performed in temples. The *buwaa* stands
facing the idol. A carpet or a silk cloth is spread for him to stand
on, and he moves on it (backwards-forwards). This carpet is regarded to be the 'seat' of Naarada and hence is sacred. Care is
taken to see that the *buwaa's* view of the idol is never obstructed.
Some distance away, the *buwaa* also places an idol or a photo of
his family-deity, etc., in front of himself and a large *thaali* near it
for the listeners to deposit rice-grain offerings, etc. It is a custom
that while going to a *darshan* of God, one should not go with empty
hands; hence the offerings.

    To the *buwaa's* left is the harmonium-player and behind the latter,
the females in the audience. To his right is the *tablaa*-player and
behind the *tablaa*-player are seated the males in the audience. In
case the *buwaa* avails of other accompanists like *zaanz*-players,
violinist, etc., they are seated behind the *buwaa*.

III

It is on this interesting backdrop that some deductions regarding
the basic drives, chief functions and developmental tendencies of
the two major *keertana* sub-traditions of Maharashtra could be
made. The two sub-traditions referred to here are the *Vaarkari* and
the *Naaradeeya*.

    Both the sub-traditions do not have the same relationship with the audience. Even though their intended appeal is to an 'audience', in the sense that both want to communicate to the collective mind, it is clear that examined performance-wise, the *Naaradeeya keertana* is inclined to be a solo. On the contrary, the *niroopankaar buwaa* and his accompanists on the *taal* in the *vaarkari keertana*, themselves form a collective of their own. In addition, the members of the audience too are encouraged to join in the *gajar* and *bhajan* so frequently that it is no exaggeration to describe the entire *vaarkari keertana* as an act of collective devotion. It is also to be noted that specific *abhangs*, their specific sequence along with their being interrupted at specific intervals by the *bhajans*, etc.—all make the audience a true participant. Compared to this deep-hued collectivity of the performance in the *vaarkari*-school, that of the *Naaradeeya* is glaringly of a solo nature. The performing group as such is confined to the *keertonkaar* and his accompanists (numbering four). Thus it is easily comparable to the operational set of the art-music tradition—as seen in a *mehfil* (a concert). In a way the unambiguous separation of the chief performer and the accompanists is a distinctive feature of the *Naaradeeya*, especially as compared to the *vaarkari*. The older custom of the art-musicians was of a singer holding the *taanpuraa* himself and to seat the *tablaa* (that is, the rhythm) accompanist on the right and the *saarangi* (that is, the tonal) accompanists on the left. This is what the *Naaradeeya keertankaar* does. Unlike the *Naaradeeya*, the *vaarkari pakhaawaj*-player sits on the left! It is likely that the *Naaradeeya keertankaar* has modelled himself (as a performer) on the Hindustani art-musician. The *Naaradeeya keertankaar* found the model irresistable because the driving forces behind both the performances, that is, the *keertan* and the *mehfil* are similar in nature. The drives are, it is suggested, aesthetic in essence. It can plausibly be argued that a *keertan* sub-tradition, slowly deviating from the older *sam-keertan* alongside the *vaarkari* sub-traditions, crystallized itself into a more art-oriented performance-style called *naaradeeya* in Maharashtra of the later Peshwa rule because the total environment was conducive to such a development.

An aesthetically oriented performance inevitably causes a performer-audience relationship of a different type. The difference is not so much due to the number of the listeners as to their quality. An aesthetically oriented performer—an artist—is pledged to win over an audience on the strength of his skill and artistry. The audience that attends the performance of an artist is, on the other hand, alertly attentive from the beginning but not necessarily appreciative in the initial stages. In other words, an art-performance is a conflict situation and the performer is to pass certain tests before the audience surrenders to him. Hence the critical or the evaluative (self-used) vocabulary of a *Naaradeeya keertankaar* often refers to the artistic success (i.e., *rang*) and failure (i.e., *berang*) of a *keertana.*

Circumstances are different in case of a *vaarkari keertan.* The *vaarkari niroopankaar buwaa* is in reality a spokesman of a religious sect. That is, he is a more vocal representative of a body of well-disciplined, philosophy-bound initiated persons. The *buwaa* and the listeners are, in a manner of speaking, links in one and the same chain. Their *keertan* is a *vaarkari keertan* because they all are followers of the *vaarkari* sect. This causal relation makes for an audience-performer relationship of mutual acceptance which could be assumed from the beginning. The audience is more homogeneous, its expectations are known and predictable as also its participation and responses. Therefore unlike the *Naaradeeya keertan*, —a *vaarkari keertan* performance is not characterized by the conflict of aesthetic sensibilities of the performer and the audience. Consequently there is less scope for individual artistry or for solo virtuosity in a *vaarkari keertan.* In it the audience is always with the *niroopankaar* while in the *Naaradeeya keertan* the audience is before him, face to face, as a sympathetic combatant to be ultimately won over. The *Naaradeeya keertan* therefore tends towards an aesthetico-dramatic presentation while the *Vaarkari keertan* is inclined to be an unilinear, homogeneously experienced, collective and devotional act. (It is to be noted that perhaps due to this less aesthetic and hence less challenging format, the *vaarkari bhajan* developed later on different lines. The solo element became pronounced, music moved nearer to art-music tradition and the audience-participation was cut down to become more of a silent appreciation. But this compensating or balancing act of the devotional—communicational channels within the sectarian corpus is altogether a different theme.)

In comparison, the artistic orientation of the *Naaradeeya* sub-tradition is unequivocally communicated. Firstly, it is named after the sage *Naarada*, perhaps the first major musician-musicologist according to the tradition. However chronology, geneology, etc., pose problems and hence the point cannot be stretched further. But even the structuring of the *keertan* asserts its aesthetic intention. The philosophical discourse in the first half is to be matched by a corresponding story-telling and judiciously interspersed are the elements of music, literature, dance and *abhinaya*, i.e., histrionics. The very components are a challenge to a skilled performer. As in a drama he needs composite sensibility and craftsmanship. In addition it is his aim to win over an audience that is not bound to him by sectarian loyalty. Therefore the *Naaradeeya keertan* is intrinsically close to a dramatic performance. It is no coincidence that the music-drama in Maharashtra found its early sustenance in the *Naaradeeya keertan* structure, music, etc. and not in those of the *vaarkari keertan*. The music-drama and the *Naaradeeya keertan* are cognate entities in so far as their fundamental aesthetic drives are concerned.

A corroborative feature is reflected in the studies that a *Naaradeeya keertankaar*s pursue diligently over a number of years. Their approach is characterized by a concern for effectiveness. Though the accent is logically on learning by heart, complete *poorvarang*s, anthologies of quotations, compositions, etc., are written down in what are known as *baad*s (i.e., bundles of papers or thick notebooks). They are secretively preserved and handed down from generation to generation according to established norms of the oral tradition. (An easy parallel is found in the field of art-music). About the *aakhyaan*s too, care is lavished to bring in elements of variety and decorative elaboration. Many *Naaradeeya keertankaar*s 'sing' songs of the *pant-kavi*s. Many are proficient in the singing of *laavani*s. (On the other hand quite a few *laavani*-singers turned to *keertan*s!). All this goes to stress the aesthetic aims of the *Naaradeeya* sub-tradition. That the present format of the *Naaradeeya keertan* should get stabilized during the later Peshwaa-rule (and not earlier) is also significant. Similarly the *laavani* was becoming more musical and sophisticated during the same time-span, a feature which cannot be ignored. A strengthening of the Hindustani art-music traditions in Maharashtra also took place during the same period.

Finally the best proof of the musical drives could be obtained in the type of musical instruments used in both the sub-traditions. The *Naaradeeya keertankaar* opted for the *taamburi* while the *vaarkari* selected the *veenaa* as well as the *ektaari*; the former soon shifted from *pakhaawaj* to *tabla* while the latter stuck to *mridang* and the *taal*. The former relied on the softer *chiplyaa* and *maanjiri*; later it did not hesitate in installing the pedal-harmonium for accompaniment. The *vaarkari* did not follow suit in these matters (at least in *keertan*-performance). In addition, the *Naaradeeya keertan* exploited the *raag*-corpus, tunes from stage-music and instruments like violin too! The *vaarkari keertan* however continued to be austere and orthodox. Both these sub-traditions changed but on account of the differences in the basic motivation they moved in different directions.

The contemporary scene in Maharashtra thus presents an interesting phenomenon of oral tradition subjected to a process of modernization. A society which turns or is turning modern encourages specialization. Taking a total view of the Indian oral tradition one detects a specialization movement with the didactic core remaining common to all differentiated channels. For ethico-didactic entertainment of the lay public it was the *puraana*, for the enlightenment of the mature men of the world, it was the *pravachana*, for a non-caste, organized and sectarian religious teaching, it was the *vaarkari keertan*, and for an aesthetic, collective and a non-sectarian ethico-didactic imparting of knowledge—it was the *Naaradeeya keertan*. As hinted earlier, these developmental stages were attained over a period of years and to that extent there exist no fixed points of chronology. Yet the phases are clear enough to be perceived and unmistakable in their import. Altogether the criss-crossing of the communication channels involved has one moral: the situation is complex and needs sensitive analysis.

NOTES

1. Koparkar, G.N., *Paayeek Naaradanche*, pub. self, Pune, 1977, p. 21 (Appendix 4).
2. Ibid, loc. cit.
3. Pathak, Yeshwant, *Caachu Keertanaache Rangi*, Continental Prakashan, Pune, 1980, p. 79.
4. Koparkar, G.N., *Paayeek Naaradanche*, pub. self, Pune, 1977, p. 54, (Appendix 5).
5. Ibid, p. 23.
6. *Saarth Shridaasbodh*, ed. Narayan Maharaj Ramdasi, K.B., Dhawale, Bombay, 1967 (Dashak 4, Samaas 2), pp. 131-134.

Part Two

Pandit Ramkrishnabuwa Vaze, 1871-1945

1

Pandit Ramkrishnabuwa Vaze
1871 - 5.5.1945

Born in Sawantwadi, Maharashtra, he went through considerable hardships while learning music from many *gurus*. He received training chiefly from Ustad Nissar Hussain Khan of Gwalher *gharaanaa*. He had a flair for playing a number of instruments but he is remembered as a vocalist. Pt. Vazebuwa composed tunes for stage-songs during the period 1920-31. In two volumes entitled *Sangeet Kalaa Prakaash* he has included some interesting compositions in rare *raags*. The prefatory pages of the first volume contain an autobiographical account which throws a fascinating sidelight on the contemporary musical scene. He had many disciples.

The author had not the privilege of listening to Pt. Vazebuwa in a *mehfil*, for he passed away in 1945 when the author had yet to acquire his musical ears. Hence, for the present assessment we fall back on four sources. They are: his gramophone records and the two volumes of art-music compositions, a few compositions from his repertoire available to the author, the tunes he had provided to Marathi music-plays and lastly the music of some of his direct disciples (namely, Pt. Haribhau Ghangrekar, Pt. Shivrambuwa Vaze, Pt. Gajananrao Joshi and Pt. Bhaskarbuwa Joshi).

Pt. Vazebuwa received intensive *taaleem* from Ustad Nissar Hussain Khan of the Gwalher *gharaanaa* though he learnt from many other learned musicians too. Like many other receptive artists he assimilated many influences from myriad exposures to music in such a manner as to generate a style that can hardly be pigeon-holed. Therefore, it seems more appropriate to analyze his music structurally rather than to examine it as a musical deduction from the Gwalher point of view.

Pt. Vazebuwa's accent was on singing of the *khayaals*. He knew many *thumrees*, *dhrupads*, etc. But then it was the general practice of the serious and well-trained musicians of those times to have a *repertoire* varied within a particular musical form as well as to enjoy a repertoire-width within the general hierarchy of musical forms. Their choice of expression through one or a few musical forms was motivated by their desire to maintain a minimum efficiency in performance. The fact of the wide-based studies and narrower specialization need to be noted because characteristics of one or more forms studied by the artist tend to prove influential in the renderings of forms he actually selects to perform. A musician who could be described thus is structurally more complex, and musically more exciting.

The first thing that one noticed about Pt. Vazebuwa's singing was the high fundamental pitch he employed. It is easily discerned that he was not at ease while singing at such a pitch. The feeling a listener received was that of hearing a voice under strain. In other words, he could not have attached any musical significance to the high pitch *per se*. In all probability he was resigned to it on account of his asthamatic condition.

However, the musical consequences were inevitable and worth-discussing. There was no sustained note-production in his music nor were there *taan*-passages, etc., of any remarkable length. The phrase-terminations as well as the pronunciation of the words were characterized by an abruptness. Of course, it is also to be remembered that performing conditions available to most of the musicians active before 1920 in India were acoustically speaking far from ideal. In the absence of any sound-amplification devices, etc., the musician's primary consideration was in the first instance to reach the audience and secondly to remain audible with reasonable musical intelligibility. As a consequence, the dimensions of voice regarded more useful were pitch and volume. It meant that high-pitched singing was to be accorded priority even at the cost of 'quality' of voice which was adversely affected due to the high pitching in many sections of the vocalized range. The point is that even if Pt. Vazebuwa would not have been an asthamatic patient he would have resorted to a high fundamental pitch under the compulsion of the prevailing performance-environment. Notwithstanding all such factors Pt. Vazebuwa had the ability to mould the circumstances to yield high musical returns and that is what should concern us.

On examination it is detected that to offset the disadvantages of too high a pitch, he employed a tempo which was on most of the occasions describable as medium. When set in this tempo, any *taal* becomes more tractable because the temporal spaces that require filling-up also become manageable on account of their shorter span. In this connection, it is to be remembered that the broader and the immediately relevant temporal frame-work for music is provided by the overall tempo of the *taal* cycle. It is therefore very important to take a proper aesthetic decision in respect of the *taal*-tempo. Further, as far as the perceptual participation of the audience is concerned it is again the *taal*-tempo that supplies the initial clue. In selecting the medium tempo Pt. Vazebuwa made a very vital musico-aesthetic strategic decision.

The matter of the *taal*-tempo cannot of course be considered in isolation. The real question is: medium tempo of which *taal*? Pt. Vazebuwa's inclination was to rely with conspicuous frequency on *teentaal* and *jhaptaal*. This preference follows almost as a corollary from the choice he exercised in respect of the tempo. As is known, the *taal*-structure essentially depends on the number and distribution of the beats incorporated in the *taal*-cycle. With its four four-beats sections, the *teentaal* is found to be suitably structured irrespective of voices, forms, etc. The *jhaptaal* is however of a different type. Pt. Vazebuwa's great predilection for it again proved his unerring aesthetic sensibility. This *taal* has only ten beats and thus has an extremely matching skeleton vis-a-vis medium tempo. In itself the *jhaptaal* is neither sprawling (hence difficult to traverse) nor is it too constricted (hence too short for any significant patterning). Further, the distribution of beats is 2 3 2 3 —a pattern which makes it rather 'difficult' when employed in fast tempo and meaningless in a slow one. However, too slow or too fast compositions in this *taal* are extremely rare in the known repertoire of Hindustani artmusic. Pt. Vazebuwa employed the *taal* very frequently; the frequency is also reflected in the corpus of compositions he has chosen to publish.

Scanning the two volumes of compositions one finds that there are 49 *teentaals* and 40 *jhaptaals*! Pt. Vinayakrao Ghangrekar, who accompanied Pt. Vazebuwa on *tablaa* for a number of years (and whose elder brother, Pt.Haribhau Ghangrekar was Pt.Vazebuwa's seniormost disciple) told the author in the course of a TV interview that Pt. Vazebuwa sang very often in *jhaptaal* and *aadaa choutaal* because everybody else was employing *ektaal* and *teentaal*! In a way, this too is an instance of Pt.Vazebuwa's acute perception. As if to provide us with supporting evidence, his recorded music includes three *jhaptaal* compositions and significantly they happen to be the best pieces. The compositions are in *raag khambaavati, khat* and *tilak-kaamod* respectively.

The abruptness evident in his singing was responsible for another important feature in his presentations: the active role of the element of pause.

Due to the high singing-pitch as well as perhaps due to his short breath, Pt.Vazebuwa had apparently developed a vocalizing technique in which (contrary to the accepted Gwalher norm, singing did *not* rely on the vowel-sound 'AA'. Instead, a variant, Aw was employed. This variety of a distorted 'AA' afforded him an opportunity to hold the breath longer. Secondly, it also provided him with more room to manoeuvre the more perceivable emphasis on notes or the desired word-units of the song-text. Immediately after an occurrence of such emphatic points in the rendering, he usually introduced a pause before taking up the melodic thread again. He did not allow the shadow of the note to linger and the resulting fractional pauses created a chiaroscuro effect of sound and silence. One has only to listen to his *jhaptaal* compositions or the famous *'Bol re papiyaraa' teentaal, miya malhaar*, to appreciate his skilful use of the pause.

The pauses adjacent to *sam*-points in all his renderings, and those located after the introduction of new and intricate musical phrasings, are worth a closer scrutiny. All such pauses allowed his music to sink in. They make one realize the truth that in music much more is achieved (than imagined) if an uninterrupted vocalizing is not equated with musicality. On account of the *taals* and the tempo the listeners became permeated with his music. Even today these features of Pt.Vazebuwa's music afford us a scope or a breathing space to establish confirmed relationships between the intricate and the non-lingering musical phrases that Pt.Vazebuwa so much excelled in.

Pt.Vazebuwa's choice of the *jhaptaal* made it easier for him to apply the chiaroscuro effect. Even a brief consideration of the *jhaptaal*-structure reveals the distribution of the sonorous and the not-so-sonorous syllables of the *tablaa*-language especially those around the *sam*-point. In a *jhaptaal* composition, an artist appears to come to the *sam* in a pouncing manner which has an appeal of its own. In this connection, the author still remembers how an old-timer described the *taals*, *jhaptaal* and *jhumraa*, in a picturesque way. He remarked in Hindi, '*jhaptaal jhapse aataa hai, aur jhumraa jhoomke*'. (The *jhaptaal* comes in a pouncing manner and the *jhumraa* in a swaying manner.) This special quality, born of the structural features, was doubly reinforced in Pt.Vazebuwa's singing because the *mukhdaas* of his *jhaptaal*-compositions never started from the *sam*-points. They invariably began from the eight and a half beat point, and the achieved effect was inimitable.

Abruptness of diction was of course not the only characteristic that attracts our attention in Pt.Vazebuwa's music. There was another aspect to his handling of the words of the song-text.

Firstly, the words were enunciated with surprising clarity: surprising because Hindustani vocalists are not generally found to exhibit this quality. It is possible to maintain that they take a dim view of the clarity of word-pronunciation because it necessarily means introducing repeated consonantal terminations in the vocal flow. Yet, Pt. Vazebuwa opted for clarity and force in the enunciation of words in the song-text. The way he accomplished this (to the accompaniment of general forcefulness), almost amounted to *carving out contours of words in sound*. This was observed in all his renderings. Whether it was a *bhajan* like '*Udho karaman ki gati nyaari*' ('O Uddhav, the ways of Karma are inscrutable') or a *drut ektaal* composition like '*Bal bal bal jainye*' (*bhatiyaar*)— the words were uttered with strength and deliberateness which underline his conviction that they were the carriers of *musical* meaning. It may be mentioned here that the style of stage-singing popularized in Maharashtra by the late Keshavarao Bhonsale, Bapurao Pendharkar and Master Dinanath also exemplified a similar tendency: it could not have been a coincidence that all the three regarded Pt. Vazebuwa as their *guru*.

Pt. Vazebuwa treated the words of a song-text as sound-patterns that invited emphasis and employment for their own sake. The role assigned to words in this manner was thus sound-oriented, not meaning-oriented. Perhaps this was the reason why he frequently ignored uttering words fully! For example, in his otherwise sensi-

tive pieces in *khambaavati, khat, bhatiyaar* and *tilakkaamod,* there
are numerous instances where words are, semantically speaking,
dismembered.

The consideration of the content of Pt. Vazebuwa's music is
intrinsically bound with the technical aspects. Hence the nature of
his *raag*-elaboration also needs to be looked into. It is in this context that his renderings of *khat* and *tilak-kaamod* are notable.

It is common knowledge that during the period Pt. Vazebuwa
was active, these *raag*s were considered *aprachalita* (rare); they were
also believed to be near-monopolies of the *khayaal*-singers belonging
to the Jaipur *gharaanaa* as represented by the late Ustad Alladiya
Khan and his disciples. A little exercise of the historical imagination would however enable us to realize that Pt. Vazebuwa's interpretations of such *raag*s at that time indicated, in reality, that the
raag-lore in Hindustani music was very much a matter of general
circulation than the impressionistic accounts of the *gharaanas* make
out to be. (Perhaps it could even be proved that Pt. Vazebuwa
preceded the Jaipur musicians in presenting the extremely complex and challenging *repertoire* of rare *khayaal-raag*s). The author
has personally heard rare *raag*s like *kankan, pradumna-kaanada,
mudrikaa-kaanadaa, nat-naaraayani, kaafi-kaanadaa, khat, saamant-
kalyaan* from stalwarts like the late Pt. Shivrambuwa Vaze, Pt.
Haribhau Ghangrekar and from the veterans like Pt. Gajananrao
Joshi and Pt. Bhaskarbuwa Joshi. The author remembers how his
guru Pt. Gajananrao Joshi responded to a query put to him by his
father (and *guru*) the late Pt. Anant Manohar Joshi. Pt. Gajanan-
raoji had learnt only a few compositions from Pt. Vazebuwa. Hence
Pt. Anant Manohar asked his son, 'What have you learnt from Pt.
Vazebuwa?' The latter replied without hesitation, 'I have learnt
from him the technique of solving the puzzle what *aprachalita raag*s
are.' (The moral of the story is that to obtain an insight into the
nature of *aprachalita raag* as a phenomenon is more significant than
learning a great number of such *raag*s).

In reality a rare *raag* can be a set of structures based on deviations from many other known *raag*s. It is therefore frequently
found that a rare *raag* involves a very subtle balancing of *raag*-
forces than a mere rendering of *raag*-phrases of many individual
*raag*s. It is sufficient to listen to Pt. Vazebuwa's *khat* to discern his
bold way of treating this rare *raag*. He conceived it as a melodic
interplay of two forces: the forces being the *gandhaar-dhaiwat*-pairs

and the overall *aasaavari*-mood-orientation in the interpretation. Such a treatment achieved two goals: it enhanced the structural appeal of the *raag* because the paired notes are consonant notes. Secondly, the *aasaavari*-orientation bestowed on the *raag* an emotional appeal otherwise inconceivable. Even today the conventional grammatical interpretation of *khat* maintains that the *raag*-name is a derivation of the Sanskrit term *shata* meaning six. The implication is that the *raag* consists of six *raags*. If strictly adhered to, this logic would lead to a rendering characterized by a mechanical doling out of phrases of the six individual *raags* in succession! Thus presented, the *raag* could turn into a colourless entity similar to many of the *patmanjiri* (i.e., *raags* reported to have five component *raags*). In Pt. Vazebuwa's treatment *khat* escaped this fate. This short analysis is of course illustrative but could be easily carried out further in respect of other *raags*.

From his conception of *aprachalita raags* to the complex *taan*-patterns is a logical passage. As soon as the basic decision about the nature of these *raags* is arrived at, the *taans* can hardly remain 'the faster rendering of *aalaaps*.' The *taans* too have to discharge the function of carrying over the structural and sometimes even the emotional musical content of the *aalaaps*. The general practice of the Hindustani musicians has been to introduce lengthy *taans* ranging over a span of two or more octaves. In contrast, Pt. Vazebuwa believed a great deal in deploying shorter passages, also in employing an element of tonal contrast. Therefore his *taans* do not appear to be an act of reeling off of *palataas* (i.e., traditionally devised scale-patterns used as musical exercises aimed at attainment of technical virtuosity). His *taans* succeed in their truer aesthetic task of becoming significant consolidations of *raag*-images and being the instantaneous recapitulations of the more important of the *raag*-themes. Pt. Vazebuwa's *taan*-units are generally found to consist of four/five component notes uttered with remarkable energy. In fact, in places he seems to have gone out of tune—but this could have been due to his advancing age. (One of the discs has a label mentioning his age to be 82 years when the disc was cut.) The vigour with which the *taans* were presented makes an impact of such a depth that to an extent, the volume seems to compensate for the lack of speed (as Pt. Vazebuwa's *taans* were not impressive in respect of the agility of movement).

What was Pt. Vazebuwa's contribution? Firstly, he enriched the *raag*-repertoire in effective circulation to a considerable extent. He also presented an alternative approach towards solving the puzzling phenomenon of the *aprachalita raag*. His singing of the *jhaptaal*-compositions showed a perceptive mind which invested these compositions with a new flexibility and also represented a new found artistic alertness that seized upon the structural potentialities of the *taal*. The vigour with which he infused his total singing was a clear 'dimensional' contribution because it carried a hint of substitution of pitch by volume—another dimension of the human voice. In the case of every great artist, his disabilities seem to possess the quality of turning into assets: Pt. Vazebuwa is one more example of such an alchemy.

Discography

Raag	Text line	Record number	Make
Kaafi Kaanadaa	Preet Puraani	GE 3189	Columbia
Bhatiyaar	Bal Bal Bal Jainye	-do-	-do-
Todi	Masiat Punchaniyaa	GE 3177	-do-
Khat	Vidyaadhar	-do-	-do-
Khambaavati	Sakhi Mukhachandra	GE 1554	-do-
Tilang	Mere Ghar Aaj	-do-	-do-
Bhajan	Udho Karaman Ki Gat	GE 1540	-do-
Barwaa	Bol Raadhe	-do-	-do-
Tilak-kaamod	Teerath Ko Sab Kare	GE 1501	-do-
Miyaan Malhaar	Bol Re Papeeharaa	-do-	-do-
Maarwaa	Taraanaa	GE 1532	-do-
Nat-bihaag	Damru Dam Damru Baaje	-do-	-do-
Gaaraa-bageshri	Joban Ras Le	GE 1579	-do-
Bhatiyaar	Har Har	-do-	-do-
Jaunpuri	Hardam Maula Tero Nam	GE 1517	-do-
Bhairav-bahaar	Daar Daar Paat Paat Koyaliyaa Bole	-do-	-do-

Ustad Abdul Karim Khan, 1872-1937

2

Ustad Abdul Karim Khan
1872 - 27.10.1937

Born in Kairana (district Saharanpur, U.P.); initially
trained by his father Kalekhan and uncle Abdullakhan.
In the 1890s, served in the princely state of Baroda for
some time; then moved through Bombay, Miraj and
Hubli successively; founded Aarya Sangeet Samaaj in
Pune (1913) and opened a branch of the same in Bombay
(1917); collaborated with M/s Clements and Deval in
carrying out research on the *sruti*-problem in Indian
musicology. He was one of the major Hindustani vocalists to win acceptance in the South. After closing the
Bombay branch of the Aarya Sangeet Samaaj in 1920,
he settled permanently in Miraj. He still has many
disciples and admirers.

In India, revaluation of musicians of the pre-1930 era by the later
generation poses special problems—the chief being the impossibility of personal exposure to the musician concerned in a *mehfil*-
situation. The acuteness of the disadvantage is however slightly
lessened in the case of artists like Ustad Abdul Karim Khan who
were recorded not too meagerly. Not only was he recorded fairly
well, having about thirtyfour pieces to his credit, but the recorded
corpus is also adequately representative of his art. In other words
it covers all the major (and also some minor) categories of his total
musical expression. The break-up of his recorded music may prove
of some interest:

*Khayaal*s	14 (including both varieties, i.e., *badaa* (6) and *chhotaa* (7))
*Thumree*s	8

Naatyageets	6
Marathi *pads*	2
Taraanaas	2
Carnatic *raags*	2

It is therefore felt with some justification that the samples of his recorded music need not be considered too insufficient for the purpose of analysis. In addition, not to discuss him at all would surely impair the attempted examination of the total musical perspective obtained in Hindustani art-music, so important has been his influence through admirers and disciples.

On this backdrop if one considers the matter of musical forms, the Ustad is heard to revel in *khayaal, thumree* and the few stage-songs he sang with relish. The three expressions could to an extent, be discussed as separate categories. However, in all these categories his renderings exhibit certain common features. It is therefore advisable to discuss the common features prior to devoting attention to the other traits of his art, specific to particular musical forms.

Irrespective of the musical form, the Ustad's singing displayed a very striking feature: the tone of voice he used. His vocal tone could be described as thin, pointed, slightly nasal and occasionally a little hollow. It also gave an abiding impression of a high fundamental pitch. His voice could be technically classified as an 'upper register voice' that excelled in accentuating those brilliant overtones usually available in abundance in the higher portion of the scale. Unless in possession of a matching lower register, such a voice is naturally weak in the lower ranges. The Ustad clearly lacked the lower register and the musical consequences flowing from this partial vocal development proved inevitable. It is therefore not surprising that most of his pieces were better elaborated in the upper reaches of the scale. The pieces in *bhairavi* (*Jamunaake teer*), *jogiyaa* (*Piyaake milanki aas*) and *tilang* (*Kaaheko nainaa lagaaye*) are worth noting in this respect. In fact the *sams* of the compositions in *jogiyaa* and *bhairavi* are on the *taar saa* (the octave note). To carry the point a step further one notices that the spots of unmistakable musical impact are also found in the upper reaches. This is not to suggest that he was out of tune in the other parts of the scale. It only means that due to an adherence to the vocal tone mentioned above, the Ustad was not able to extract the results which he could obtain in the upper reaches. A similar lack of appeal was also evident in his execution of the progressions in faster tempi. Apparently, an exception is detected in the tonal space around *madhya gandhaar*. Even though this note is located in the lower stretches of the scale, the Ustad was surely able to invest the singing with appeal while he was engaged in elaborations around the note. In this connection the author has a hypothesis which can accommodate the present exception. Due to the fascinating acoustical qualities (inadequately analyzed so far) the last string of the *taanpuraa* (which provides the drone to all Hindustani musicians) produces a *gandhaar* which is known to Indian musicology as *swayambhu gandhaar*, i.e., the self-existent *gandhaar*. It is suggested here that by virtue of the Ustad's nasal and upper registered voice-production, the overtones of the note received reinforcement: this enabled him to retain the musical appeal in an area which would have otherwise remained out of his effective orbit.

The vocal tone so uniformly applied by him was further characterized by superimposition of the compound vowel-sound 'ou' on the entire vocalizing process. Pressed into service in this manner the vowel-sound proved a very reliable aid in maintaining *aas* in his renderings. The importance of this quality in a solo, melodic tradition can hardly be overestimated. It was due to the *aas* that the Ustad was able to keep vocal connection between the successive musical phrases. The slow fade-out quality realized through the *aas* prevented occurrence of breaks in the intended vocal flow. Of all the vowel-sounds, 'O' has the maximum resonance except in the tonal area above the octave (where in fact all the vowel-sounds tend to lose their individual identities). The total situation obtained in the Ustad's music could therefore be interpreted as an application of a two-fold strategy: use of a uniform vocal tone and reliance on a compound, resonant vowel-sound. From the dual strategy two musical consequences followed directly: the experience of continuity and evocative quality.

The formulae served him well in slow tempo singing and at least in respect of the higher notes. In addition, it also blurred the consonantal edges of the words of the song-texts and in the process made the words sound rounder. Unfortunately the operation made all the words non-starters in the etching of their individual sound-contours. Therefore, whether it was a Marathi stage-song (*Ugich kaa kaantaa*), an art-music composition in *bilaawal* (*Pyaaraa najar naahi awandaa*) or a *thumri* (*Kaaheko naina lagaaye* or **Paani** *bhareli)* the projected words were unfailingly appealing though utterly indistinguishable from one another.

The foregoing argument has an interesting counter-proof available in the performing techniques of some of the other major followers of the *Kiraana gharaanaa*. As is known, of Ustad's male followers the late Pt. Sawai Gandharva and Pt. Behrebuwa 'sounded' appealing a la their *guru*: one could easily detect in them the same vocal techniques as the Ustad had applied: the superimposed compound vowel-sound, abundant use of the upper register and the uniform vocal tone. On the other hand, Roshanara Begum (now in Pakistan) and Pt. Bhimsen Joshi (a well-known disciple of Pt. Sawai Gandharva) do not possess the same type of appeal because they do not sound like the Ustad. The reason is that these singers use a two-registered voice and a multiple-vowel-sounds strategy. Such changes were imperative. Without introducing them, the latter two artists would not have been able to execute the fast *taans*, an act they perform so effectively. It is in fact a vindication of a performer's logic to see the same artists also abandon the use of a uniform tone.

Another commonly traceable feature of the Ustad's singing was his total reliance on the *bol-aalaaps* and the proportionate paucity of the use of *aa-kaar* (utilization of the vowel-sound 'AA') in the musical elaborations. This was causally connected with the continuity of tone that he so firmly believed in. Musical continuity of the type described earlier would not have been possible if the vocalization was to depend on vowel-sounds (and especially on that of 'AA'). The simple and unexceptional reason is that vowel-production by itself means spending more breath than is necessary for producing consonants. Even a non-technical, commonsense definition tells us that vowel-sound is heard when an uninterrupted, outgoing, air-flow is used for producing voice, while a consonant-sound is created when the flow is stopped at various points in the oral cavity in various ways to produce linguistic sounds, etc. The Ustad's accent on the *bol-aalaaps* is to be viewed in this context. Words were used copiously because using them meant exploiting the consonants as devices for shaping and also maintaining the voice-flow. However, this manner of giving importance to words is not the same as the other two modes of according recognition to words as musical forces. (The two other modes of giving musical importance to words are to pay heed to them as meaningful units and to use

them as sound-patterns). As the Ustad used them, they were more
of voice-savers and colouring agents than being vehicles of meaning
or patterns in sound. Almost as a rule, words were formed tentati-
vely rather than definitively in his music and their aura was regarded
more important than their clarity. There was a pervasive blurring
of sound-contours of the individual words and in place of their
purposeful differentiation (either meaning-based or sound-based)
listeners became conscious of a continuous musical flow.

The third recurrent characteristic of his music was the Ustad's
notion of the role of *taal*. To judge from his music, the Ustad
definitely assigned a subservient role to *taal*. He took the first
step towards making the *taal* less important and less obtrusive,
perceptible and rigorous when he slowed down the tempo of the
accompanying rhythm. Nothing could have been more effective in
attenuating the impact of the individual pattern of any *taal*. It is
significant that those responsible today for a further slowing down of
the tempo of *khayal* music are also followers of the *Kirana* ideology.
Today the tempo has been slowed down to such a (crawling) pace
that it has caused a near-total obliteration of the design of individual *taals*. Slackening of the general tempo of the *taal* was further
followed in the Ustad's music by a reduction in the variety of the
taals kept in circulation. The Ustad confined himself to a very few
taals and in the process totally ignored the effect of the diversity
of patterns made available to us by the structural peculiarities of
individual *taals*. In sticking to *ektaal* and *teentaal*, he proved logical, in the sense that his usage exemplified his position: if the
pattern of a *taal* was not worth noticing, there was no need to use
a variety of *taals* as basic frames. This same scant respect for the
taal-entity was also evident in his noticeably sparing use of *taans*
and *bol-taans* with pronounced rhythmic orientation. His avoid-
ance of the conventional tempo-doubling at the closing stages of
thumree-singing could also be traced to his basic reluctance to allow
any scope to the *taal*-element in music. It is known that the doubling of the tempo in *thumree*-singing ensures a shift of emphasis to
the *taal*-frame which is otherwise kept dormant. The Ustad did not
concede to *taal* even this momentary glory! He was reported to
have stated that if a musician lost in respect of *taal*, it was comparable to a mere loss of hair but if he went out of tune, it was like
losing the head itself!

It was on this background that irrespective of the form of music presented, the Ustad's music recognized only those beats which were adjacent to the *sam*-point. As far as other sub-sections of the *taal* or other contributory time-points like *khaali*, etc., were concerned, no special care was taken to build any relationship with them. It was obvious that *taal* was regarded as a constraining force rather than as a co-operative component of the patterning activity that music ceaselessly tries to be. *Taal* was treated as less than equal, though peaceful co-existence with it was not totally ruled out. For the Ustad, it was the tempo and not the *taal* which was material. He was traditional enough to employ a *taal*, yet he was a rebellious soul in the sense that he voluntarily denied himself the exciting possibilities and appeals of rhythmic variations as well as their interplay with the changing tempi. Listening to him one always gets a feeling that had he been living today, he would have hardly hesitated to banish the *taal* completely, even at the risk of making music unvaryingly smooth and therefore undesirably satiating. It is no secret that between the tonal and the rhythmic variations, the latter are conveyed and perceived with more facility. In fact, even in the case of transcending the intercultural or crosscultural barriers, the element of rhythm crosses them with more sureness. The stakes involved in playing down the role of *taal* were therefore very high. It may of course be possible that on the Ustad's part this was more of an intuitive choice than a conscious aesthetic decision. Yet the consequences were aesthetic and are to be considered as such.

Finally, his entire music was also imbued with a spirit of non-academism. The observation perhaps needs some explaining.

In this context two terms must be clearly distinguished. They are: academism and pedantry. Pedantry is a dry (or puritanical) adherence to the scholastic tradition of music. In contrast with it, academism is a positive recognition of the scholastic tradition. Academism views scholastic tradition as a musical force that stabilizes the performing tradition and provides a continuous base for deviations. Having a wider perspective, an academic musician becomes the chief protagonist in an effort to realize the aesthetic paradoxes. An academic strikes a balance between conformity and innovation, stability and dynamism and lastly between craftsmanship and creativity. For example in the matter of *raag*-renderings an academic musician tries to project a grammatically correct image of a *raag* and yet takes care to suggest deviations. It is in

this sense that the Ustad lacked the academic outlook. The grammatical outlines of his renderings were often confused or lacked
definition. For instance, his *sarparadaa* could hardly be endorsed
by the established interpretation of the *raag*. It also happened that
his *taan*s would disagree with the *raag*-interpretation as put forward in *aalaap*s (e.g., his *basant*). All these musical *faux pas* could
take place not because he was *not* aware of the core-deviation
phenomenon but because he had accorded an aesthetic priority to
the particular general tone of his music and because he regarded
individual notes as more important than the collective *raag*-image
that the notes stood for. In other words effectiveness of the musical tone reigned supreme in his musical logic and correctness-core
and the deviational periphery remained on the sidelines. It is
therefore not surprising that his recently published correspondence
with disciples reveals his preference for intensive practice as opposed to the theoretical concern for the correctness of *raag khambaavati*. Of course to have such preferences was not unique in his
times. A majority of musicians always regarded effective performance as more relevant to musicianship than the possession of
theoretical insights. Though exonerable, the sort of either/or
attitude exhibited towards musical matters in such preferences was
surely a lop-sided response to the total musical reality. It is *naive*
to equate grammatical correctness with pedantry and to dissociate
knowledge of music from its practice. However, as such opinions
were almost universally detected in his times the Ustad need not
be singled out for censure.

Discussion of these general characteristics of the Ustad's music
prepares us for a more technical analysis of two particular musical
forms the Ustad selected as vehicles for his musical expression:
khayaal and *thumree*.

Even a cursory hearing makes it clear that in his renderings
khayaal and *thumree* came so near that they became practically
indistinguishable.

To start with, the singing of a composition in both the categories
was replete with the same uniform, appealing tone, described earlier. The consequence was predictable. In this connection it must
be remembered that one way of keeping musical forms separate is
to vary the emotional appeal with which they can be infused. It
can be safely generalized that those art-musical forms categorized
as 'classical' in India are cooler, less sensuous or less emotional

than those categorized otherwise. The classical forms tend to attract the listeners by the arabesque quality of music. The Ustad's strategy of investing both *thumree* and-*khayaal*-singing with the uniform tone resulted in uniform appeals and similar musical appearances. The act was a musicological taboo as it was an aesthetic risk. But the choice was, in the final analysis, his to make and he made it unequivocally.

There was also the possibility that the forms could have been kept separate by keeping a watchful eye on the 'definition' of structures of the individual *raag*s. This would have made the contours of *raag*s a little more resistant to effacement. In each *raag*, the primary building-blocks of set melodic phrases are clearly identifiable. Such phrases are often exclusively attached to a particular *raag*. Thus to emphasize these phrases is a very efficient course open to a musician interested in *raag*-individuation. Of all other distinguishing factors, it is the *raag*-individuation that effectively separates 'classical' from the 'non-classical' music in India. It could be seen that on account of his overall musical strategy both tone-differentiation and the *raag*-individuation were denied to the Ustad. His *khayaal* and *thumree* therefore produce a near-identical musical impact.

In addition, the Ustad also refrained from employing the words of the *thumree*-text in a meaningful manner. A *thumree*-singer (as contrasted with a singer of *khayaal*) could be said to orient all his musical elaborations on the lines suggested by the emotive drift of the *thumree*-text. There are many *thumree*-types in vogue but all of them agree on the point of putting emphasis on the words of the text. For example, in one type of *thumree*, the words are arranged, rearranged and distributed in the main stream of music. This type is aptly known as *bol-baant*. In another type the singer of *thumree*s laces the emotive appeal of the words with matching tonal and gestural variations. This type is appropriately known as *bol-banaav*. *Thumree*-singers are also prone to recite matching lyrical couplets in between the main elaborations. All such devices undoubtedly bring the word-meaning to the fore. In fact, *thumree*-singers are so conscious of their use of words that they are also aware of the sameness of musical effect that the word-orientation might produce. This unrelieved dependence on one single element of music they seek to diminish by bringing in the elements of tempo (through the *dugun*-phenomenon), rhythm (through the centering of the *laggi*-pieces reeled off by the *tablaa*-player during the *dugun*) and *taan* (through the flourishes coming at the phase-terminations during the presentation).

One finds that all such features were absent in the Ustad's renderings. In their place was installed a uniform, enveloping tone which blurred the word-contours as well as the structural lines of the presentation taken as a whole. *Thumree* as a musical form had already crystallized when the Ustad was active. (Even the *thumree-gharaanaa*s had come into their own.) Under the circumstances the Ustad's neglect of the accepted conventions of *thumree*-singing needs to be explained. Was it the Ustad's lack of academic outlook that led to the 'blurring'-effect referred to?

To be fair to the Ustad, another possibility may also be considered. That possibility was of deliberately introducing the 'blurring' as a measured step towards modernity. It is known to all students of arts that merging art-forms or initiating processes that accelerate their overlap is very often regarded as a major characteristic of modernity. The Ustad's music could be construed as a prominent example of such a phenomenon in *Hindustani* music of the present century. His tendency to blur the dividing lines existing between two forms could be interpreted as an operation that denied the validity of the traditional hierarchy of musical forms. For him musical forms were only carriers of musical messages. His music had one message: hence followed the equality of treatment and temperament in respect of *khayaal*s and *thumree*s.

The Ustad's preference for the 'blur' effect was also discernible at one more level. It has already been seen how he had burnt his boats as far as *raag*-differentiation (according to structural features) was concerned. He adopted a similar attitude in respect of the emotional or the evocative identities of individual *raag*s. In this context it is instructive to examine the way he handled the matter of *raag*-dynamics which is a very effective device of *raag*-individuation. *Raag*-dynamics can be described as the cumulative result of volume-variations and the condensation-rarefactions of the note-clusters involved in a particular *raag*. The Ustad was deprived of these devices because his motto was fidelity to every note in an equal measure and also because he was insistent on maintaining a high degree of melodiousness *throughout* a rendering. Sincerely pursued, the resultant policy placed him in a predicament of a lyricist who insists that every word in his composition should be lyrical! Such a literal 'single'-mindedness achieves artistic success of a 'monochrome' variety. Inevitably, *bilaawal, shankara, basant* or *jogiyaa* all sounded alike in the Ustad's music. Irrespective of one's position on the interrelationship of *rasa*-theory and *Hindustaani* music, it is clear that *raag shankara* has a mood that is different from that of *raag jogiyaa* or that *raag basant* possesses an atmospheric effect of its own which is qualitatively and radically different from that of *bhairaavi*! In the Ustad's music, however, there is only one deep hue of anguish all over and in all *raag*s. In view of the vocalizing techniques he adopted unvaryingly, the general attitude he held about the nature of musical appeal and the treatment he reserved for words in all categories of music —it was inevitable.

Of his musical personality one facet needs to be considered before a settled opinion about his contribution can be recorded. The matter of his responses to *Carnaatic* music deserves special mention. His responses were more positive and deep-seated than the responses of other musicians of his times. To 'import' *Carnaatic raag*s into the *Hindustaani* fold, to author new compositions in them and in this manner to totally acclimatize *Carnaatic raag*s is perhaps too obvious and easy a response to merit analysis. What the Ustad tried was however more fundamental and subtle. What he did was to incorporate certain *Carnaatic* patterns of phrasing the *sargam* (i.e., the sol-fa singing) in his *Hindustaani* elaborations and to employ them *without* the colour of the *Carnaatic gamak*-style. To all purposes a major way of enriching a total, available, musical *repertoire* of any culture is to induct new patterns into it, and this was what the Ustad achieved. The patterns he brought in were well assimilated because they were not accompanied by the *Carnatic* way of intoning them. At the same time, the quality of novelty was unmistakable because they did not belong originally to the *Hindustaani* progressions and were an outcome of a deft removal from their original matrix. He had transplanted them and placed them in a different but conducive context. His act was therefore not an act of wholesale borrowing of *Carnaatic* structures, nor was it a fashion or a 'gimmick'. It was a skilled act of introducing new resources by way of recreation. As a result, the new patterns could serve him as generative moulds which were neither restricted to the particular instances of their original appearance nor to *Hindustaani* musical examples similar to them in structure, *raag*-phrasings, etc. In other words, the Ustad's *sargam* with the *Carnaatic* contours was a veritable feat of musical bisociation. It was logical that these moulds were used in all forms of music he selected to perform.

Ustad Abdul Karim Khan surely belonged to the category of the non-conformists. His musical accomplishment was twofold. Firstly, he was responsible for throwing a strong challenge to the dry (though grammatically correct) *khayaal*-singing that was in vogue. When most of his contemporaries were interested in systematizing the available corpus of *Hindustaani khayaal*, he stressed the role of 'appeal' in music. It is true that many other musicians too would have sworn by the same credo. But in reality very few took the risk of changing the traditional orientation in pursuance of the musical ideals they preached. The other form he chose to perform was *thumree*—and in his singing of it he registered an interesting deviation. He chose *not* to cling to words in an obvious, literal fashion in the name of emotional appeal. Under the circumstances he could be credited with liberating the *thumree* from its word-dependence. Without having recourse to the word-meaning, he succeeded in retaining the emotional quality of music by virtue of his 'tone' and his attitude towards musical material in general. His achievements as a *thumree*-singer stand out as a valuable addition to the established dimensions of the form. He could be emotional without being sentimental and sweet without being cloying in his *thumree*s. This was not a minor feat to perform.

Discography

Raag	Text line	Record number	Make
Shuddha Pilu	Soch Samajh Naadaan	BEX 260	Columbia
Shuddha Kalyaan	Maunder Baaje	-do-	-do-
Maalkauns	Peer Naa Jaane	SS 4020	Odeon
Gujri Todi	Dim Dara Dim	-do-	-do-
Jhinjhoti	Piyaa Bin Nahi	SS 4001	-do-
Basant	Phagwaa Brij	-do-	-do-
Gaaraa (thumri)	Jaadu Bhareli	SS 4007	-do-
Mishra Kaafi	Baawri Ram	-do-	-do-
Mishra Jangalaa	Raam Nagariyaamen	SS 4010	-do-
Jogiyaa	Piyaake Milanki Aas	-do-	-do-
Bilaawal	Pyaara Najar Nahin	SS 4009	-do-
Sarparadaa	Gopaalaa Meri Karuna	-do-	-do-
Darbaari Kaanadaa	Jhanak Jhanakwaa	SS 4017	-do-
Gujri Todi	Begun Gun Gaawe	-do-	-do-
Patdeep	Dhan Dhan Ghari	SS 4026	-do-
Lalit	Bhaavandaa Yaardaa	-do-	-do-
Abhogi Kaanadaa	Banraa Rangiraa	SS 4012	-do-
Adaanaa	Bandhanawaa Baandhore	-do-	-do-
Marwaa	Taraanaa	SS 4413	-do-
Gauri	Atahi Prachand	-do-	-do-
Saaveri	...	SS 4015	-do-
Karharpriyaa	...	-do-	-do-
Shankaraa	Aaj Sohag	BEX 252	Columbia
Tilang (thumree)	Saajan Tum	-do-	-do-
Devgaandhaar	Chandrikaa Hi Janu	SS 4008	Odeon
Bhimpalaas	Premsevaa Sharan	-do-	-do-

Malkauns	Aataa Rampaayi	SS 4001	-do-
Khamaaj	Taari Raamraayaa	SS 4001	Odeon
Basant	Aah Maine	BEX 259	Columbia
Bhairavi	Jamunaake Teer	-do-	-do-
Sindh kaafi	Nach Sundari	BEX 254	-do-
Aanad bhairavi	Ugich Ka Kaanta	-do-	-do-
	Dehaataa Sharanaagatta	SS 4018	-do-
Jaunpuri	Prembhaave Jeev Jagi	-do-	-do-

Ustad Faiyaz Hussain Khan, 1886-1950

3

Ustad Faiyaz Hussain Khan
1886 - 5.11.1950

Born in Agra; spent his growing and impressionable age surrounded by families of musicians; received training mainly from Ghulam Abbas (grandfather) and Kallan Khan (granduncle) – both of Agra *gharaanaa*.

Appointed state-musician in Baroda in 1912, awarded the title of *Aaftaab-e-mousiki* by the Maharaja of Mysore in 1925; known for his ability to sing a variety of musical forms; immensely successful in *mehfils*.

Since 1925, Ustad Faiyaz Hussain Khan was popularly known as *Aaftaab-e-mousiki*, 'sun in the world of music.' For once, the praise was not hyperbolic—though it did describe a musician! The *Ustad* belonged to that rare category of musicians who not only won admiration but also earned affection from the audience because he brought so much cheer to them through his music.

Does cheer as a quality belong to the extroverts among musicians? It might be so, because in a very marked way, the Ustad's music displayed an unmistakable outgoing quality. His music was very openly directed at the audience with an express purpose of involving it in the musico-cultural processes that every musical concert in India promises to be. For the Ustad, the number of listeners hardly mattered. The mere presence of attentive ears was enough to spur him on. At the same time the Ustad (like Prime Minister Pt. Nehru, who was an improviser in speech!) loved crowds. In the participating company of the audience the Ustad's music acquired an easy flow and a conquering edge. Very aptly he was also called *Mehfil ka baadshah* (king of concerts).

How did the Ustad achieve this intense and qualitative involvement of his audience? His first asset was an unabashed projection of a bass, booming voice. To describe his use of the bass, as 'unabashed' has a special propriety because in his times and among his contemporaries, the employment of a high fundamental pitch by vocalists was a religiously followed custom. To a certain extent the absence of sound-amplifying gadgets certainly made the practice necessary. It is also true that to sing in a low key was not highly regarded! To do so was almost taken to be an admission of some weakness in the musical make-up of the artist. It is on this background that the Ustad's decision to select to sing in a low-keyed fundamental could be regarded as courageous.

Of course as a performer he was not interested in empty heroic gestures! He used the bass and in doing so exploited the volume-dimension of the voice (as opposed to the pitch-dimension utilized by a majority of his contemporaries). It followed logically that in his music the aesthetic principle of musical contrast came into operation. Whether it was the *nom-tom* (e.g., *lalat* and *darbari*), his famous rendering of the *antaraa* in *raag barawaa* or his pieces in *bhairavi*, it was the *fortissimo-pianissimo* effect that was repeatedly employed. As an expressive dimension the volume of human voice has less potentialities than the dimension of pitch. In the light of this acoustic fact the Ustad's choice spelt an aesthetic risk. In all probability he accepted it because he was aware of the limited pitch-range of his voice, weighed the total consequences and decided in favour of a low-keyed but strongly projected voice as against a high-keyed but strenuously produced voice. The Ustad's use of the voice was validated by his music. He could reach the audience to the last man and could also envelope the listeners by a surging-forward music. It was the sense of power that one primarily experienced in his music. As his expression was directed at the audience the power-element was entirely in place. His aim was to gain ascendency over the audience, either by conquest or through persuasion. To achieve an 'effect' was of primary importance to him and he was hardly satisfied by an aesthetic realization of musical ideas.

The low-key base and the accompanying projection in vocalization were also associated with a marked superimposition of the vowel-sound 'a' (approximate to 'a' in 'man'). This must have proved to be a valuable aid in projecting voice effectively because the vowel-sound 'a' is certainly less open than 'A'—the vowel-sound, customarily advocated in *Hindustaani* vocalization. Consequently, the vowel-sound 'a' was easier to control. It is clear that what was involved here was a performer's musical logic, not an accidental choice.

An important clue to his musical logic is to be found in the *dhrupad*-orientation of the Agra *gharaanaa*. Ustad sang *dhrupad-dhamaar* in accordance with all the established norms. However, listening to him in between the notes one found that of his *dhrupad-dhamaar* renderings, the weakest was the *dhamaar*—it was uninspired. On the other hand, he seemed to relish the singing of *nom-tom* to such an extent that he went on to record *nom-tom*s alone in *raags darbaari*, *raamkali* and *lalat*. The deduction is that he valued *nom-tom* singing as an unfettered way of elaborating the *raag*s or of creating the *raag*-mood in a more immediate manner. In this context it is interesting to note that he did not restrict the *nom-tom* to the *dhrupad-dhamaar* genre. He employed it even before rendering a *bhairavi dadraa* (*Banaavo batiyaan*) or prior to presenting a *drut khayaal* composition (*jaunpuri: Phulwanki gajare*). This only strengthens the view that he had divined the wider potentialities of the *nom-tom*: it could evoke a *raag*-mood and allowed the musician a free hand in doing justice to the thematic complexities of a *raag*. It is no exaggeration to say that he sang *dhamaar*s, etc., out of a sense of musicological loyalty to the accepted *repertoire* of the *gharaanaa* and in conformity to the performance-norms of the genre. Yet the artist in him keenly felt the aesthetic possibilities of *nom-tom* which could be brought to the forefront only when this phase was employed in isolation. This was the reason why he employed it irrespective of the form presented.

The Ustad's penchant for the *nom-tom* and the superimposition of the vowel-sound 'a' were intrinsically and mutually related features. As a detailed elaboration of *raag*, *nom-tom* aims at constructing a complete structure with the help of a perceptive use of meaningless syllables. In other words, this phase is also marked by a vocal flow which is intermittent in contrast to the *raag*-elaboration presented with the help of the vowel-sound 'AA'. In *nom-tom* the interest is not therefore centered on an experience of continuity but on making us feel the tonal movement realized through succession of units. It was this punctuated phrasing which was facilitated by the vowel-sound 'a'.

The discussion of the Ustad's ability to involve the audience is directly related to the projection-techniques he pursued. However, the projection-techniques were not the only tools he had. His success in establishing a rapport with his listeners was also greatly aided by his mastery in presenting a variety of musical forms. He was at home in *dhrupad-dhamaar, khayaal, taraanaa, thumree* and *daadraa*. In fact it was due to his versatility that he was called a '*choumukha*' artist, i.e., an artist who could see in four directions like the lord Brahmadeva of the Hindu pantheon! His *repertoire* of *raag*s too was very wide. He relied heavily on the *prachalita raag*s like *darbaari, yaman, kedaar, basant, todi, lalat, jaunpuri* but equally expert was his exposition of *raag*s like *paraj, nat-bihag, gaaraa-kaanadaa,* s*uhaag, narwaa, bhankaar,* etc. To have *aprachalita raag*s in one's repertoire and yet to insist on presenting the *prachalita raag*s was undoubtedly an indication of his desire to bring music nearer to the general audience. Presenting *prachalita raag*s was to all purposes a musical strategy he used for taking the audience into confidence. But whenever the occasion demanded he sang the rare *raag*s with a stamp of authority that only deep knowledge could bring out. In this context it becomes more important to study how he managed to create and sustain the listener's interest in the *prachalita raag*s he sang so frequently.

In order to achieve this he used a number of devices. A very distinctive device was the pronunciation of the words in the song-text in *khayaal*-singing. The author is inclined to characterise his manner of pronunciation as 'speech-oriented' or 'conversational'. That is, the pronunciation was so realized as to convey the meaning through patterns of intonation, inflexion, etc. As already said, he used the volume-dimension of the voice by making it sound soft, loud, tender or vigorous, etc. He brought this same skill to the utterance of words according to the requirements suggested by the linguistic meaning of the word-units. The actual process was in fact comparable to clothing dramatic categories of speech with musicality and use the resulting phrasing as a part of the musical idiom. For example, in his *drut khayaal* in *lalat* (*Tarpat hun jaise jal bin meen*) the vocal tone-modulations introduced after the word '*sainyaa*' (meaning 'beloved') are expressive in a manner reminiscent of a dramatic presentation. Remaining true to his perception of the musical appropriateness of a dramatic tone, he is heard to repeat the device with a telling effect in *thumree-daadraa* renderings too. For instance, the words *'vahin jaavo'* (lit. go only there!) were almost spoken and not sung (*bhairavi*). In addition one also encountered the use of words like *'are'* *'haan'*, etc.—words which are the distinguishing marks of day-to-day conversation. Employment of such exclamatory class of words moves music closer to the first, intuitional impact which is so vital for a deeper and better understanding of music. His way of rendering made music more concrete because his presentations contained inbuilt clues useful for initiating a listener into music.

These and similar devices are in fact used abundantly by *thumree*-singers. Their incorporation in *khayaal*-singing was a daring if not an altogether original act of intra-formal transfer of musical devices. Perhaps a rarer feat of a similar quality was the Ustad's resorting to speech-tone for the *nom-tom*. The meaningless syllables of the latter were articulated as if they had definable and communicable meaning (viz., *nom-tom* in *lalat*). Treating them as 'words' enabled him to combine freedom from the worldly meanings of the words and yet simultaneously suggest shadow-meanings through 'tones'. When meanings were hinted at in this manner they did not become shackles on musical manifestations: both for the musicians and the listeners. This could be taken as an emotive use as against the more obvious emotional use of words and the material they are made of. Poets are known to have taken pride in their stylistic achievements because of their success in realizing linguistic approximation to the colloquial. The Ustad could have made similar claims. He brought the musical experience nearer to speech-tones without sacrificing the distinctive elements of the musical act.

Under the circumstances it was very logical on his part to stress the *bol-aalaap* portion in his elaborations. In fact a musical chain-reaction was observed here. He could afford to give short shrift to *aalaap*s in *aakaar* because of the extremely detailed presentation of *nom-tom* which preceded his singing of *khayaal*. Further, during the singing of *khayaal* he could switch over to *bol-laya* (i.e., rhythmic variations on the words of the song-text in slower tempi) and then to *bol-taan* and the *taan*. For the climactic *taan*-portions he usually employed a not-so-fast-rendered *drut khayaal*. The total situation was therefore an example of judicious transplantations and intermixtures of musical genres or specific vocal techniques associated with them. His *khayaal* used *dhrupad* techniques for laying bare the total structure of *raag*, exploiting in the process the special attributes of his natural voice: low-keyed fundamental and sonority. His *khayaal*-singing also employed speech-tones to make the words dramatically appealing. Finally he rounded off by improvising extraordinarily varied rhythmic patterns in *bol-taan*s and *taan*s.

This brings us to the discussion of his *bol-taan*s and *taan*s regarded as specialities of the Agra *gharaanaa* even to-day. The *taaleem* of the *dhrupad-dhamaar* genre imparted with a syllabic regularity in this *gharaanaa*, obviously helps the followers in conceiving and executing *bol-taan*s and *taan*s which possess astounding variety and power. Some of the easily identifiable *dhrupad-dhamaar* orientations in the *bol-taan*s and *taan*s can be enumerated as follows:

i) Majority of *bol-taan*s employ the method of '*pat*' while formulating a *bol-taan*s. *Pat* is doubling, trebling, etc., of tempo associated with the original setting of the units (i.e., in the present context, *bol*s).

ii) There is an abundance of *tihaai*s designed in the manner of *dhrupad*-singing.

iii) As in *dhrupad-dhamaar* idiom, *gamak* is used in profusion. *Gamak* is an act of intoning every specific note with the context of the adjoining notes. Thus intoned, the individual notes are less sharply defined.

iv) Very often the *taan* patterns begin from successively changed starting points of the *tal*. Consequently, the whole *taal*-cycle undergoes a process of re-segmentation. This too is a *dhrupad*-feature employed in that genre in respect of *bol-taan*s. (The genre does not allow the use of *taan*s.) By merely changing the point of beginning the rhythmic pattern gets a new look and the sin dreaded by all musicians, that of repetition, can be easily avoided on account of the new patterns put into circulation.

v) The overall bearing of Ustad's singing was comparable to the singing of *dhrupad-dhamaar*. This was so because he relied more on robustness of expression and a ponderous musical movement. Listening to Ustad's *taan*s it becomes evident that they were not dazzling in speed. Their main impact was one born out of a controlled dynamics. Gradations in volume were so discriminatingly used so that the lack of speed was not felt.

Foregoing analysis helps in understanding the logic that motivated his use of *prachalita taals* and moderately slow/fast tempi.
Music of his extroversion did not allow pauses. His *bol-taan*s and
word-play also could not afford inordinately distanced *taal*-points.
Even during *aalaap*s his non-use of a clear *aakaar* denied him continuity. Altogether there were no chinks in the Ustad's performing
armoury!

All these virtuoso characteristics were matched by a unique sense
of freedom in his demeanour on the stage. He was not inhibited
and enjoyed to have a 'presence'. Neither was he shy of using facial
expressions, hand/head gestures to underline a musical effect.
Perhaps this was what helped him in establishing an immediate
contact with his heterogeneous audience. He loved every moment
in the process of music-making and was eager to openly invite
others to sense it and to participate in it. Like a *thumree*-singer,
the Ustad sometimes sang with his body! All said and done, not
everything that a vocalist wants to convey is understood by the
audience through the actual singing. A lot more could be communicated through the accompanying factors. Ustad Faiyaz Hussain
Khan could communicate his musical involvement, his happiness in
music-making as well as his considerable ascendency over the
abstract material of his art. If there was any secret of his artistry,
this was perhaps the clue.

Discography

Raag	Text line	Record number	Make
Darbari	Nom-Tom	H 1166	Hindustan
Darbari	Kaahe	-do-	-do-
Sugraai	Nain So Dekho	H 1093	-do-
Daadraa	Mere Joban Par	-do-	-do-
Bhairavi	Chalo Kaaheko	H 355	-do-
Natbihaag	Jhanjhan Jhanjhan	-do-	-do-
Kaafi	Vande Nandkumaram	H 793	-do-
Jaunpuri	Phulwanki Gend Naa	-do-	-do-
Ramkali	Aalaap	N 38050	-do-
Ramkali	Un Sang Laagi	-do-	-do-
Lalat	Aalaap	N 861	-do-
Lalat	Tarpat Han	-do-	-do-
Poorvi	Mathuraame Jao	H 1331	-do-
Chhaayaa	Pavan Chalat	-do-	-do-
Todi	Garwaa Maisan	H 2494	-do-
Paraj	Manmohan Brij	-do-	-do-
Desi (dhamaar)	Ari Mero	N 36614	-do-
Jaijaivanti	More Mandar	-do-	-do-
Bhairavi	Baajuband Khul Khul Jaye	H 41	-do-
Pooriya	Mai Kar Ayi	-do-	-do-

4

Surashree Kesarbai Kerkar
13.8.1892 - 16.9.1977

Born in Keri (Goa); received training from Pt. Vazebuwa and Ustad Barkatulla Khan (*beenkaar*); however, her intensive *taalim* was from Ustad Alladiya Khan of the Jaipur gharaanaa, for about fifteen years from 1920 onwards.

She was awarded the title *Surashree* by Ravindranath Thakur in 1938; was also receipient of many other honours.

Smt. Kesarbai Kerkar was one of those artists who exercised an undisputed sway over at least two generations of musicians in this century. The lay listeners, equated her with majesty and strength; for the discerning she was a measure of greatness and excellence. To practicing vocalists she was puzzling and challenging and to students of music she was a model. How could she register victories on such diverse fronts?

Perhaps the foremost striking feature of her singing was an almost masculine breadth of voice. The impression one received was of a very low natural key being used as the fundamental. However, even a casual check revealed an interesting fact: her fundamental key-note was always between G and G-sharp. This means that in reality her singing-pitch was *not* low. Female singers in India usually employ the same key. Hence, the impression of the low singing-pitch was to be explained by some non-pitch factor. A little attentive listening revealed the reasons for both of the easily and primarily perceived qualities: breadth and the low-pitch. The reason was her undistorted vowel-sound 'AA'.

Irrespective of the tempo of music, the part of the octave-range

Surashree Kesarbai Kerkar, 1892-1977

under exploration, and the *raag* presented, she employed a flawless, unattenuated 'AA'. The special acoustic qualities of this vowel-sound are well-known. It has a better reach, allowing greater continuity of musical effect; it is also more maneuverable according to the changes in tempi and especially for *taan* and other 'fast' executions. The primary consideration of the reach needs no explanation. The continuity and the conduciveness to speed *vis-a-vis* Kesarbai's music are the features to be taken up for discussion a little later.

We come back here to the breadth-low-pitch syndrome. Kesarbai was interested in *projecting* her voice; she could achieve this only by singing in an undistorted 'aa'. It is an acoustic fact that the perception of pitch is weakened by the perception volume. Taken all in all it provides us with the total causation of the syndrome. A point to note is the distaste she felt for the microphone: she made it a point to 'forcefully request' the organizers to remove it! The power and the breadth of her vocalization would have been distorted by a conventional and unimaginative setting of the double-edged weapon that the microphone is—and apparently she was well aware of the truth.

The Jaipur *gharaanaa* to which Kesarbai chiefly belonged stresses, through its usage, the significance of *aprachalita raag*s and complex *taan*s. In fact, the followers of the *gharaanaa* lay so much emphasis on including such *raag*s in their performance-repertoire that their insistence has created a specialization-effect. Rare *raag*s and Jaipur musicians have come to be equated with each other! However, as far as Kesarbai's recorded music is concerned her *repertoire* is not adequately reflected. It is true that from the disc-music, *raag*s like *nand, nat-kaamod, maaru-behaag*, etc., can be categorized as *aprachalita*, but she was heard in *mehfil*s to present *raag*s like *badhans saarang, suhaa-kaanadaa, triveni, khokar, saavani-kalyaan, basanti-kedaar, hindol-bahaar, jaun-bahaar, khat, sampoorna-maalkauns, jayat, meeraabaai ki malhaar, poorbaa* and *megh*. Even this illustrative listing is sufficient to prove the depth and variety of the *aprachalita* component in her repertoire.

However, the inadequate representation of the *aprachalita* component in the available disc-music should not stand in the way of musical analysis. Her approach to even *prachalita raag*s carried a hint of the *aprachalita*! She conceived and presented them in such a way that they proved more intricate than their familiar faces would otherwise suggest. She achieved the effect most of the times through an introduction of complexity in the phrasing but sometimes she also used the age-old trick of somewhat arbitrarily employing notes conventionally considered weak in the *raags* concerned. For example, in *raag jaijaivanti* she used to introduce the komal *gandhaar* in a phrase like '*saa re saa ga re*'—a phrasing that was not very common. Similarly, in the case of *raag desi* she used to employ both the varieties of the *dhaivat* note in a way that could be considered arbitrary when subjected to musicological scrutiny. The flexibility and the boldness unfolded in such usages are qualities not generally associated with the Jaipur *gharaanaa*. The author still remembers a concert in which she sang *raag poorvi* but phrased the two *madhyama* in such a way as to cause a minor (*raag*) identity-crisis amongst the listeners! Her rendering of the simple-looking *durgaa* was another instance of her approach which exhibited a marked propensity to puzzle. The pentatonic *raag* would acquire another character and would seem full of potentialities as she wove her intricate patterns.

Her *taan*s too exemplified the characteristic of complexity. Some of the procedures she relied on could be easily identified. For instance, she used to group musical notes in varying numbers— odd and even numbers sometimes alternating. Another, rather scarcely heard principle of constructing a *taan* was to sustain an intermediate (and not the initial or the final) note longer than the others -- which were kept moving fast. A third specific effect specially associated with the Jaipur *gharaanaa* was a vigorous and weighty execution of a 'double-stranded' *taan*. In this variety of *taan*, the progressions would go as follows: "*Ga Ma, Ga Ma, Ga Pa, Ma Pa; Ma Ni, Pa Ni; Pa Saa, Ni Saa,*" etc. It was of course apparent that much of the complexity of her *taan*s was to be traced to the basic, original movement of the *raag*—which in this case when examined structurally was itself a complex entity. Thus, even the slow-tempo *aalaap*s were complex. As the *taan*s are a retracing of the musical map already etched in the *aalaap*-phase —the principle of musical consistency could not have possibly allowed her the luxury of simpler *taan*s. This, however, was only a partial explanation of the complexity of the *taan*s. She also used some supplementary devices which magnified the intricacy of the original design. For instance, very frequently she utilized a triadic patterning, wherein she initiated and completed a pattern of few notes—the pattern itself being complex. After that she immediately went on to repeat the same pattern in the two succeeding halves of the scale. Presented in this manner, the pattern was registered thrice within a span of about one and half octave and the outcome was a certain magnification of the pattern. Perhaps the triadic design was also necessitated by the original or the intrinsic movement of the *aprachalita raag*. This sounds plausible because almost without exception such *raag*s are examples of '*vakra chalan*', that is, convoluted movement. They cannot proceed straight —along the line of the gamut—without running the risk of distorting the *raag*-identity. In the same context, Kesarbai's *taan*s could not be described as fast; yet they created an impression of speed. This could happen because due to the intricate patterning she managed to cover wider tonal spaces. While we are at the speed-aspect another possibility may also be mentioned. In all probability the breadth of voice she maintained throughout a performance without any taper-off effect also contributed to the speed-illusion created by her so capably. In other words, the overall effect was of speed *because* a musical mass was kept moving continuously. It was as if the medium pace appeared as fast pace on account of the broader singing line.

Discussion of her *taan*s can hardly be exhausted easily. At least one more subtlety may be mentioned. During the *taan*-progressions she was wont to make a skilful change of pattern that was being followed *before* a listener could get accustomed to it and begin to expect it with certainty so inimical to the aesthetic impact. The dangers of initiating a complex pattern and dragging it through the entire *taal*-cycles, etc., are two-fold. Firstly, too regular an appearance of a pattern kills the golden goose of surprise. By itself this is enough to blunt the aesthetic sensibility of the listener. Secondly, a rigid regularity of patterns verges on affecting the listeners as mechanical practice-exercises. Such exercises do not decorate the music that is presented—they tax it. Incidentally, it is an example of musicological and terminological appropriateness to know that patterns which could decorate music are called '*alankaar*' (lit. ornament) and those which are expected to help in attaining technical virtuosity through intensive practice are called '*paltaas*' (lit. reversal). However complex the pattern in a *taan* might be, its repetition could be overdone: Kesarbai avoided it by a mid-way change of pattern-types. On numerous occasions, the immaturity of a musician is easily detected through his reluctance to leave a pattern and take up another (without of course violating the law of musical coherence). By unerringly picking up the right moment for introducing a change Kesarbai eliminated the possibility of parading adherence in place of creative coherence.

And to cap it all, she displayed enough aesthetic flexibility to loosen the shackles of the constraints imposed by the concept of grammatical, musicological correctness—especially in her *taans*. She ignored the unbending syntax of phrasing she so assiduously used to maintain in the *aalaaps* and repeatedly executed straight *taans* moving towards musical climaxes by brushing aside the strict protocol of phrase-succession. In fact, this is a device which the Gwalher *gharaanaa* singers have developed to perfection. Just as nothing is as eye-catching in cricket as a straight drive past the bowler, similarly, there is hardly anything as ear-filling in music as a straight *taan*. The climactic effect achievable (only) through such a *taan* could hardly be dispensed with. Therefore, Kesarbai's performance-logic came unhesitatingly into operation. She reasoned that if and when an atmosphere of a *raag* is adequately built up by meticulous and detailed *aalaaps*, nothing could damage the edifice even when grammatical fidelity is relegated to the background. The author remembers in this context the way Pt. Anant Manohar Joshi (a prominent disciple of Pt. Ichalkaranjikar of the Gwalher *gharaanaa*) differentiated between the respective roles of *aalaaps* and *taans vis-a-vis raag*. He said, '*aalaaps* shape the individual *raags* into their individualities, *taans* bring out the unity of all *raags*'. It was clear that Kesarbai subscribed to the view. In the final analysis, every rendition of a *raag* is a matter of balancing unambiguous projection of the musicological with the interpretation aspect, which represents the essential freedom of the creative mind. It is to Kesarbai's credit that she could achieve the rare feat most of the times.

There is nothing like correct or incorrect music. Music is either relevant or irrelevant. Whether in *aalaaps* or in *taans*, Kesarbai used to step out of the *raag*-frame: this going across the border was well-calculated. The aesthetic justification for the deliberate contravention of 'rules' was not far from the dictates of musical commonsense. If a *raag*-frame is to be established properly, it must be loosened intermittently. Without the graces of flexibility, a *raag* will become a musical strait-jacket instead of being a mould of suggestive musical guidelines. The content of any musical endeavour is finally determined not only by an artist's particular presentations at a point of time; also by what he manages to suggest. Depending on the training, temperament and the risk-taking ability of the artist concerned, this loosening of the *raag*-frame can be actualized in various ways. Kesarbai achieved it largely through arbitrariness in the matter of conformity to the *raag*-grammar and by straightening out the contours of the *raag* in the *taans*. To anyone who had heard the other prominent Jaipur vocalists—the individuality of Kesarbai's approach would be easily recognizable.

A marked feature of her music was her eclecticism. This came out in a personal discussion the author had with her some time during 1968-69: she accepted this position, though with great reluctance and in a somewhat round-about manner. In that memorable 'encounter' she questioned the author very closely about an article he had published earlier. In it, the author had pointed out that even though Kesarbai followed the ideology of the Jaipur *gharaanaa*, she was able to go beyond the confines of the *gharaanaa* much more significantly than a majority of the other vocalists belonging to the Jaipur fold: it was this touch of rebellion which made her a better musician. The author had also argued further that she was able to carry the non-conformist banner effectively because she displayed an alert absorption of the salient and selective features of other *gharaanaa*-philosophies like Gwalher. The author had added that this was apparent in her treatment of *raag*s like *yaman* as opposed to her treatment of *raag*s like *nat-kaamod*. She was more imaginative and free in the former and scintillating but disciplined in the latter. Secondly, the author had also pointed out that on occasions she presented *alaap*s which were so elaborate and gradual that they could not have been bettered even by a direct disciple of the Kirana *gharaanaa*! And finally the author had maintained that unlike many others of the Jaipur *gharaanaa* (with the exceptions of Manji Khan, Pt. Mansoor and Smt. Padmavati Gokhale) she had not shied away from musical forms like *thumree* and *bhajan* and this too had helped in toning down the austerity of her music. The author had then concluded that all these features separated her from the Jaipur hard-core. (In support of the arguments the author had quoted specific *mehfil*s and specific *raag*s that she had presented, as evidence.) Her responses, as they emerged during the discussion, ranged from 'very vocal to the equivocal'! The Gwalher-touch she was not too reluctant to admit;

in respect of her occasional, detailed *aalaaps* she credited them to the *taalim* she had received from Bak Barkatullah Khan (*beenkaar*) and the third point she ignored. But in spite of all those admissions to electicism she averred that she had *not* overstepped the confines of her *gharaanaa*! The musical paradox of a musician's eagerness to leave behind the territory of the initial *gharaanaa* and yet to claim an unswerving loyalty to the same *gharaanaa* holds no mystery. In all probability it is a clannish hangover from the days when the concept of *gharaanaa* was tied to family-fidelities.

However, all the rich content of her music and her abundant powers of presentation would have been of no avail in the absence of that rare quality she displayed in all its glory: precision. The most important manifestation of her preciseness was her conception of the content. On no occasion did she leave behind an impression of tentativeness in the formulation of her musical ideas. One was never compelled to guess or deduce. Her thoughts were spelt out with great clarity. There was no fumbling with words, no half-hearted enunciation of the vowel-sounds, no excruciating suspense on account of a protracted process of reaching the tonal levels. In spite of the complexity of design there was no obscurity in her music. A very perceivable instance of the quality of precision is the manner in which a musician attains the *sam*-point. In Kesarbai's music this was always a moment to remember. It was as if she crammed the entire available temporal space of the *taal*-cycle with music—almost to the last fraction of a second—before she took up the *mukhdee*. She seemed to create the *taal*-space which no listener could have suspected to be there. This sort of precision invariably invested her *sam*s with extraordinary weight. She never came to the *sam*, she arrived at it regally!

It was not surprising that the cumulative effect of her music was the sense of immense authority she brought to bear on everything she did. One instinctively accepted the position that she could do no wrong. Udayanaachaarya, one of the ancient Sanskrit grammarians, is believed to have said, 'The correct in grammar is what Udayanaachaarya says. The east is where the sun rises.' Kesarbai was imbued with a similar confidence and she communicated it as an assurance to the audience. To a great extent, this was possible because of the sound structuring of her music. Even in her musically weak moments her performances did not fall below a certain level which itself was pitched quite high. There was *a guarantee in her music* that due to its firm backbone it would never go limp and hence at least a 'standard' musical fare could be hoped for. This made her an ideal artist for a student, a safe performer for a connoisseur and an admirable phenomenon for a musician.

Discography

Raag	Text line	Record number	Make
Lalat	Ghatan Laagi Rain	EALP 1278	HMV
Todi	Haare Daiyaan	-do-	-do-
Kukubh bilaawal	Devi Durge	-do-	-do-
Desi	Mhaare Dere Aavo	-do-	-do-
Bhairavi	Jaat Kahaan Ho	-do-	-do-
Lalitaa gauri	Preetam Saiyaan	-do-	-do-
Nat kaamod	Nevar Baajo Re	-do-	-do-
Gaud malhaar	Maan Na Kariye	-do-	-do-
Maalkauns	Main San Meet	-do-	-do-

5

Pandit Omkarnath Thakur
24.6.1897 - 29.12.1967

Born in Jahaaj (district Khambat, Gujarat); had his training in Gandharva Maha Vidyalaya, Bombay, 1910-16;
headed the Lahore branch of the Vidyalaya before return-
ing to Bharoch in 1919; ran a music school in the town
till 1923; later, shifted the school to Bombay (1934) and
then to Surat (1942). He was primarily responsible for
instituting the Faculty of Music in the Benaras Hindu
University in 1950, and was its Dean till 1957.

He represented India in many international conferences
(Florence, 1933; Budapest, 1953; Germany, 1954), awarded Padmashri (1955); also received many other honours.

Delivered a lecture-series on 'raag and rasa' (M.S.
University, Baroda, 1950) and on 'Mahaa Gujaraat kaa
sangeet tatva' (University of Bombay, 1962).

Important published musicological works include six
parts of Sangeetaanjali which came out during the period
1938-1962, and Pranav Bhaarati in 1956.

Pandit Omkarnath Thakur worked in many areas connected with
Hindustaani music. He was a performer, composer, educationist
as well as theoretician. However, we deal with him only as a
performer.

According to all accounts Panditji had his musical training from
Pt. Vishnu Digambar Paluskar of the Gwalher gharaanaa. However,
both immediate and considered responses to his music compel one
to categorize him as a major deviationist with a firm base in the
Gwalher gharaanaa. His voice and the uses that he put it to, provide a convenient starting point in assessing his contribution.

On comparison with all other stalwarts of the Maharashtra

Pandit Omkarnath Thakur, 1897-1967

branch of the Gwaalher *gharaanaa* like Pt. Vinayakrao Patwardhan and Pt. Narayanrao Vyas, it is realized that Panditji used his voice more evocatively. In the case of the other two vocalists, the entire vocalization was marked by a certain sameness of tone irrespective of the scale-range traversed, musical form rendered or the *raag* elaborated. In their cases there was only a negligible trace of modulation of voice—an effect which is described in Indian musicology as *swar kaaku*.

On the other hand, Panditji had sensed the importance of the dimension of timbre as indispensable and also judged it as a quality to be purposefully explored and exploited. Therefore he used a tender voice in *neelaambari*-rendition, and a forceful one to the point of harshness in the vigorous *taan*-patterns in *raag sughraai*. He was solemn in his *maalkauns* and *shuddha kalyaan*, and serene but joyful in *shuddhanat*. He could also be melodramatically emotional in his *bhajan*s (e.g., '*Mat jaa jogi*') and full of fervour in the rendering of the '*Vande maataram*'. The point of recording these descriptive or, to an extent, impressionistic statements is to suggest that correlating them with the specific instances from disc-music would bring out the contention that more than any other singer of his times, Panditji employed tonal colour with variety and purposefulness.

He was a very conscious vocalist. Technically, he employed both the lower and upper registers of his voice faultlessly and effectively. While Ustad Abdul Karim Khan relied on the upper register, Ustad Faiyaz Hussain Khan employed the lower register. But Panditji used both the registers: this enabled him to traverse a range of about two and half octaves without sacrificing musical quality at any point. (This was not so in the case of the other two vocalists.) Panditji's voice was full of resonance. Due to the exceptionally well-matched registers his music-flow suffered no breaks even in the staccato *taan*s (e.g., *sughraai*). It could easily avoid abrupt cutting up of words (e.g., *shuddha kalyaan* and *shuddha nat*). This was because his vocalization succeeded in leaving behind a tonal shadow even after the progressions had moved ahead or even when they were punctuated by short pauses.

However, the possession of a good voice and a faultless technique of bringing the third voice-dimension into play alone would not have made a significant musician of Panditji. These features were only contributory to another and a more basic characteristic: his attitude towards the meaning of the art-song taken as a whole and also towards the individual words of the song. Firstly, he was careful to see that words were pronounced clearly—so clearly that a listener could take them down just by listening to him. In fact, in the initial portions of many of his discs he surrounded the individual words with deliberate pauses and in this manner brought the words into an aural relief. This was obviously very much intentional because in the later portions of the same records he showed a cool disregard for the same words—to the extent of dismembering them during the elaborations! In *bol-taans* and the *tihaais* he broke the words nonchalantly according to the necessity of the rhythmic patterns. For example, in his *shuddha kalyaan*, the phrase *'bolan laage'* is broken up as *'Bo bo bo lan laage'*! A similar unhesitating cutting-up was also evident in his *shuddha nat*.

The obvious deduction is that he surely believed the words to be important as a base for all elaborations; hence he insisted on their clear pronunciation—but only till the listener had received them as words. Once this was achieved, he treated words as any other item of the musical material. As compared to the positions adopted by his contemporary vocalists, this two-pronged policy itself was a deviation. Unlike Panditji, the other vocalists either considered the words to be dispensable or treated them as something to be deliberately camouflaged! On the other hand Panditji regarded them worthy of notice but not through the entirety of the progressions. This was surely aesthetic opportunism!

Panditji accorded recognition to words also for their emotive power and content. Solicitude for their clarity alone would have befitted a phonetician rather than a musician! The most potent and moving illustration of his regard for the evocative power of words is his rendition of *raag neelaambari*. Throughout this presentation he had pronounced and employed the word *'mitwaa'* ('beloved') with great emotional charge. Sometimes he took the word to high notes, sometimes he just repeated it or sometimes isolated it from the adjacent words—and thus cajolingly brought out all the persuasive, emotional atmosphere that could be associated with it (and not its meaning alone!) This surely added a dimension to the music.

Though with less consistency, he showed a similar awareness in other presentations too. *Maalkauns* ('*Peer na jaani*'), *shuddha nat* ('*Karat ho nehaaki batiyaan*') or *Devgiri bilaawal* ('*Banaa Byaahan aayaa*') are some other pieces relevant in this respect. As has been pointed out earlier Ustad Abdul Karim Khan and Ustad Faiyaz Hussain Khan had also employed an emotionally coloured pronunciation of the song-words. But their tonal colouring lacked subtler shades. The former lent an unvaryingly yearning and anguished tone to his entire music while the latter relied on the manly erotic touch. Panditji was more mindful of the emotive subtleties: this enabled him to project a wider spectrum of feeling-tones through his use of words.

At this stage it would be proper to comment on the virtuoso element in Panditji's music. Bearing in mind the usual and convenient division of early, middle and the later years of his career, it can be maintained that the virtuoso element was to the fore in his singing in the early phase and (surprisingly) in the later phase. Yet there was a noticeable difference of character between the two manifestations. In the former phase the virtuoso element was fully backed by a matching faultless performance while in the later phase it had been almost reduced to a shadow of the musical intent. In fact it will be more appropriate to say that the earlier manifestation was a real virtuosity while the later one was more inclined to be exhibitionist. The distinction between the two was not so much the ability to execute difficult musical feats of vocalization. It was a distinction in respect of the content-orientation of the virtuosity present or absent in the supporting presentations. For example, one can examine the two major expressions of virtuosity: execution of fast, complicated *taan*s and the actualization of quick transitions from high to low notes (and *vice versa*) to establish tonal contrasts. An earlier piece, *sughraai* was notable because Panditji did justice to both these modes with remarkable ease and fluidity. His precision in coming to *sam* proved that he was completing a design, not trying to convince listeners of his vocal abilities. This is not what happened in his later piece in *devgiri bilaawal*. The loose ends of the musical progressions and the lack of tautness in design were obvious. It seemed that this content-oriented emptiness compelled him to divert the listener's attention to the difficult things he was executing on his way to the *sam*-point!

However, an artist is to be judged by his best. Hence if and when he was heard and examined in his element, Panditji surely proved to be a satisfying virtuoso. His *taan*s exhibited ample variety of the technical category. For example, he executed *sattaa*s (straight *taan*s), *jabdi taan*s (fast *taan*s executed with the manipu-

lation of the jaw-movements), *gamak taans* (in which every component note in the melodic line is provided with the context of the
adjacent note), and *tappaa* type *taans* stringed with *khatakaas* (i.e.,
groups of stressed and separated component notes). His effective
vocal range too was more than average—spanning over a gamut of
two and half octaves. And what was more important was that he
could traverse over the whole range with rapidity, forcefulness and
yet with full resonance. Faults like shrillness, nasality, flatness or
a single reed thinness never reared their heads in his music which
therefore remained aurally satisfying.

A major evaluative question can now be posed. What sort of
musical imagination did he possess to make him a successful deviationist? It is perhaps possible to answer the question in one word:
'dramatic'. The category is obviously drawn from the critical vocabulary of the group of performing arts: dance, drama and music.
The dramatic quality would often be expressed in performing arts
through the operation of the principle of contrast. Contrasts in
music are of various types. For instance they may be tonal (i.e.,
those realized through the use of timbre); positional (i.e., those
depending on the positions of the notes in the scale); rhythmic (i.e.,
those expressed through density and sparseness of the stresses
grouped together); tempi-based (i.e., those experienced through
juxtapositions of tempo-variations). In addition, words and gestures may also be employed to build up a further array of contrasts.
Panditji's music was full of all these contrasts as may be easily
illustrated from his disc-music: tonal contrasts (*neelaambari*); positional contrasts (*shuddha kalyaan*) rhythmic contrasts (*sughraai*);
tempi-based contrasts (almost all discs).

A dramatic touch of a very special nature pervasive in his music
could be described as a speech-like phrasing of musical content.
The method in which he proceeded to accomplish this variety of
contrasts could be easily perceived. He used to select certain operative words (or phrases formed with them) and 'sang' them while
keeping their speech-orientation intact. For instance, in the rendering of his *khayaal* in *shuddha nat*, he selected the phrase '*Karat ho*'
as an isolatable, speech-based unit and used it in varied and
various musical contexts. He was wont to use the minimal sentence
'*Mat jaa*' from the famous Meera-*bhajan* in a similar manner. It is
obvious that this device of distributing words in a meaningful
manner and also to lace them concurrently with matching musical

phrases can be described as a *thumree*-like exploitation of musical resources. Employing it in *khayaal* helped Panditji in reaching the audiences because the semantically channelized music provided them with a comparatively familiar clue to follow musical progressions. Further, the speech-oriented musical phrasing acquired a dramatic quality in his music because the contrast between the musical and the spoken expression became vivid and as a consequence made the listeners aware of an additional dimension: the musico-dramatic.

In Ustad Faiyaz Khan's music it was the tone of the speech which was brought into music while in case of Panditji it was the speech-phrasing that was pressed into musical service. The process was well-realized in Panditji's performances and the audience felt a possibility of sharing and participating in the total musical activity. Those who had attended his 'live' concerts will remember his tendency to launch forth into rhetorical speech-sallies during a performance. These were symptomatic of his dramatizing proclivities. Unfortunately, the 'speechifying' was overdone in the later years of his career when his creative faculties could not strike a balance between the counteracting forces of the cognate performing arts. It is worth noting that in spite of his flexible voice and meaning-oriented music Panditji did not sing *thumrees*. This was because of the discerning operation of the performer's logic. As he was already blending *thumree*-elements in his *khayaal* singing, presenting *thumrees* separately would have surely resulted into a glaring example of musical tautology.

While we are discussing the dramatic quality of Panditji's musical imagination it may not be out of place to mention some slightly extra-musical features because they corroborate the conclusions suggested here. Panditji was a performer amongst the vocalists and a showman amongst the performers! In other words, he exploited all types of non-musical means unabashedly to create an atmosphere conducive to his concert. For instance, he would have his own carpet spread over the concert-platform; he would always be preceded—almost ushered in—by his disciples and accompanists; he would have four *taanpuraa*s instead of the usual two . . . and then he would make his entry! This was followed by a very elaborate bow to the audience. In fact all his movements and gestures were just so much exaggerated as to ensure an all-round noticeability! Peter Ustinov, the English actor, has somewhere noted that the great Laurence Olivier's tone and demeanour would suddenly and totally change in character the moment he became aware that somebody might be watching him! Panditji was not much different. He would not hesitate even to weep, speak in a tremulous voice or make wide dramatic gestures with his hands, head, etc., if he felt that such actions would help to ensure an immediate rapport with his audience. Even in the case of his accompanists, he 'acted' out his encouragement to them and commented picturesquely on their contribution. It is safe to say that these extra-musical devices formed a part of his total presentation-technique. It is to be regretted that they were overplayed in the less authentic years of his career.

One more dramatic manifestation of his musical imagination also needs to be noted. In his otherwise traditional presentation of *khayaal* in *maatkauns* ('*Pag ghungroo baandh mira naachi re*') he was heard to employ meaningless syllables of the *nom-tom* type. One construction that can be put on the unusual improvisation is that the syllables were used to represent the devotional dancing of Mira referred to in the composition. The other possible interpretation is that this was an attempt to introduce the *taraanaa*-element in *khayaal*-singing. Whatever may be the interpretation accepted finally, the longish passage certainly created a contrast rarely used. Though *Hindustaani repertoire* does possess musical forms incorporating elements of both *khayaal* and *taraanaa*, e.g., the *chaturang*—to improvise the *taraanaa*-aspect because the song-text carried an appropriate semantic suggestion or alternatively use it as an improvisation a la *taraanaa* was certainly unusual and hence hinted at the dramatic quality Panditji possessed in abundance.

Panditji's contribution in respect of the repertoire-enlargement had two aspects: firstly, he composed plentifully. More importantly, however, he reinterpreted *raag*s of *Carnaatic* origin so completely as to leave no trace of their genesis. What made his efforts more praiseworthy was his choice of *raag*s to be thus brought into the *Hindustaani* fold. Most of the *raag*s to be thus transplanted were mood-oriented. It is to be remembered in this context that in the early decades of the present century, music-education was getting standardized in India and the adverse effects of the standardization procedures were already leaving their impact. For example, the *raag*-movements were excessively simplified, interpretation was being subjected to regimentation and due to the onset of the methodical singing, dry pedantic performances were becoming

ing more general. Occurring at this juncture Panditji's interpretations of *raag*s like *neelaambari, saraswati, gorakh kalyaan* assume importance. These *raag*s are mood-oriented in essence because their identity does not depend on strict succession and structuring of phrases following a rigid sequence. Panditji's rendering of *raag neelaambari* is a fine example of mood-oriented *raag* and Panditji's outlook in the matter of rendering such a *raag*. Therefore, it is instructive to mark that his *neelaambari* did *not* proceed to incorporate all the features associated with conventional *khayaal*-singing. A special mention must be made of the near-total elimination of *taan*. Absence of *taan* can surely be taken as the strongest indication of the mood-oriented character.

Panditji did not sing *thumree* but accepted the *thumree*-effects. As a dominant form of *Hindustaani* art-music, *khayaal* has been increasingly threatened or challenged by forms like *thumree, ghazal,* stage-songs throughout the present century. Those who believed in the inherent adequacy of the *khayaal*-form on account of its quality of combining classicism and individual freedom of the artist, have tried to stand by the form and have also attempted to enhance its appeal. Panditji's contribution lay in this direction.

Panditji was a deviationist of a major stature and this was reflected in his music as well as in his communicative techniques. He tilted dangerously towards exaggerated importance of showmanship in his later life and paid the highest penalty for it by 'parodying' his own musical self! But this does not diminish the worth of his accomplishments. After all, an artist is to be judged by that which is his best.

Discography

Raag	Text line	Record number	Make
Neelaambari	E Meetwaa	VE 1014	Columbia
Sughraai	E Maai Kantha	-do-	-do-
Deshkaar	Jhaannjhariya Jhanke	VE 1013	-do-
Champak	E Mag Jainyo	-do-	-do-
Gujri todi	Garwaa Main San	VE 1016	-do-
Bhajan	Raajaa Thaari	VE 1015	-do-
Ghazal (Guj)	Sharu Sharu Man	-do-	-do-
Shuddha Kalyaan	Bolan Laagi	GE 3117	-do-
Tilang	Nanadiyaa Kaise	?	-do-
Shuddha nat	Karat Ho	?	-do-
...	Vande Maatram	GE 3132	-do-
Multaani	Surjan Matwaalaa	BEX 201	-do-
Tankshri	Maalan Laai	GE 3178	-do-
Desi	Kadamb Ki Chaiyan	GE 3187	-do-
Maalkauns	Peer Na Jaani	BEX 270	-do-
Maalkans	Pag Ghungaru	BEX 271	-do-
Bhajan	Maiyaa Mori	?	-do-
Bhajan	Amar Woh Deswa	SEDE 3302	-do-
Bhajan	Re Dib Kaise	-do-	-do-
Devgiri	Yaa Banaa Byaahan	33EC3751	-do-
Bhajan	Jogi Mat Jaa	-do-	-do-

6

Ustad Bade Ghulam Ali Khan
1901 - 23.4.1969

Hailed from Kasoor in the Punjab; received training chiefly from Kale Khan (uncle); initially earned his living as a *saarangi*-player; regarded today as the main exponent of the Patiaalaa *gharaanaa*; migrated to India after 1948; possessed good knowledge of folk-musics of Kashmir, Sindh and the Punjab regions.

The author heard him for the first time in a Bombay concert in 1948. He opened with *raag kedaara* and within seconds touched the *mandra maadhyama* with such clarity, strength and sweetness that the audience burst into a spontaneous and overwhelming applause! To anybody familiar with the *mehfil*-protocol the uncommonness of the event would be apparent. During the initial phases of a *mehfil*, praise is more polite than deserving and more gestural than vocal. This is not because the audience is hostile or a reluctant listener, but because the warming-up period required by the artist is usually considerable.

It was not so in the case of Ustad Bade Ghulam Ali Khan: he had a unique voice, a very wide range, effortless production, all-round sweetness, extreme flexibility and ease of movement in all tempi. These parameters were ever present in his case. Consequently his music possessed an exceptional and unmatchable lucidity. Perhaps the quality sought to be described here is better explained by a term from Sanskrit poetics: *prasaad*. Mentioned as one of the major qualities of style, it means clarity in addition to serenity or calmness. This is the quality that enables us to have an unobstructed experience of art-work (e.g., a poem). This was what hap-

Ustad Bade Ghulam Ali Khan,1901-1969

pened in Ustad's vocalization due to his voice. The voice was so transparent that the musical design came through as originally conceived. The veil of a faulty voice-production was totally absent in his musical endeavours.

The welcome non-presence of musical obscurity in Ustad's music came to fruition in many ways. For instance, Ustad's enunciation of words was very clear. In addition, his approach to pronunciation was marked by an element of leisure. The formulation of the vowel-sounds and consonants was completed with unhurried attentiveness. Even the joint-consonants of the words were not glossed over (e.g., the words *'premki'* in *sohoni thumree;* *'tatsat'* in *bhajan;* and *'swaami'* in *khayaal maalkauns*). What was more amazing was his ability to maintain the same quality even when words were pitched on high notes. Generally speaking, vowel-sounds tend to become indistinct on higher notes in case of most of the vocalists because the voices are operating under strain. The fact that Ustad could maintain the phonetic outlines of the vowel-sounds indicated an extraordinarily well-coordinated voice-production. The quality was equally evident in his *taraanaa*-singing. The grouping together of unusual, prosaic and often unintelligible consonant-weighted *taraanaa*-syllables have often compelled vocalists to sound forced and harsh and consequently utterly unmusical. However, Ustad could maintain his 'sing-at-ease' quality along with a firm shaping of the phonetic units in *taraanaa*s due to his rare voice-qualities. Therefore edges of the words were never lost or rounded off in his singing. They were carefully chiselled into their individual shapes —unblunted and yet without strain.

Another important manifestation of the *prasaad*—quality in his singing was the care he bestowed on the tonal values of individual notes treating them as full-fledged musical entities. Nobody of course denies that all the component notes of melodic expressions like *aalaap, taan,* etc., have significance as individual entities. But a careful listening of various musicians (including many instrumentalists) frequently reveals the fact that in most cases only those notes which are regarded as structurally important are given their full values. For instance, it might be seen that very often the initial or the final note of a phrase receives due attention and (therefore) its full value while the others are only endowed with approximate values. In particular, most of the musicians tend to do so in *taan*s—where speed is impressed upon and note-values are merely suggested. Employment of *gamak*s too displays a similar approach.

Ustad's work were free from these defects. In his music, the values of the individual notes remained intact irrespective of the length, the tempo of the *taan*s and proportion of *gamaks*. He was never 'slippery' in *taan*s and never remained merely sonorous in *gamak*s. The melodic line was always clear, the component-notes received their full values and the termination-points never remained abrupt dots. This was all the more creditable because in the Patiaalaa *gharaanaa* (which he so ably represented) fast and intricate *taan*s are accorded a special status and weightage.

In the *taan*s, speed was given a place of pride. As is usual with vocalists in possession of a light and flexible voice, Ustad excelled in *sattaa taan*s. The distinctive feature of his *taan*s, however, was the use of speedy movement in case of short spiralling patterns spanning the entire range of vocalization. While a *sattaa taan* impressed due to its power and evoked surprise due to its miraculous and instantaneous shortening of the tonal space, the spiralling variety featuring in Ustad's singing registered two achievements: creating greater awareness of the tonal space and accentuating the intricacy of the design involved. The spatiality of the tonal gamut was accentuated because the octave note or any other terminal note was approached with a gradualness into the spiralling design. The intricacy of the design was also brought into relief because the very nature of a spiral involves repetition. The chances of the complexity of design being clearly perceived rose considerably as it was repeated on progressively higher pitch-levels. The total effect was of a flashy or dazzling surprise.

It was here that a very salient characteristic of the Patiaalaa *gharaanaa* came to the forefront: the influence of the *tappaa*, a non-classical form in *Hindustaani* art-music. The form is flashy, intricate in intent, fast in movement, and light in touch. It therefore excels in producing an impact of an aural dazzle rather than an effect of any sustained musical power. Punjab is reputedly the home of this form and it was not surprising that Ustad should have incorporated aspects of *tappaa* in his *taan*s. Significantly, he did not sing *tappaa*. It is obvious that it would have been a musical repetition to have *tappaa*-oriented *taan*s in *khayaal* and again present *tappaa* as an independent musical item. The *tappaa*-oriented sections in his music were prominent in the *chhotaa* *khayaal*s. The placement of the *tappaa*-oriented elaborations were inevitable because to fill up the large *taal*-spaces of the *badaa-khayaal* with the fast *tappaa*-patterns would have been both diffi-cult and unaesthetic. Ustad's *chhotaa-khayaal*s in *todi* ('*Bhor bhai*'), *maalkauns* ('*aaye pi more mandarwaa*') are good instances of how frameworks—which were themselves set in fast tempo originally —could facilitate an effective emergence of fast and intricate *taan*-patterns.

Repertoire-wise, Ustad was also known for his singing of *thumree*s. In fact, in the opinion of many, his place as a *thumree*-singer was to be considered higher than his rating as a *khayaal*-singer. Though this opinion may not be considered tenable, the argument creates an interesting situation.

It seems that in Ustad's case three musical forms exerted mutual influence (even though all the forms were not 'playing' members of his team!). Curiously, it was the form not included in his active repertoire, the *tappaa*, that deeply impressed both *khayaal* and *thumree* in his music. His *thumree*s borrowed the flashy elements from the *tappaa*. It was arresting to note that in spite of the strong musicological convention in favour of eschewing *taan*s and intricacy from the *thumree* in the interest of sustained and unimpaired emo-tional appeal, Ustad succeeded in combining both flashiness and emotionality in his *thumree*s. A little more explanation of his con-tribution to *thumree*-singing is therefore in place.

When he appeared on the Indian musical scene as a major musi-cian in the late forties, the two well-established *gharaanaa*s in *thumree*-singing were the Benaras and the Lucknow *gharaanaa*s. (The two other minor variations were exemplified by the *Agra* and the *Kiraanaa* musicians: the former consolidated the mainly-erotic type and the latter *khayaal*-oriented.). In brief, it may be stated that the Benaras *gharaanaa* with its high seriousness and poise, and the Lucknow *gharaanaa* with its minute delicateness and *ghazal*-orientation, had created types that were in danger of becoming too rigid. The sets of the *thumree*-texts in circulation, the procedures of presentation and even the norms to be followed by the accom-panists were about to degenerate into musical stereotypes. Under the circumstances, a new interpretation was rendered difficult if not impossible. The *impasse* had to be met with musical ingenuity and towards this end, Ustad intuitively chose the option of impressing his *thumree* with the *tappaa*-orientation. He was an ideal artist to attempt such a task because his voice was well-equipped to do so. Any laboured introduction of the *tappaa*-features in the *thumree* would have made it impossible for anyone to keep the spell of the words intact. As Ustad could interweave the complex, abrupt and fast *tappaa*-patterns in his *thumree*s effortlessly, the evocative power of the words was not adversely affected. Naturally his *thumree*-compositions were themselves set in a faster tempo and their texts were also different. In both these respects his *thumree*s therefore acquired an independent identity—distinguishable from both the other major *gharaanaa*s mentioned earlier. Perhaps Ustad himself too might have felt that his contribution to *thumree*-singing could be considered original and ostensibly to extend the scope of the form, he sang a *thumree* even in a *raag* like *sohoni*. The suggestion is that he was more inclined to treat *thumree* as a legitimate and pervasive point of view of looking at all musical material instead of merely regarding it as a member of the hierarchy of musical forms.

Referring back to the mutual influencing act among the three forms, it can be concluded that while the *tappaa* influenced both *khayaal* and *thumree* in Ustad's music, the *thumree* too influenced the *khayaal* to an extent. The *tappaa* remained unsung but not without representation. It surely cast effective long shadows.

Ustad never made any claims to being a 'learned' musician. He repeatedly stated that he really knew only a few *raag*s. This was also borne out by his rather limited effective repertoire. His emphasis was on the *prachalita* and mood-oriented *raag*s. Most of his 'patent' *raag*s have fortunately been recorded. Apart from these *prachalita raag*s the author heard him present *shukla-bilaawal*, *khat* (*Punjab ang*) and *gunji kaanadaa* but it was obvious that they were second-class citizens in his realm. He was also reported to have known about fifteen varieties of *pahaadi*—a folk-melody used conspicuously for 'lighter' compositions (and etymologically connected with the music of the people living in the mountains, i.e., *pahaad* in Hindi). A recording of his folk-repertoire would have certainly thrown better light on his creative process. It seemed that though he knew a number of traditional song-texts of *Hindustaani* art-music he did not have them in plenty or perhaps many of them left him cold. The deduction follows from the fact that he composed under the nom-de-plume *'Sabrang'* and also from the fact that he presented the same compositions again and again. One salutary effect was that the listeners could become familiar with his music in a limited number of exposures. Instead of novelty he had therefore to bank on originality in music.

This is important and warrants some attention. By the fifties, standardization of music-education had been well under way, the mass-media had already established their hold over the lay listener of music. During the period, musicians were therefore trying to attract and hold audiences through various stratagems. One of the easiest devices they employed was to puzzle and dazzle the listener into captivity. These ends were sought to be achieved through musical acrobatics and through emphasizing one's knowledge of *apprachalita raag*s. Ustad did not follow this easy road to recognition and insisted on *creating new music from the known*—in matters of *raag, taal* and compositions alike. In fact he never seemed to address himself to the connoisseur. His unspoken faith was: if you can move the musical common-man then the learned will also be moved. He had also grasped one more truth about the common man: a common man likes music which fills his 'ears'. Ustad relied on continuous sweetness to carry out the task. This was also the way in which his *swarmandal* seemed to contribute to his performance. It helped him in creating a musical aura. It provided an unbroken, subdued but a rich circle of sound matching his voice more than a bowed string-instrument like *saarangi* could have hoped for.

He perhaps suffered from one major defect as a performer. There was a certain degree of casualness in the music he presented in larger conferences. In such gatherings, he tended to repeat what he had already popularized through his discs. He did not seem to take any creative risks whatsoever on such occasions. On the other hand, in smaller *mehfil*s, he was a totally changed and better musician. In such select gatherings he exhibited an earnestness of purpose that transformed his music.

He used to remark that music should be likened to playing, dancing or rhythmic movements of the sea-waves. The impressionistic attitude reflected in such remarks was also perhaps symptomatic of his deeper desire: to de-ritualize music and in a way to make it less serious and more enjoyable. Perhaps he did not want to be serious about music all the time. His music certainly held a mirror to his views.

Discography

Raag	Text line	Record number	Make
Gunkali	E Kartaar	EALP 1258	HMV
Maalkauns	Eree Kab Ab Yaahi Bhed	-do-	-do-
Gujri todi	Bhor Bhai	MOAE 50044	-do-
Desi todi	Manwaa Larje	-do-	-do-
Bhimpalaas	Begun Aaye	-do-	-do-
Kaamod	Chaand De	-do-	-do-
Pahaadi	Hari Om Tatsat	-do-	-do-
Kedaar	Naveli Naar	-do-	-do-
Jaijaiwanti	Binati Kaa	-do-	-do-
Darbaari	Bhaj Re	-do-	-do-
Adaanaa	Jaise Kariye	-do-	-do-
Maalkauns	Mandir Dekh	-do-	-do-
Paraj	Latak Chale	-do-	-do-
Thumrees	Kankar Maar	MOAE 5005	-do-
	Aye Na Baalam	-do-	-do-
	Saiyaan Bolo	-do-	-do-
	Yaad Piyaaki	-do-	-do-
	Prem Ke Phande	-do-	-do-
	Prem Ki Maari Kataar	-do-	-do-
	Kaatenaa Birahki Raat	-do-	-do-
	Tirachhi Najariya Ke Baan	-do-	-do-
	Prem Agan	-do-	-do-
	Naina More Taras	-do-	-do-

Glossary

Aalaap: An important elaborational, slow or a medium-tempo rendering of melodic ideas in Indian musical tradition. Conventionally it is insisted that the vowel-sound 'aa' be employed to realize the *aalaap*. However, analogous musical elaborations in instrumental melodic music are also called *aalaap*.

Aarati: The term refers to a song-type as well as a ritualistic act. Chiefly, it denotes collective devotional singing in praise of a deity, preferably in front of the idol, *guru*, etc. The ritualistic content involves clockwise movement of a circular metal plate with a wicker lamp in it. Often the devotees place their offerings in the plate at the conclusion of the ritual. The ritual is observed in certain *keertana* performances, as well.

Aas: A lingering tonefulness of a sound felt by the hearer even after the physical act of producing the sound has virtually been completed.

Aavritti: Literally meaning repetition, it is regarded as an important technique of musical studies in which texts, melodic and rythmic patterns, etc., are repeated in their entirety on appointed days, etc.

Abhang: A traditional prosodic and melodic mould, prevalent in the devotional literature and music of Maharashtra.

Alankaar: Refers to permutation-combination patterns of melodic and rhythmic components or units introduced in musical elaborations for decorative effects.

Antaraa: In Hindustani art-music tradition, *antaraa* is the second half of the song-text; generally designed to highlight that part of the relevant scale which remains unexplored in the first half known as *sthaayi* or *asthaayi*.

Aprachalita: Literally means 'that which is less known'. In the *raag*-lore of Hindustani tradition, may also mean a *raag* with more intricate basic design needing a convoluted movement in rendering.

Bol: The units of meaningful or meaningless text of the compositions in vocal or instrumental melodic or rhythmic musical forms.

Bol-aalaap: Rendering of *aalaaps* with the help of *bols*, that is the letters in the text of a musical composition.

Bol-laya: Rhythmic variations carried out by vocalist with the help of words from the song-text.

Bhajan: A song-type or a way of collective rendering of lines or songs of devotional content with or without the accompaniment of musical instruments or other aids like clapping of hands, etc.

Bhakti-sangeet: A term of wide connotation, connoting music composed and practiced by the followers of the *Bhakti*-cult prevailing in India from the 800 A.D., if not earlier.

Bukkaa: Black, scented powder applied in ritualistic acts on the foreheads of devotees, also scattered in the air.

Band: The term refers to less sonorous and resonant sound-productions in playing instruments like *tablaa*, etc.

Chaturang: A musical form having 'four colours', that is, four composition-parts of different characters: *sthaayi*, *antaraa*, *sargam*, that is, sol-fa singing and rhythmic pattern of *bols* in *tablaa*-compositions suitably set to tune.

Cheeze: Any song-text in its entirety (in manifestations of art-music).

Chillaa: Prevalent chiefly among Muslim musicians, *chillaa* is practicing music at appointed hours (for forty days) with a ritualistic vow at the end of the action.

Choumukhaa: A musician versatile enough to render, skilfully four music forms, viz., *dhrupad-dhamar*, *khayal*, *thumri* and *taraanaa*.

Dohaa: A popular prosodic mould consisting of couplets, used for memorizing *raag*-characteristics and other features of musical grammar.

Dugun: An important rhythmic device used in vocal and instrumental music and musical forms. It consists of introducing a part of the composition or elaboration, in a tempo which is twice as fast as the original tempo.

Gajar: A collective and loud rendering of short devotional phrases couched in simple melodic formulae.

Gamak: A special vocal and instrumental technique in which every specific note is produced along with the text of two adjoining notes, one lower and one upper. There are sixteen varieties of the *gamak* mentioned in the ancient texts.

Gandabandhan: A ritual in which the *guru* accepts a person publicly as his disciple in music. The ritual includes distribution of sweets and the tying of black thread by the *guru* around the wrist of the intending disciple. It chiefly prevails amongst Muslim musicians.

Gharaanaa: A statement of a closed and coherent musical point of view that governs reinterpretation and redistribution of

	musical elements, their interrelationships and the derived details within the system.
Graam:	Modal arrangement of musical notes prevalent in India till the medieval times.
Guru pournimaa:	The auspicious full moon day of the first half of the month of *ashadh* according to the Hindu calendar when the *guru* is worshipped and offerings are made to him by his disciples.
Improvisation:	To conceive, execute and receive successive musical patterns and the corresponding musical responses while performing.
Jabdee (taan):	A particular variety of *taan*: the jaw movement of the singer and the resulting percussive vocalization play a dominant role. The technique is found to be conducive for fast-tempo renderings.
Javaaree:	The special rounded quality of sound resulting from the manipulation of a thread inserted between the string and the bridge-surface in drone and concert string-instruments like *taanpuraa* and *sitaar*.
Khaali (in tablaa-taals, etc.):	A beat which indicates the less sonorous or the more 'silent' spaces in the pattern of a *taala*.
Khatkaa:	A type of musical ornamentation in which groups of isolated and stressed component-notes of a melodic progression occur.
Kafnee:	A one-piece long robe, white, black or ochre in colour, worn by monks or ascetics.
Khayaal:	Prominent form of vocal art-music in Hindustani tradition: a composition in a particular *raaga* and *taala* with two main parts called *sthaayi* and *antaraa*. A slow-tempo *khayaal* is called *badaa* or *vilambit* and a fast-tempo composition is known as *chhotaa* or *drut*.
Keertana:	A devotional story-telling heavily interlaced with music, employing dance and *abhinaya* to some extent.
Khulaa:	As opposed to *band* (→) means a playing technique or style, resulting in a sonorous, resonant sound in vocal or instrumental music.
Lakshangeet:	A song describing the grammatical characteristics of a *raag* and composed in the same *raag*.
Lavanee:	A semi-folk dance-song in Maharashtra often erotic in content.
Luggee:	A fast-tempo rythmic pattern for *tablaa*, etc., introduced while accompanying lighter musical forms after the *dugun* (→) portion of musical elaboration has begun.
Mehfil:	Concert.

Melaa-song: Song of varied musical quality and literary content composed for variety entertainment programmes called *melaa* in the late nineteenth century Maharashtra.

Mukhdaa: Short melodic or textual portion of compositions in vocal and instrumental music repeatedly rendered almost identically before attaining the *sam* (→).

Muth: Seat of a religious order, where the ascetics or followers, etc., can stay and pursue the penances or studies.

Nom-tom: The pre-*taala* phase of *raag*-elaboration, rendered with the help of meaningless syllables, nasal consonants, vowels and clusters of all these.

Ovaalane: A ritualistic act of devotees in which the idol or the *guru* is worshipped and a circular metal plate with a wicker-lamp in it is moved clockwise in front of the worshipped.

Ovee: An ancient prosodic and tonal mould popular in literary tradition, folk as well as the sophisticated.

Paltaa: Traditionally devised scale-patterns used as musical exercises aimed at attainment of technical virtuosity in vocal or instrumental melody-based music.

Pant kavee: Poets of the Marathi literary tradition during the 17th and the 18th centuries. They wrote profusely in sanskritized narrative poetic idiom on themes from the great Indian epics. The poets were also referred to as *pandit kavee* on account of their deep studies in Sanskrit rhetorics.

Paran: Rhythmic compositions for *Pakhawaaj*: the ancient two faced horizontal drum in India.

Pasaaya daan: *Pasaaya* is from the Sanskrit word meaning *prasaad*, that is the auspicious edible/potable items or sacred things which a devotee receives back from the priest after making offerings to the deity.
In the *vaarkaree* tradition of *keertana* in Maharashtra, the compositions sung at the conclusion are equated with *prasaad*.

Phetaa: A long white or coloured cloth wrapped tightly around the wearer's head skilfully to form a tightly bound turban.

Prachalita: See *aprachalita*.

Pad: A musical composition half way between verse and lyric. It has a refrain and may run into many stanzas.

Raag: A basic melodic and grammatical construct born out of the entire gamut of musical notes subjected to a process of intentional selection and further exploited with a view to enable the artist to produce melodic patterns of infinite variety.

Rang: A term which alludes to the undefinable aesthetic and ultimate success of an artist's creative efforts in musical renderings.

Saint poets: Saints of the *bhakti*-cult who were seers, poets, composers and performers, all rolled into one.

Sam (in taala): The first beat of the *taala*-cycle in Hindustani music-tradition.

Saashtaang (Namaskaar): The ritualistic offering of respect to idols, *gurus*, etc., in which the disciple, devotee lies down prostrate on the ground in front of the idol, etc., ensuring that the eight body-components touch the ground. The components are hands, knees, feet, chest and the forehead.

Sattaa: The straight, ascending or the descending fast-tempo progression moving at least over a range of one octave. It is a variety of *taan.*

Shaaheer: A bard-like poet of folk-songs.

Sthaayi: See *antaraa.*

Swarakaaku: Modulations of vocalization in accordance with the dictates of the ancient musicological texts.

Swaramandal: A harp-like, plucked string-instrument.

Swarasaadhanaa: Early morning exercises of a vocalist chiefly exploring the lower octaves. The only accompanying instrument allowed in it is the *taanpuraa.*

Taalpaani: A person delegated the task of marking *taala* with hand-claps, etc., according to the procedures laid down in the musicological texts.

Taaleem: Rigorous, inter-personal music-training carried on for long years according to the norms in the *guru-shishya* tradition.

Taan: A fast-tempo, melodic, musical elaboration which mainly recapitulates and repeats the musical content of the *aalaap* (→).

Tamaashaa: A musico-dramatic folk-form of Maharashtra.

Tappaa: A non-classical form in Hindustani art-music tradition, characterized by an abundant use of fast movement, intricate phrasing and lightness of touch.

Tihaai: A melodic or a rhythmic triplet, the use of which indicates the performer's ability to achieve instant and intricate temporal calculations and pre-setting of the total musical design with precision.

Uparane: A long white or coloured cloth used by men to cover the shoulders or for tightly binding of the waist.

Vakra chalan: A convoluted musical progression.

Index

LIBRARY OF DAVIDSON COLLEGE

Books on regular loan may be checked out for **two weeks.** Books must be presented at the Circulation Desk in order to be renewed.

A fine is charged after date due.

Special books are subject to special regulations at the discretion of the library staff.